Spotlight
on CAE

WITHDRAWN

Francesca Mansfield and Carol Nuttall

Teacher's Book

HEINLE
CENGAGE Learning

Brazil • Japan • Korea • Mexico • Singapore • Spain • United Kingdom • United States

Spotlight on CAE Teacher's Book
Francesca Mansfield and Carol Nuttall

Publisher: Jason Mann

Commissioning Editor: John Waterman

Development Editor: Amanda Cole

Product Manager: Ruth McAleavey

Content Project Editor: Amy Smith

Manufacturing Buyer: Maeve Healy

Cover Designer: Lisa Sjukur

Text Designer: Echelon Design

Compositor: Q2AMedia

ISBN 978-1-4240-1681-5

Heinle, Cengage Learning EMEA
Cheriton House
North Way
Andover
Hampshire
SP10 5BE
United Kingdom

Cengage Learning is a leading provider of customised learning solutions with office locations around the globe, including Singapore, the United Kingdom, Australia, Mexico, Brazil and Japan. Locate our local office at:
international.cengage.com/region

Cengage Learning products are represented in Canada by Nelson Education, Ltd.

Visit Heinle online at **elt.heinle.com**
Visit our corporate website at **cengage.com**

Photo credits

The publishers would like to thank the following source for permission to reproduce their copyright protected text:

'Getting a message across the universe: would E.T. send a letter?' http://www.nsf.gov/discoveries/disc_summ.jsp?cntn_id=106711
Credit: Nicolle Rager-Fuller, National Science Foundation.

Illustrations by: Michael Perrin and KJA Artists

Printed in Singapore
1 2 3 4 5 6 7 8 9 10 – 12 11 10

Contents

	Teaching in Practice	Background	Spotlights (1)
Unit 1 **Beginnings**	• Using the Vocabulary Organiser • Referring back to previous material	• Celebrities • Edwin Hubble	• Reading • Interpreting context from vocabulary • Similar meaning in transformed sentences • Key word transformations
Unit 2 **A child's world**	• Motivating class discussion • Predicting information • Using the Grammar Reference section • Classroom management for speaking practice • Showing your class examples • Word limit reminder	• Outdoor nurseries • Children and colour	• Identifying connectors • Verbs with passive forms • Predicting information
Unit 3 **Are you game?**	• Motivating students to respond to visual stimuli • Listening strategies • Classroom management for speaking activities	• Pete Goss • Nikos Magitsis	• Understanding the writer's/ narrator's attitude • Speculation and suggestion • Understanding the speaker's attitude
Unit 4 **Eureka!**	• Skills practice in text reading • Helping reticent speakers • Listening again	• Eureka! • Dinosaurs	• Scanning texts for information • Future time in subordinate clauses • Developing topics for discussion • Listening for gist
Unit 5 **Safe and sound?**	• Explaining their choices • Eliciting information	• Anti-virus software	• Following a line of argument in a text • Supporting points in an argument • Text organisation features • Grammar
Unit 6 **Hale and hearty**	• For and against points in discussion • Justifying answers by reference to the text • Checking conditionals • Helping your students talk for a minute	• Naturopathic medicine	• Understanding written texts • Text analysis • Analysing unknown words • Using idioms in speech
Unit 7 **Wish you were there ...**	• Reading poetry • Understanding cloze tests • Inversion in writing • Making tasks active	• 'Second Life'	• Interpreting the question • Contrast and negative ideas in the text • Interpreting context to identify the speaker
Unit 8 **Making our mark**	• Paraphrasing texts • Mixing pairs • Noticing word patterns	• Straw bale construction • The three little pigs • Easter Island	• Understanding opinion • Reaching a decision through negotiation • Interpreting context • Reduced relative clauses
	Teaching in Practice	Background	Spotlights (1)

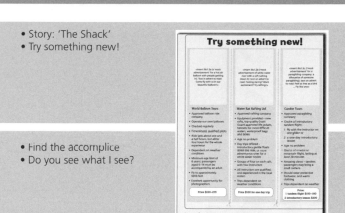
v

	Teaching in Practice	Background	Spotlights (1)
 **Unit 9 Brushstrokes and blueprints**	• Eliciting language • Gauging students' level of interest	• Scissors and the corkscrew • *The Dark Room* • Vasilis Kapodistrias • Colour in different cultures	• Understanding tone and implication • Understanding stated opinion • Key word transformations
 **Unit 10 The good life**	• Understanding gapped texts • Reporting verbs	• Long-distance families • The Freecycle Network™	• Text structure, paragraph cohesion and coherence • Paragraph cohesion • Odd paragraphs • Focus on questions • Direct speech to reported speech
 **Unit 11 Making ends meet**	• Speculating about a reading text • Maintaining good habits	• *Brick Lane* by Monica Ali	• Literary devices • Listening for dates, figures or statistics • Plans, predictions, criticism, annoyance, resignation
 **Unit 12 Behind the silver screen**	• Skimming and scanning • Emphasis on *quite* • Reading the titles • Reading reviews	• Academy awards • 'Penguin' films	• Understanding humour, irony and sarcasm • Emphasising adjectives • Understanding purpose and function • Participle clauses
 **Unit 13 Getting the message across**	• Developing what is done in class • Consolidating language learned in the unit	• Charity organisations	• Predicting information • Reference words • Making educated guesses
 **Unit 14 Gaia's legacy**	• Pictures and idioms • Eliciting answers from the class	• The age of the Earth • Gaia hypothesis	• Matching gist to detail • Adjectives followed by particles • Unreal past • Focused listening
 **Unit 15 Our global village**	• Teaching in multicultural versus monocultural groups • Preparing for part 1 of the Speaking Paper • Writing in pairs	• The global village • Morris dancing • Some traditional ceremonies	• Texts from different sources • Attitude and opinion
Unit 16 Endings ... and new beginnings	• Contextualising discussion questions • Make it active! • Approach to this text • Eliciting students' ideas • Ways of revising vocabulary		• Looking for specific information • Intensifying comparisons • Consolidation of things to look for in this part

Spotlights (2)	Extension	Photocopiable activities	
• Justifying choices	• Reading: commenting on household gadgets • Grammar: emphasis and meaning	• Creative compounds	
• Reported speech to direct speech • Organising a larger unit of discourse • Lexical contexts • An information sheet • Using register	• Getting started: 'free rice' website • Reading: checking comprehension level • Listening: pre-teaching tapescript vocabulary	• Scruples questionnaire • Reporting the news	
• Words of similar meaning, different uses • Being concise	• Language development: stories about credit card fraud • Listening: discussing credit card safety measures	• Fiction or fact? • Monopoly token personality quiz	
• Participles as adjectives • Exchanging ideas • Identifying parts of speech • Planning your review • Writing reviews	• Writing: preparing additional plans	• Film images • 'Ellie' award ceremony night	
• Sustaining interaction • Doing multiple tasks at once	• Reading: reading further • Use of English: building up a list of word groups • Speaking: researching charity organisations	• Reading skills worksheet • Charity balloon debate	
• Making choices • Suffixes • Discussing issues that surround a topic	• Reading: brainstorming memories • Language development: art competition	• Odd animal out! • Ideal world	
• Clauses of time, purpose, reason, concession and result • Using description and anecdote	• Reading: researching for homework • Grammar: extra practice with adverbials	• Home exchange holidays	
• Recognising agreement and disagreement • A letter of reference • Final reminder – check your work!	• Reading: commenting on what has been read • Listening: checklist for the Listening Paper	• Just a minute! • Advanced particles dominoes	

What are the differences between the old exam and the revised exam?

You're probably wondering what the differences between the old and revised exam are. There are still five papers, but overall time has been reduced in length by approximately one hour. It is now four hours and forty minutes. The new exam will also contain new and improved task types, and is designed to be more 'user-friendly'.

Revised Exam

1 Paper 1: Reading [Four parts, 34 questions]
1 Themed texts (6 questions) **NEW**
2 Gapped text (6 questions)
3 Multiple choice (7 questions)
4 Multiple-matching (15 questions)

2 Paper 2: Writing
1 Write one of the following: an article, a report, a proposal, a letter (compulsory task).
 Answer reduced to 180–220 words
2 Write one of the following: an article, a competition entry, a contribution to a longer piece, an essay, an information sheet, a letter, a proposal, a report, a review.
 Answer to be 220–260 words (1 task from a choice of 5)
 Possible set texts option. **NEW**

3 Paper 3: Use of English
1 Multiple-choice cloze (12 questions)
2 Open cloze (15 questions)
3 Word formation (10 questions)
4 Gapped sentences (5 questions) **NEW**
5 Key word transformations (8 questions) **NEW**

4 Paper 4: Listening
1 Short extracts (6 questions) **NEW**
2 Sentence completion (8 questions)
3 Multiple choice (6 questions)
4 Multiple matching (10 questions)

5 Paper 5: Speaking
1 Spoken questions between the interlocutor and each candidate (3 minutes)
2 Individual 'long turn' for each candidate and a brief response from the other candidate (1 minute + 30 seconds)
3 A two-way conversation between candidates with written and visual stimuli used in a decision making task (4 minutes) **NEW**
4 A discussion on topics related to the collaborative task (4 minutes)

Differences

Introduction of three texts in part 1, each with two four-option multiple choice questions.
A broader text range used (for example, fiction and reports are now introduced).

Candidate is given less material as a writing prompt.
Candidate's response is reduced from 250 words.
Tasks added: 'Contributions to longer pieces', 'essays' and set texts.

In part 4, the candidate now needs to complete a gap in a set of three sentences with the same word removed.
In part 5, the candidate needs to rewrite the first sentence into the second, using three to six words, including the 'key' word given.
The old section, error correction, has been removed.

Introduction of three extracts of interacting speakers in part 1, each with two three-option questions.
Candidates can now listen twice to all parts.

Candidate to candidate interaction removed from part 1
Written prompts with visuals now used in parts 2 and 3.

Introduction

What will I find in this Teacher's Book?

In this introduction, you'll find an overview of the new CAE exam, key differences between the old and new version, and some remarks about the differences between general English teaching and teaching exam classes.

In the main body of this Teacher's Book, you'll find notes and guidance for each unit with an easy access answer key at the end. The notes often contain suggestions for alternative approaches and ideas. Teaching tips feature throughout, as well as suggestions for extension activities. There are also tapescripts of all the listening passages. Each unit has photocopiable material. This may contain activities and games to practise vocabulary and grammar learned in the unit, or freer activities to practise speaking skills. Lastly, there is a literature photocopiable after Unit 16 aimed at students choosing to study the optional text in Paper 2, part 2 (question 5).

Why do students do the exam?

The Cambridge Advanced Examination is an internationally recognised qualification, which follows on from the First Certificate. The new version is more closely related to the First Certificate and develops skills taught at that level. Students are attracted to it because it proves to prospective employers and educational institutions around the world that the holder's knowledge of English grammar and vocabulary is of a high level. It also shows that they can display a corresponding level of ability across the skills. It acts as a significant bridge between FCE and CPE, helping students adjust to what is otherwise a very big jump! In today's terms, it is considered a C1 level by the Council of Europe.

What does CAE show?

Students who successfully complete a Cambridge Advanced preparation course will finish with a useful and very solid knowledge of grammar, vocabulary and skills. In particular, they will be confident speakers of the language in most situations, and many businesses and institutions of further education view this certificate as a valuable asset when considering a candidate for a position. Students themselves may also use this course as a solid foundation on which to base their studies for the Cambridge Proficiency Examination.

What do students need to pass the Advanced Examination?

To pass, students need:
- a sufficient level of language
- a clear understanding of how the exam works and how they will be tested

- practice in all skills
- exam skills
- regular and extensive practice of all question types

What's in a name?

Spotlight on CAE is the second book in the Spotlight series, and follows on from the highly successful *Spotlight on FCE* book. It works with the same principles in mind as the FCE book, emphasising the importance of focusing and shedding light on the language and skills students need for success.

WHAT ARE THE SPOTLIGHTS?

The Spotlights throughout the course give these areas prominence by focusing on key areas of language and examination skills development. They draw the student's attention to what is being tested and illuminate problem areas such as understanding a writer's tone in a reading passage, or a speaker's opinion in a listening task. They give authoritative and useful advice on grammar, vocabulary and skills that is then practised. Exam spotlights are particularly useful for teaching students about the nature of the exam and examination technique. They may help learners avoid common pitfalls and traps.

How does *Spotlight* help?

Spotlight on CAE helps by being both challenging and cohesive in its development. It contains a lot of language and information, presented in an engaging thematic framework. While offering fully comprehensive preparation for the CAE examination, the course also provides consolidation and development of all the main grammatical structures and language areas needed to develop the learner's general English. It does this by providing the following features:
- a Grammar Reference section at the back of the Student's Book
- a Language Development section in each unit, where vocabulary items are prioritised and developed
- a key word feature within this section, which aims to encourage students to examine the different ways a single word can be used
- an 'In other words' feature appears either in the Writing or the Speaking Papers and focuses on useful ways students can vary their vocabulary when using the English language actively
- a Vocabulary Organiser at the end of each unit, which helps students organise, develop and consolidate vocabulary as it is learned in the unit. Ideally, each exercise should be completed alongside the relevant tasks in the unit, so that students can transfer useful information to their notebooks.

To the new teacher: how is teaching an exam class different from general English?

If you haven't taught an examination class before, here is some advice on how to adapt your teaching style and approach effectively. You need to consider the following points:

- the emphasis of a CAE class
- the content and balance of what you teach
- the way you teach and the demands you place on your students.

Quite rightly, general English classes often focus on developing students' fluency and confidence and developing their overall communicative competence; that is, maximising successful communicative outcomes from what they know. In general English classes, teachers may prize fluency and spontaneity over accuracy and reflection. In a general English class there is always the temptation to allow speaking and discussion activities to run on as long as they need. In an examination class, you need to be more vigilant about optimising your use of time.

Who are our students?

Advanced learners in language schools vary widely. You may find yourself with a class of students who have been studying together for several years, and have just successfully completed an FCE course. In this case, they will be familiar with most of the task types that appear in the CAE. However, it is quite likely that you will have students who are new to the school, or some who are returning to their English studies after a break of several years. The latter group may have studied English in a traditional manner, with emphasis on grammar, reading and writing, and so their speaking skills may be relatively weak.

Conversely, students who have acquired English from living in an English speaking community, or who have studied in institutions where fluency and communicative competence are favoured over accuracy, may often be weaker at writing and formal grammar. Should you have a class of students with such mixed experiences in their language learning, you will need to take some time for everyone to become 'acclimatised' to the current learning environment.

What do students need?

CAE students will have already achieved a B2 level standard of English, and so should have sound knowledge of grammatical structures and vocabulary to this level. If, however, they are returning to English after a break, this knowledge may need refreshing. It will also need developing in order for them to attain the necessary standard to sit the Advanced examination. This development should be balanced across the four skills of listening, speaking, reading and writing. Be warned: even students who have just passed a B2 level examination have a surprising habit of forgetting how to use basic grammatical structures! For this reason, the Grammar Reference section in the coursebook is particularly useful. Finally, successful candidates will need total familiarity with all the aspects of the examination coupled with good exam technique.

TEACHING IN PRACTICE

A few tips:

- Be strict about time-keeping and disciplined about how classroom time is spent. Don't allow speaking activities or discussion to drag on.
- Set homework after every lesson. Contact parents if it is not done.
- Encourage students to be aware of their problem areas, and to correct their mistakes, while also praising their achievements.
- Once students are about two thirds through the course, organise a full mock examination. Make sure this is carried out under exam conditions. Then, give students individual tutorials telling them what they need to focus on.
- Use a lot of simulations of the Speaking Paper, as students often find this the most stressful part of the exam.
- Also give plenty of practice in exam style listening tasks, as this is another stressful area for language students.

As the exam approaches, be more and more strict about respecting time limits and doing more work under exam conditions. Check students' writing by getting them to produce a piece of writing in the classroom without preparation. Students are often appallingly lax about checking their work. Stress the importance of doing this.

'CAN DO' SUMMARY

Typical abilities	Listening and Speaking	Reading and Writing
General ability	Can contribute effectively to meetings and seminars within own area of work or keep up a casual conversation with a good degree of fluency, coping with abstract expressions.	Can read quickly enough to cope with an academic course, and can take reasonably accurate notes in meetings or write a piece of work which shows an ability to communicate.
Social/Tourist	Can pick up nuances of meaning/opinion. Can keep up conversations of a casual nature for an extended period of time and discuss abstract/cultural topics with a good degree of fluency and range of expression.	Can understand complex opinions/arguments as expressed in serious newspapers. Can write most letters (s)he is likely to be asked to do; such errors as occur will not prevent understanding of the message.
Work	Can follow discussion and argument with only occasional need for clarification, employing good compensation strategies to overcome inadequacies. Can deal with unpredictable questions.	Can understand the general meaning of more complex articles without serious misunderstanding. Can, given enough time, write a report that communicates the desired message.
Study	Can follow up questions by probing for more detail. Can make critical remarks/express disagreement without causing offence.	Can scan texts for relevant information, and grasp main topic of text. Can write a piece of work with a message that can be followed throughout.

Certificate of Advanced English: Paper by paper

1 Paper 1: Reading

Four parts testing a range of reading skills: candidates must answer all four parts; there are 34 questions in total; candidates receive two marks for each correct answer in parts 1, 2 and 3 and one mark for each correct answer in part 4.

Part 1: Multiple choice

Candidates have to read three short themed texts from a range of sources. Each text is followed by two multiple choice questions with four options each. Emphasis is on the understanding of detail, tone, purpose, implication, attitude and also text organisation features.

Part 2: Gapped text

Six paragraphs have been removed from a longer text and placed in a jumbled order, together with an additional paragraph. Candidates have to choose the missing paragraph for each gap. Emphasis is on understanding how texts are structured and following text development.

Part 3: Multiple choice

A longer text followed by seven four-option multiple choice questions. Emphasis is on the understanding of a long text, including detail, opinion, tone, purpose, main idea, implication, attitude and organisation.

Part 4: Multiple matching

A text or several short texts is preceded by 15 multiple-matching questions. Emphasis is on locating specific information, detail, opinion and attitude in texts.

2 Paper 2: Writing

Two parts: candidates must answer both parts (a compulsory one in part 1, one from a choice of five in part 2).

Part 1: One compulsory question

Candidates may be asked to write any of the following: an article, a letter, a proposal, a report. They must use the input material and write 180–220 words.

Part 2: One from a choice of writing tasks

Candidates can choose one task from a choice of five questions (including the set text options). They may be asked to write any of the following: an article, a contribution to a longer piece, an essay, an information sheet, a letter, a proposal, a report, a review or a competition entry. Candidates must write 220–260 words.

3 Paper 3: Use of English

There are five parts with 50 questions in total.
Parts 1, 2 and 5 test both grammar and vocabulary. Parts 3 and 4 test vocabulary.
Parts 1, 2, and 3: each correct answer receives one mark.
Part 4: each correct answer receives two marks.
Part 5: each answer receives up to two marks.

Part 1: Multiple-choice cloze

A modified cloze test containing 12 gaps and followed by 12 four-option multiple choice items. Candidates must choose the option that correctly fills the gap.

Part 2: Open cloze

A modified open cloze test containing 15 gaps. Candidates must write one word to fill each gap.

Part 3: Word formation

Candidates must read a text containing ten gaps. Each gap corresponds to a word. The stems of the missing words are given beside the text.

Part 4: Gapped sentences

There are five questions, each of which contains three separate sentences. Each sentence contains one gap, which must be completed with one appropriate word.

Part 5: Key word transformations

There are eight separate questions, each with a lead-in sentence and a gapped second sentence to be completed in three to six words, including a given 'key word'.

4 Paper 4: Listening

Four parts: each part contains a recorded text or texts and corresponding comprehension tasks. Each part is heard twice. There are 30 questions in total.

Part 1: Multiple choice

Three short extracts, from exchanges between interacting speakers. There are two four-option multiple choice questions for each extract.

Part 2: Sentence completion

A monologue with a sentence completion task which has eight items. Candidates must complete each sentence with a word that heard in the recording.

Part 3: Multiple choice

A longer dialogue or conversation involving interacting speakers, with six multiple choice questions.

Part 4: Multiple matching

Five short themed monologues, with ten multiple-matching questions. There are two tasks to complete.

5 Paper 5: Speaking

Four parts: there will be one interlocutor and one invigilator; there will be two or three candidates per group. Candidates are expected to respond to questions and to interact in conversational English.

Part 1: Introductory questions

A conversation between the interlocutor and each candidate (spoken questions).

Part 2: Individual long turn

An individual 'long turn' for each candidate with a brief response from the second candidate (visual and written stimuli, with spoken instructions).

Part 3: Two way conversation

A two-way conversation between the candidates (visual and written stimuli, with spoken instructions).

Part 4: Extension of discussion topics

A discussion on topics related to part 3 (spoken questions).

Pre-CAE quiz

How much do you know about the CAE? Answer the following questions by choosing A, B or C.

1 What does CAE stand for?

A Cambridge Advanced Examination

B Certificate in Advanced English

C Cambridge Advanced English

2 What is its rating with the Council of Europe?

A C1

B B2

C C2

3 How many Papers are there in the exam?

A six

B four

C five

4 Which skills do the Papers cover?

A Listening, Speaking and Writing

B Reading, Writing and Speaking

C Reading, Writing, Listening and Speaking

5 What do the exams mainly test?

A the ability to think in English

B the ability to communicate in English

C the ability to write in English

6 When was the first CAE offered?

A 2002

B 1985

C 1991

7 What's the pass mark?

A more than 60%

B 70%

C less than 60%

8 What's a good reason to take CAE?

A to travel

B to gain employment

C to pass the time

9 All CAE Papers are worth the same in marks.

A true

B false

10 What is Paper 4?

A Use of English

B Listening

C Speaking

11 How many parts are there in Paper 4?

A two

B three

C four

12 How many times a year is the exam offered?

A once

B twice

C every two months

13 Is the Grade D a fail?

A yes

B no

C maybe ...

14 How many parts are in the Reading Paper?

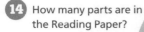

A four

B three

C two

15 A multiple matching task means:

A there is more than one question on the text.

B there is more than one extract to read.

C each question corresponds to a different text.

16 How many candidates take the Speaking Paper together?

A two

B two or three

C between two and four

17 In the Writing Paper, you must produce:

A two pieces of writing of equal length.

B one letter, and two discursive pieces of writing.

C two pieces of writing, of different lengths.

18 You will lose marks for spelling mistakes:

A always.

B never.

C sometimes.

19 How many parts are in the Use of English Paper?

A five

B four

C three

20 Your CAE course should offer you:

A development in general English.

B development in a range of communicative skills.

C a balance of development in skills and exam preparation.

Congratulations! You've now completed the Pre-CAE quiz. Good luck with the rest of your course!

Beginnings

Lesson planner

Fast lane: 3 x 1.5 hour lessons = 4.5 hours per unit
(total course = 72–76 hours)

Lesson	Time	Classwork	Exam Booster (EB) homework
1	1.5 hours	Getting started, Reading + Vocab. Organiser (VO)	Getting started + Reading
2	1.5 hours	Check homework, Lang. develop., Grammar, Listening + VO	Lang. develop., Grammar + Listening
3	1.5 hours	Check homework, Use of English, Speaking, Writing + VO	Use of English, Speaking + Writing

Slow lane: 4 x 1.5 hour lessons = 6 hours per unit
(total course = 96–100 hours)

Lesson	Time	Classwork	EB homework
1	1.5 hours	Getting started, Reading, VO + photocopiable 1	Getting started + Reading
2	1.5 hours	Check homework, Lang. develop., Grammar + VO	Lang. develop. + Grammar
3	1.5 hours	Check homework, Listening, Use of English + VO	Listening + Use of English
4	1.5 hours	Check homework, Speaking, Writing + photocopiable 2	Speaking + Writing; Coursebook Writing task

Before you begin

If you are starting with a new class, try to break the ice by doing a warm-up activity. Write out or photocopy the '*Find someone who ...*' activity top right, and give one copy to each student. They should move around asking other students

questions. When they find someone for whom an item is true, they should write their name next to that item.

Find someone who ...

1 ... is wearing something new.

2 ... has joined the class for the first time.

3 ... likes the same kind of music as you.

4 ... likes dancing.

5 ... enjoys eating the same food as you.

Topic: starting things, beginnings, starting again

This unit aims to focus on new vocabulary, especially verbs and phrases, which are associated with *beginnings*. As students are *beginning* a new book, they are probably *beginning* a new course (Advanced) and they may well be *beginning* a new school year or period of their education.

Unit 1 Wordlist

activate	found	minuscule
animation	frustrated	notion
auspicious	generate	originate
blissful	hoarse	postulate
breathtaking	humble	predecessor
coin	hypothesis	produce
complex	ideal	prompt
crisp	inaugurate	proportional
demonstration	indefinably	propose
descent	in earnest	protestor
dimension	infinite	provoke
distinct	inherent	rejection
download	initiate	reluctant
effortlessly	instigate	resounding
elated	institution	revelation
embark (on)	intriguing	spawn
engender	invaluable	speculation
establish	launch	stimulate
excerpt	massive	trigger
extract	material	ultimate
fledgling	matter	vulnerable

Getting started

1   Elicit what the pictures show the beginning of. Place students in pairs and encourage them to think of other beginnings as quickly as possible.

2   Students should have a go at the quiz according to their own knowledge and then check their answers at the back of the book. Ask students to underline the verb in each sentence and ask them to explain in what context they think it means *start*.

3   Draw the students' attention to the box of verbs. Ask them to identify words they already know and ask which of the meanings below might apply. Help them with unknown words by writing example sentences on the board.

TEACHING IN PRACTICE

Using the Vocabulary Organiser

The purpose of the Vocabulary Organiser is for students to be able to arrange, organise, consolidate and revise vocabulary as it comes up in the unit. It is not meant to be set as a test and students should be encouraged to refer back to the corresponding unit pages as much as possible in order to complete the exercises.

→   Vocabulary Organiser 1.1 + 1.2, page 10

Reading: reading for specific information

As this is the first unit, aim to do at least the first, if not all three texts and their accompanying tasks in class, in order to guide your students and assess their individual abilities.

BACKGROUND: CELEBRITIES

Charlie Chaplin

In 1910, Charlie Chaplin moved to America. By 1914 he had made 35 films. He made another 14 the following year, and 12 short films between 1916 and 1917.

Chaplin's most notable films include *The Gold Rush* (1925), *Modern Times* (1936), and *The Great Dictator* (1940). Chaplin was married four times, and had a total of 11 children. He died in Switzerland on 25th December 1977.

Sean Connery

Sean Connery was born on 25th August 1930 in Edinburgh, Scotland. His mother was a cleaning lady, while his father was a factory worker and truck driver. Connery had various jobs before becoming an actor. He also showed potential as a footballer, but turned to acting aged 23.

Connery's most famous role was as the first James Bond. Other notable films Connery starred in include *The Name of the Rose* (1986), *The Untouchables* (1987), and *Finding Forrester* (2000). Connery has married twice and has a son from his first marriage, as well as a grandson.

Oprah Winfrey

Arguably the world's most famous talk show host, Oprah Winfrey was born on 29th January 1954 in Kosciusko, Mississippi, USA. Her upbringing was poor and abusive, and she had a troubled adolescence, but was determined to change her life. She became the first African American woman television news anchor to work in Nashville at the age of 19. This eventually led to her world-famous talk show. *The Oprah Winfrey Show* has become one of the most successful TV talk show programmes in history, and Oprah herself is not only a TV personality, but also an extremely successful businesswoman and philanthropist.

1   Ask students to look at the two small photographs and the large one of Charlie Chaplin, and elicit information about any or all of them.

> Who are they? What are they famous for?

> Where do they come from? Do you know anything about their background?

2   [Text A] Allow students time to read the text. Tell them to underline the relevant information which shows the answer.

SPOTLIGHT ON READING

3   Draw the students' attention to the Spotlight on Reading. Ask them to read sentences a and b carefully, and compare them to the text.

4   Ask students to do this task individually. Ask them to check their answers with a partner, before eliciting the answers as a class.

→   Vocabulary Organiser 1.3, page 10

5   [Text B] Allow students time to read the text before asking them about their answers.

6   [Text C] Find out why the writer initially gave up her activity. Then, students could do exercise 9 in class or at home.

7   Ask the students to write down their answers to the questions before discussing together as a class.

8 The aim of this task is to make students take note of slight differences in the phrasing of options which can change their meaning. Tell them to pay careful attention to the wording of each sentence. Allow them time to choose their answers. Elicit, and give feedback.

→ Vocabulary Organiser 1.4, page 10

9 Instruct students to write the options using their own words as far as possible.

10 Discussion. Elicit words such as *nervous, excited, anxious, enthusiastic*, for something new. Then elicit words such as *nervous, fearful, afraid of making mistakes*, for anyone returning to an activity. The idea is that, for many people, it is more difficult to go back to something, than it is to start something new.

Language development:
starting again

1 Ask students to think about what usually happens at a drawing board (elicit words such as *architects, designers*). Ask them to guess why someone might have to go 'back to the drawing board'. Then tell students to skim the text again to find the other phrases. There are two more.

TEACHING IN PRACTICE

Referring back to previous material
Throughout *Spotlight on CAE*, students will be directed to 'look back' at previously read texts or exercises. The purpose of this is to make sure students continue to look at language in context and revise it correctly.

2 Ask students to have a go at the exercise. They will probably be able to answer most of the questions. If they have trouble, ask them to refer to their dictionaries.

3 Do this as a class activity.

4 Tell students that this is an exam-type questions. Ask them to read all three sentences in each question before they write the answer. Check the answers with the group.

5 Ask students to refer back to the texts to find the phrases and read them in context before they attempt the task.

Key word: *make*

6 Ask students to use the context of the sentences to guess the meanings. They should not use dictionaries to help them with this task.

7 Allow students time to guess some of the items here, before asking them to use a dictionary.

→ Vocabulary Organiser 1.5, page 10

Grammar: review of tenses (past and present)

1 Discussion. This is an opportunity for students to use a mixture of tenses. Accept a variety of answers and encourage discussion to lead into the theme of the grammar section.

2 Students should read the text and underline examples of the tenses. Check their answers with the class.

Grammar extension

Write on the board or ask the class to listen as you read the options aloud.

Which of following sentences best summarises the text?

a We have learned all there is to know about the history of the universe but still want to know more.

b No matter how much we learn about the universe, we cannot answer all the questions.

c We do not understand most of the things we have learned and scientists always disagree.

The answer is b.

3 This exercise offers an opportunity to revise the uses of different tenses and is probably best done as a class activity.

4 This text provides an opportunity to revise the past tenses, and compare them to each other. Students should read the text first by themselves all the way through to understand the meaning.

→ Grammar Reference 1.1, page 169

5 Students should attempt this exercise by themselves. Tell them they can refer to the Grammar Reference section if they need to. Check the answers with the whole group.

BACKGROUND

Edwin Powell Hubble (1889–1953) was an American astronomer. He profoundly changed astronomers' understanding of the nature of the universe by demonstrating the existence of other galaxies besides the Milky Way. He also discovered that the degree of redshift observed in light coming from a galaxy increased in proportion to the distance of that galaxy from the Milky Way. This became known as Hubble's law, and would help establish that the universe is expanding.

6 Students can refer back to the text if necessary.

7 Students should attempt this exercise by themselves. They should read the whole text first in order to understand the context of each gap and the tense required.

→ Grammer Reference 1.1, page 169

8 Ask students to form pairs so they can practice talking about the text and asking each other questions.

Listening: short extracts

1 Try to generate discussion. Prompt with questions such as:

> Why might someone prefer reading a book to watching a film?

SPOTLIGHT ON LISTENING

Interpreting context from vocabulary
2 Explain to your students the value of reading task questions before they listen in order to anticipate what they are going to hear. They should learn to pinpoint key vocabulary that indicates the subject, speaker's attitude and opinions expressed.

3 Ask students to read the questions and underline the key words in each option. Elicit other words the students think they might hear connected with each one.

4 🎧 1.1 Play the recording once and allow students to choose their answers. Play the track again and ask them to check. Check answers before allowing students to look at the tapescript on page 204.

5 As this is the first unit, you may like to do this exercise as a class. Ask students to read the questions, and brainstorm ideas about what they are going to hear. Write the students' rubric on the board.

6 🎧 1.2 Play the recording and give feedback on the rubric the students chose. Then play the track again, and allow the students to answer the questions in exercise 5.

7 Play the track again, and allow students to write down words connected with feelings. Ask students to turn to the tapescript on page 204, and underline the words that show the speaker's feelings.

8 Ask students to do this task individually without listening again.

9 Refer students back to the table in exercise 2, and ask them what words they expect to hear.

10 🎧 1.3 Play the recording and allow students to answer the question. Play the track again so they can check their answer.

Use of English: key word transformations

EXAM SPOTLIGHT

PAPER 3, PART 5 Similar meaning in transformed sentences
1 Ask students to read the information in the Spotlight and elicit the answer from the class. Tell them that sometimes in this task several changes need to be made in order for the second sentence to have a similar meaning to the first. Don't give definite feedback on this at this stage, as the students will need to mark off the checklist on the next page.

2 Tell students to do this task individually. Ask for explanations about why the other options are wrong.

3 Students should attempt the exercise individually in class or for homework.

EXAM SPOTLIGHT

PAPER 3, PART 5 Key word transformations
4 This should be done in class. Go through the checklist with the group. Elicit the reason for each answer.
5 Ask students to look back at exercise 3 and match each question to a rule in exercise 4.

Speaking: talking about new experiences

1 Allow students to comment freely as a class on the pictures before focusing on the question.

2 Ask the class to contribute questions and write them on the board.

SPOTLIGHT ON SPEAKING

PAPER 5, PART 1 Social talk
Read the information in the Spotlight with the group. Tell your students that although they don't have very long to answer the questions in part 1 of the interview, they should avoid giving one-sentence only answers.

3 Allow students time to complete this task individually.

4–5 For the Speaking task, you may find it useful to elicit the full question for student A, and write it on the board. Draw students' attention to the 'In other words' box first, and ask them to complete exercise 5.

Writing: planning a descriptive or narrative piece of writing (letter)

2 Students should read the exam question in the box. Stress that whenever they do this they should check what type of writing they are being asked to create and how many things they are being asked to do. There is usually more than one thing.

3 Encourage your students to spend a few minutes thinking of ideas. Tell them you want each student to try and think of at least three different experiences.

4 🎧 1.4 Play tapescript 1.4. Do this activity with the class and check the answers.

5 🎧 1.5 Do this activity with the class and check the answers on the tapescript.

6 Students should read the letter individually. Check their answers with the class. Ask them to suggest paragraph breaks.

→ Vocabulary Organiser 1.7, page 10

7 Students should spend a few minutes writing a suitable ending that explains why the balloon ride was significant.

8 Students should do this exercise alone, in pairs or as a group.

9 Ask students to look for grammatical errors, spelling mistakes, punctuation errors, paragraphs, linking words, appropriate vocabulary etc, in each other's work.

10 Ask students to plan the letter in class and check their plans with them. Don't let them spend more than five minutes on this.

Vocabulary organiser 1

Photocopiable activity instructions

1 Activity 1.1 Story: The Shack

Aim: To awaken students' imaginations and storytelling abilities in English.

Instructions:

1   Photocopy 'The Shack' and fold the paper so that only the beginning of the story is showing.

2   The first student should read the start of the story and then write their own answer to the second part. The next student should do the same. Each student should fold the paper before passing it on.

3   When everyone has finished, the last person should read the (probably strange and wonderful) story aloud.

2 Activity 1.2 Try Something New!

Aim: To get students to begin to make suggestions and convince others of their ideas.

Instructions:

1   Photocopy the advertisements so that you have one for every two students. Separate the prompts at the bottom of the page and hand these prompts to three 'volunteer pairs'. These pairs should persuade the class to sign up to their activity.

2   While the pairs are preparing their presentation, tell the rest of the class to think of questions to ask about each activity.

3   Once the presentations have been given, and questions have been asked, the students can vote on which presentation was the most convincing.

Tapescript 1

Listening 1.1

Husband: Mandy! This one sounds good for Joey.
Mandy: Go on, then. What have you found?
Husband: 'A Child's First Clock ... Most children don't learn how to tell the time until they are in first grade, or beyond, but with this lovely 'no-numbers-needed' clock, even toddlers can learn the basics of timekeeping.'
Mandy: Mm. Sounds interesting. Tell me more ...
Husband: 'Developed by two mothers – a children's television presenter Noni Anderson and artist Alison Perrin – the woodland clock features a slow painted turtle for the hour hand, a faster grey rabbit for the minute hand, and a speedy red-breasted robin on the second hand' ... Blah, blah, blah. 'You can assemble a clock much like ours by <u>printing out</u> the art materials attached, and applying them to a clock from <u>a do-it-yourself kit.</u>' So, Mandy, what do you think? <u>Shall we download the attachment?</u>

Listening 1.2

Woman 1: So, what's brought this on, then?
Woman 2: Yeah, well, <u>Bill's just had enough of living in the city. It's all the stress, you know. Not only at the office itself, but when he's to-in' and fro-in' in all that traffic!</u> He's just sick of it. So, he suddenly decided to pack it all in, and make a fresh start. So, we're off to the Isle of Man, in the middle of the Irish Sea. <u>Middle of nowhere, if you ask me!</u> Still, at least it's not like moving abroad. He's taking up sheep farming, of all things! God knows if

it'll work. But you know Bill, when he sets his mind to something, there's no stopping him.
Woman 1: Well, I never! It seems a bit drastic, though.
Woman 2: He reckons it'll be good for us, like starting over. <u>All I can think of is sitting alone, with the wind howling outside. I mean, how many people stay there in the winter? We're used to the noise of the traffic. But, I've told 'im I'll give it a go. Who knows, it may be the making of us!</u>

Listening 1.3

Oliver: So, what do you think of our ideas, Jane?
Jane: Well, overall, quite acceptable, Oliver, but I'm not happy about some of the omissions. I mean, ignoring the details in the first two <u>chapters</u> means that members of the audience who haven't read the book will be left in the dark. They won't understand the reasons behind the protagonist's actions in the film.
Oliver: Yeah, but most people have read the book! It was a blockbuster, after all!
Jane: We shouldn't take that for granted, though. I feel that, as it stands, your proposal threatens to focus too much on action and <u>special effects</u>, leaving little room for character development.
Oliver: Huh! Yeah, well, you know, this is only a rough outline of the <u>scenes</u>, as yet ...
Jane: OK. But, personally, I would prefer the opening scene to include some sense of Jim's confusion and fear about what he's about to do.

Oliver: OooKaay!... But don't you think hitting the audience with the murder straight away creates suspense?

Jane: Perhaps. But it also looks like a cold-blooded, calculated murder rather than ... Look, I don't know what you got out of the book, but I wrote a psychological thriller, Oliver, and I'd like some element of the psychology to come through in the film, and not just the thriller aspect! Jim's character is a complex one, and your plans for him threaten to reduce it to a wooden stereotype!

Listening 1.4

Teacher: OK, let's brainstorm some ideas. What new experiences have you had that you clearly remember?

Student A: I tried <u>bungee jumping</u> once. I'll never forget that!

Student B: Really? That must have been terrifying. I don't even like heights. But I did <u>travel to America</u> – a totally new experience for me.

Teacher: Good – don't forget you also need to tell us why it was memorable or significant for you.

Student B: I was very impressed by the lifestyle there and I decided I wanted to improve my English enough to go and study over there.

Teacher: Excellent! What about you Vasilis?

Student C: I've been <u>swimming with dolphins</u> in the water. It was amazing. I would love to write about that, because it made me respect animals and nature.

Teacher: How wonderful! I can't wait to read about it. Massimo, what about you?

Student D: I, er, haven't had any new or exciting experiences that I can think of.

Teacher: Well ... maybe you could make one up?

Student D: Mm, well I suppose I could say <u>I have been to a rock concert.</u>

Teacher: Yes, and why would that have been memorable or significant to you?

Student D: Er – I could say that it changed my life and made me want to become a rock star.

Student A: Oh, I almost forgot. <u>I have flown in a helicopter too.</u>

Teacher: Well, we've certainly got a few ideas there.

Listening 1.5

Teacher: Ok, so you've brainstormed some ideas for your writing and chosen one. Now we need to outline the structure. What's the best way of doing that?

Student D: With paragraphs?

Teacher: That's right, Massimo. But you need to have an idea about what to say in each paragraph, and they should link together well. What's an easy way to do that?

Student D: You need to decide what the main purpose is of each paragraph.

Teacher: Good. Claudine, what would be the main purpose of the first paragraph?

Student A: Um, I think I would have to write about what made me decide to go bungee jumping in the first place.

Teacher: Ok, so for planning purposes, we could say: '<u>What led to the experience.</u>' What else could you call that ... Svetlana?

Student B: I would talk about how I prepared for my journey to America, and the hopes and fears I had.

Teacher: Good, so you could write about <u>the preparations and the background to the experience</u> then. Right, now, what about the main body of our piece? What would we need to focus on?

Student C: It would have to be about <u>the experience itself. Describing it, our feelings, what happened.</u>

Teacher: Very good Vasilis, and very important too. And what mustn't we forget?

Student B: An ending? <u>And the reason why it was significant.</u>

Student D: I would say <u>what happened afterwards, and how I felt about it later, and why it changed my life.</u>

Teacher: Excellent – so a good, strong concluding paragraph. Now we're getting somewhere.

Answer key 1

Getting started p1

1 beginning of a race; seeds germinating; launch of rocket; kickoff; swimmers diving in; marriage; ship setting sail.

2 Quiz: 1b; 2c; 3b; 4a; 5a; 6c

3 a incite, inspire, trigger, prompt, initiate, instigate, stimulate, activate, bring about, provoke; b spawn, conceive, generate, conceive, produce, engender; c set about, embark on, launch into; d set up, found

Reading pp2–3

1 Charlie Chaplin, Sean Connery, Oprah Winfrey. They are from fairly poor backgrounds but they all became very successful.

2 Chaplin first performed at the age of five. He had to work hard because neither of his parents could support him.

3 aS; bD

4 aF; bT; cT; dF; eT

5 It is also about something that had a humble beginning but became very successful.

6 The writer was put off by a teacher who tried to force her to draw in a particular way, which she found she was unable to do.

7 a They experienced mixed feelings, as in some cases, they feel their trademark is being misused. b They based it on a term coined to represent the number one followed by 100 noughts. They wanted it to signify their intention of organising information on the Internet. c at least five

8 "Google' is a play on the word 'googol', in itself a relatively young word'; b 'Coined by Milton Sirotta in the mid-twentieth century, googol refers to the number one followed by 100 zeros'; c 'Google, the company, has taken exception in some cases to what it calls "inappropriate usage of its trademark"'; d 'Google, the company, has taken exception in some cases to what it calls "inappropriate usage of its trademark".'

9 1 She felt frustrated that she couldn't satisfy her teacher/She felt that her teacher had destroyed her creative inspiration
2 To teach students to change the way they look at things

Language development p4

1 *'Back to the drawing board'* means to begin something again, usually because the first attempt has failed or is unsuccessful. Here it can also be used literally to mean to return to drawing sketches. Other phrases in the text are *'make a fresh start'*, *'start from scratch'*.
2 a fresh; b leaf; c square; d scratch; e slate
3 They all convey the meaning of starting again from the beginning.
4 1 leaf; 2 scratch; 3 fresh
5 1 made his debut; 2 make a name for himself; 3 make ends meet
6 a '(I found it hard to) be (heard)' b '(That) means there are (two of us)' c '(No) I'd like to change that to (a large one)' d '(... flooding) was important enough to be written about in (the national newspapers)' e '(He) forced me to (stay in)'
7 1 made it; 2 made like; 3 make or break; 4 make a go of; 5 made the best of it; 6 make do with

Grammar p5

2 a Present simple: we know, is still only speculation; It seems to be
b Present perfect simple: there have been countless theories; we have collected, we have been able to offer; have only led
c Past simple: the universe began, we once called
d Present continuous: is still being questioned
e Present perfect continuous: we have been searching
3 a present perfect continuous; b present simple; c past simple; d present perfect simple; e present continuous
4 1 past simple; 2 past continuous; 3 past perfect simple; 4 past simple; 5 past simple; 6 past perfect continuous; 7 past simple; 8 past continuous; 9 past simple; 10 past

continuous; 11 past continuous; 12 past simple
5 a He had been looking/had looked at the stars but he hadn't found any new planets. b He realised that the universe had been growing for 13 billion years. c It all started/It had all started with a big bang, according to some scientists. d We have been searching for answers and we are still looking. e The universe started to expand a very long time ago.
6 The notion that the universe had always existed in the same state, because he realised that the universe was actually getting bigger and so it couldn't have always been the same.
7 1 was expanding (possibly also 'is expanding'); 2 had been put forward; 3 had postulated; 4 had sprung; 5 has no dimensions; 6 exploded; 7 is still going on; 8 has been expanding; 9 was coined; 10 was trying; 11 stuck; 12 is

Listening p6

2 Books: front cover, first edition, chapter, paperback, extract, scene
Cinema: trailer, animation, excerpt, special effects, scene, soundtrack
Internet: web page, online, surfing, download, extract, print out
3 1 advertisement, for, book, design, do-it-yourself kit; 2 reading from, magazine, catalogue, Internet
4 1b 2c
2 '... by printing out ... (materials) attached ... Shall we download the attachment?'
5 + 6 Answers will vary. Something like: 'two people talking about moving (house)' 1 the husband wants to change their lifestyle 2 sceptical and uncertain
7 'middle of nowhere, if you ask me!', 'of all things!', 'God knows if it'll work!', 'All I can think of is sitting alone ...'
8 aF; bF; cT; dF
9 Any of the words from the cinema, and any of the words from the book section.
10 c

Use of English pp6–7

1 The second sentence indicates that he started to learn to drive when he was 17 and is still learning to drive,

whereas the first sentence suggests that he started and finished learning to drive when he was 17.
2 1b; 2a;
1a = incorrect. It means 'I want a short break, but not a change of job.' c = incorrect, as it means 'I've been teaching for some time, and I'm looking for another *teaching* position.'
2b = incorrect. He didn't go to live on an island *because* he was successful. c = incorrect. We don't know if he was successful on the island.
3 1 has been driving since
2 deliver an urgent message to
3 make up your mind
4 not been easy to
5 had not/hadn't expected the test to
6 is suspected of killing/having killed
7 has taken up fishing as
8 is she taking karate lessons
4 1T; 2F; 3T; 4T; 5F; 6F; 7T; 8F
5 1 = 2; 2 = 4; 3 = 3; 4 = 2; 5 = 8; 6= 7; 7 = 3; 8 = 6

Speaking pp7–8

1 They all depict the start of a new activity.
2 Why did you decide to do that? What was it like? Did you like it? Were you scared?
5 1g; 2b; 3a; 4d; 5e; 6c; 7f

Writing pp8–9

1 1 brainstorming 2 outlining 3 selecting vocabulary 4 writing 5 checking
2 A letter. A description of a new or unusual experience and the reasons why it was memorable or significant.
4 Five
5 Paragraph 1: Introduction: the preparations and the background to the experience
Paragraph 2 Main body: the experience itself – description/ feelings/outcome
Paragraph 3: Concluding paragraph: reasons why it was significant/ what happened afterwards/how I felt about it later/why it changed my life.
6 There are no paragraphs. It ends abruptly and doesn't answer second part of question.

8 a It was a beautiful summer's day with a fresh crisp wind blowing from the east – ideal weather for a balloon ride.
b the airfield getting smaller and the horizon expanding as we ascended over the nearby village. It was amazing to see how quickly it started to look like a toy town. Before long, everything below was just a patchwork of fields and roads. c I had expected to be frightened but as the balloon rose gently into the air I was amazed at how safe I felt. We were floating effortlessly in a blue sky with only the sound of the wind buffeting round the balloon itself. It was breathtaking. We were reluctant to return to earth.

Vocabulary organiser p10

1.1 a launched; b inaugurated; c set off; d launched/set up/ established; e initiated; f originated; g instigated; h embarked on
1.2 a inaugurate; b embark on; c set off (on); d originate; e instigate
1.3 1 invaluable; 2 hoarse; 3 resounding; 4 establishments
1.4 1 fledgling; 2 coined; 3 trademark; 4 predecessor; 5 curb the tide
1.5 a make it up to; b make for; c make up; d make off; e make out; f make up for; g make into; h make something of
1.7 1 crisp; 2 expanding; 3 ascended; 4 patchwork; 5 buffeting

Bank of English

1 material: N.COUNT.: sewing materials, artist's materials N.UNCOUNT.: writing material ADJ.: material world, material evidence, material witness
2 matter: N.UNCOUNT.: printed matter, grey matter, subject matter N.COUNT.: a business matter, personal matter, trivial matter PHRASES: what's the matter?, a matter of concern/importance/ urgency/principle, it's no laughing matter

Story – The Shack

Beginning	Billy and Jo always walked home from school along the footpath that ran through the old wood, but one day, as they were walking, they noticed a small wooden shack that seemed to have suddenly appeared in the middle of the path. It definitely hadn't been there the day before and there was definitely something strange about it.
Why did it look strange? Describe it.	
What did Billy say to Jo?	
What did they do next?	
Where did they suddenly find themselves?	
Who or what did they meet there?	
How did they react?	
What did Jo say?	
What did they do next?	
How did it end?	

Try something new!

Come fly with us in our beautiful balloon!

Feeling daring? Want excitement? Try rafting!

Feel free as a bird... fly like one!

World Balloon Tours

- Approved balloon ride company
- Operate our own balloons
- Checked regularly
- Experienced, qualified pilots
- Ride lasts about one and a half hours, but allow four hours for the whole experience
- Dependent on weather conditions
- Minimum age limit of 6 years; passengers aged 6–14 must be accompanied by an adult
- Fly to approximately 6000 feet
- Excellent opportunity for photographers

> **Price $220–275**

Water Rat Rafting Ltd

- Approved rafting company
- Equipment provided – new rafts, top quality Coast Guard approved life jackets, helmets for more difficult waters, waterproof bags and boxes
- Age no problem
- Day trips offered – introductory gentle floats down the river, or more adventurous ones for a white water novice
- Groups of four on each raft, with two instructors
- All instructors are qualified, and experienced in the local waters
- Trips dependent on weather conditions

> **Price $100 for one day trip**

Condor Tours

- Approved paragliding company
- Choice of introductory tandem flight:
  1. fly with the instructor on one glider or
  2. a one-day introductory lesson
- Age no problem
- Choice of coastal or mountain flight, lasting at least 20 minutes
- Amazing views – tandem passengers may bring a small camera
- Should wear protective footwear, and warm clothing
- Trips dependent on weather

> **Price:**
> **1 tandem flight $150–180**
> **2 introductory lesson $200**

2 A child's world

Lesson planner

Fast lane: 3 x 1.5 hour lessons = 4.5 hours per unit
(total course = 72–76 hours)

Lesson	Time	Classwork	Exam Booster (EB) homework
4	1.5 hours	Getting started, Reading + Vocab. Organiser (VO)	Getting started + Reading
5	1.5 hours	Check homework, Lang. develop., Grammar, Listening + VO	Lang. develop., Grammar + Listening
6	1.5 hours	Check homework, Speaking, Use of English, Writing + VO	Use of English, Speaking, Writing + Coursebook Writing task

Slow lane: 4 x 1.5 hour lessons = 6 hours per unit
(total course = 96–100 hours)

Lesson	Time	Classwork	EB homework
5	1.5 hours	Getting started, Reading, VO + photocopiable 1	Getting started + Reading
6	1.5 hours	Check homework, Lang. develop., Grammar + VO	Lang. develop. + Grammar
7	1.5 hours	Check homework, Listening, Speaking + VO	Listening + Speaking
8	1.5 hours	Check homework, Use of English, Writing + photocopiable 2	Use of English, Writing + Coursebook Writing task

Before you begin

Aim: To get students thinking and talking about their early childhood, and to provide oral practice without preparation. You may like to record what the students say.

Prepare slips of paper with each containing a suggested topic beforehand. Ask students to randomly choose a slip, and have each present a one minute spontaneous speech about the topic.

Suggestions: Your earliest memory; Your favourite toy; A frightening experience you had as a small child; Your first day at school; An exciting experience you had as a small child; Learning to ride a bike; Your favourite children's story; Your favourite children's TV programme; Things you didn't like as a small child; An important person in your childhood.

Topic: children, playing, childhood experiences

This unit discusses children's activities and childhood experiences.

Unit 2 Wordlist

antidote	imply	poisonous
bishop	incentive	reflect
bound	inept	retreat
braces	infer	revolutionary
childminder	innovative	rigours
clamber	inspirational	sedentary
commune	invoke	skip
conception	jump	slide
curriculum	lottery	snugly
detrimental	march	squally
disinclination	mundane	sterilised
donor	nondescript	stride
downplay	nursery	stroll
drench	oblivious	thrive
egocentric	offspring	tiptoe
envisage	outplay	trampoline
evoke	paddle	underlying
exhibit	perception	wade
fungus	pioneer	wander
heave	playmate	waterproof
hop	playwright	welly boots
horseplay	pledge	wheelbarrow
		wrestle

Getting started

1   Photos show children doing a variety of activities, leaving plenty of scope for your students to use the target vocabulary in discussion.

2   🎧 2.1 Tell students they are going to hear one man speaking. Ask them to read through the words in the box from exercise 1 again. Play Listening 2.1, and allow students time to note the words they hear. Give feedback.

3   Class discussion. Aim to allow students to develop their arguments if one particular statement seems to arouse their interest. However, encourage students to express a view on each of the statements.

Motivating class discussion

Students are often reluctant to speak in the early stages of a new course, particularly if the teacher is new to them. One way of getting them to respond is to tell a story of your own experience as a child that your students may relate to. For example, in this unit, telling them tales of you and your siblings or friends playing outside, and the kinds of games you used to play, would encourage them to respond in kind.

→ Vocabulary Organiser 2.1, page 20

Reading: gapped texts

Outdoor nurseries

The idea for outdoor nurseries first developed in Denmark in the 1950s and has spread across Scandinavia to Germany and Switzerland. In Germany there are 700 Waldkindergärten, or woodland nurseries. None of the countries where they've taken off experience anything like 'tropical weather', but they are increasingly popular with parents worried about the cloistered, sedentary lifestyle of the modern child.

1   If students haven't already done so in the Getting started section, ask them to look at the photographs and describe what they can see. Ask them to look at the newspaper headline and predict what they think the article will be about.

Reading extension

Give help with vocabulary if necessary. Ask them questions such as:

What is a nursery?

What kind of building or location are nurseries usually run in?

Why do you think the parents are enthusiastic about it?

What is an antidote to something?

Why might it be used here?

Predicting information

Being able to predict what a text is about is a useful skill that students should aim to develop. Looking at clues such as key words, headlines, pictures or headings can help students predict the content of a text or a listening tapescript.

2   Ask students to read the paragraphs before and after the gap and summarise the content of each. Ask them to

Identifying connectors

Direct students to look at the Spotlight. After they have read it, ask them to complete exercises 3, 4 and 5. This will help them identify the connectors in the paragraphs, before attempting exercise 6. Check the answers with the class.

6   Students should now attempt this task individually or in pairs. Stress that they must read all three options before making their choices. When they have finished, take a class vote – how many people chose A, B or C? Ask students to justify their reasons.

7   Ask students to read the rubric. Explain that normally in this part of the exam, students would need to find the paragraph that fits each gap, but first, they are being asked to choose between two headings, a or b, which best summarises what might be missing in each gap.

8   This exercise is meant to test students' understanding of the text so far. You can either give it to them now as a class activity, or after they have read the whole text (i.e., after exercise 9).

9   Ask students to look back at their answer for exercise 7, paragraph 1 – Monimail Tower. Ask them to quickly scan the missing paragraphs to see if they can find one that matches this theme. Explain that 'scanning' is another useful technique to use when you are looking for specific information in a longer text. They should be able to find G quite quickly as the first word of the paragraph stands out.

10   Ask students to read the remaining paragraphs more carefully, and employ the techniques they've already learnt, to find which paragraphs go where. This could be done in class as a timed activity, or set for homework.

→ Vocabulary Organiser 2.2, page 20

Language development:
'parts of the body' idioms

1   Ask students to look back at paragraph D on page 13. Elicit how the children seem to feel about playing outside in the rain. Demonstrate how students can guess the meaning of unknown words and phrases by using the context.

2   Allow students time to look at the cartoons and relate them to the phrases in the captions.

3   Tell students there are many 'parts of the body' idioms. Ask them to look at the ones in the box, then see if they can complete the sentences with one of them.

→ Vocabulary Organiser 2.3 + 2.4, page 20

Language development extension

→ Vocabulary Organiser 2.5, page 20

Draw the figure of a person on the board, with arrows off it. Write in the phrases from exercise 2 on page 14. Then, elicit the other idioms covered in exercise 3. Ask students to draw the figure in their vocabulary notebooks, and add the idioms around it.

Find out more body idioms by asking student pairs to use their dictionaries – *pull someone's leg, play it by ear, lose heart, put someone's back up, pay through the nose, an eyesore, off someone's head* etc.

Phrasal verbs: *pick up*

4   Encourage students to look back at the text again to find the phrasal verb. They should then try to find the closest match.

5   Students should do this exercise individually or in pairs. Encourage them to use a dictionary whenever they need to.

→ Vocabulary Organiser 2.6, page 20

Key word: *run*

6   Read the sentence from the text. Ask the students to think how many other things can *run* or *be run*. Get them to tick their answers off in the box. Remember, when looking at common or well-known words such as *run*, students should make notes of any new meanings or usages that they come across, especially in idioms or fixed phrases. Such obscure meanings of common words can be tested in Paper 3, parts 1, 2 and 4.

7   This exercise can be done individually or in pairs.

Grammar: passive forms

1   Read through the sentences with the class. Elicit the passive structures. Make sure that students notice there are two in the first sentence.

2   Ask students to look back at the text on page 13. The sentence appears in the final paragraph before gap 6. Allow students time to consider the contextual meaning of *can* here.

3   Ask students to complete the task individually before checking the answers as a class.

Verbs with passive forms

Tell your students that there are some verbs that take more than one passive form. Tell them to look at the Spotlight. You may like to direct them to the Grammar Reference section now, for further examples before they do exercise 4.

4   Ask them to complete exercise 4, by rewriting the sentences in two different ways.

5   Tell students to rewrite the sentences using a suitable passive form.

→ Grammar Reference 2.1, page 170

Passive form with *have* and *get*

6   Elicit the uses of *have* in each case. Explain that *get* can be used to replace *have* as a causative form.

Grammar extension

Draw some 'before' and 'after' pictures on the board, or prepare and photocopy some, of such things as:

(before) someone with long hair → (after) the same person coming out of a hairdresser's with short hair

(before) someone with a lot of shopping and her handbag on the ground → (after) a man running off down the street with the handbag

(before) a shop owner cleaning his shop window → (after) the broken window (perhaps from a brick being thrown at it).

Ask students to talk about them, using *have* or *get* to describe the 'after' pictures.

7   Elicit the answers. Make sure that your students understand that *let* has to become 'be allowed' in the passive, and that 'make someone do' becomes 'be made to do'.

Using the Grammar Reference section

Encourage your students to make use of the Grammar Reference at the back of their books whenever they address the Grammar section in each unit. They may also find it useful for reference when attempting the exercises in the Exam Booster.

Listening: sentence completion

PAPER 4, PART 2 Predicting information

1 Read through the rubric and questions with students. Make sure they understand what the task requires of them. For exercise 1 point out that several answers are possible. Read through the tips and discuss the different ways that the answer can be narrowed down.

2 Again point out that there are many possibilities here. The point is to get students to focus on various options, so they know what to listen out for.

3 🎧 2.2 Ask students to read the rubric and then read through the questions in the same way as they did for exercise 2. Check to see what information they can predict. Then they should complete questions 1–8.

Speaking: using visual prompts

1 Ask the students to look at the pictures on page 193, and consider whether small children (aged one to five) should be allowed to do the activities shown.

Expressing opinions

2 Having discussed the pictures in exercise 1, students should have had the opportunity to collect their thoughts and form their own clear opinion. This exercise gives them the chance to place themselves in the examination situation, and gain an idea of the timing. Make it clear to them that the examiner will only allow them a specific amount of time to speak, before interrupting them. Students should not worry if they are stopped before completing what they want to say.

TEACHING IN PRACTICE

Classroom management for speaking practice
A lot depends on whether you have access to a language laboratory or not. This section lends itself to the lab, as students will be able to tackle the task simultaneously, with the teacher monitoring them. If a lab is not available, you will need to conduct exercises 2 and 3 pair by pair. Ask the rest of the class to note down useful phrases and words that each pair uses in their answers, and elicit these to make a list to add to their Vocabulary Organisers at the end of the session.

3 🎧 2.4 Allow students time to look at the pictures on page 193, then play Listening 2.4 with the questions. Each pair should practise answering the questions, and the rest of the class should note down any useful language they hear.

Use of English: multiple-choice cloze

PAPER 3, PART 1 Recognising option types
The aim of this Spotlight is to highlight the different task types commonly found in a multiple-choice cloze test. Read the rubric and go through the tasks with the class. Encourage students to make notes in their vocabulary notebooks.

1 Focus on how these words have a similar meaning but are not all used in the same context.
2 Focus on how these words look or sound similar but have quite different meanings. For b, ask students to consult their dictionaries and find the meanings of the words before writing their own sentences.
3 Focus on the lexical contexts of these words.
4 Focus on the grammatical requirements of the sentence (singular and plural verbs).

Use of English extension

Ask students to find an article or piece of writing in English of a suitable length (about 250 words) and to choose ten items of vocabulary within the text that could be tested. For each word they choose they should use their dictionaries and find one correct synonym that can be used to replace it, and one word that is similar in some way, but which would be incorrect if used in the same context.

5 Ask students to read through the passage. Encourage them to expand on the subject, by talking about their own experiences with colour when they were small. Did their parents try to dress them in particular colours, or paint their walls in blue or pink, for example?

BACKGROUND

Psychologists believe that colour is very important to children. Children respond to bright colours at an early age, particularly the primary colours – red, blue and yellow. As they get older, their awareness and appreciation of colour broadens. Very young children respond to colourful objects, and learn to associate particular colours with certain things. For example: yellow – sun, bananas, lemons; red – apples, tomatoes; green – grass, trees.

Ask your students to attempt the task individually, then compare their answers with a partner. Don't expect students to know them all, as some of the items are difficult. Elicit the meanings of known words and distractors, and explanations of why they are wrong. Then ask students to use their dictionaries to find the items that were difficult, and explanations of why the distractors don't work in this context.

Writing: a review

Showing your class examples

It is often a good idea for students to see examples of authentic pieces of writing relating to the kind of task they are going to do. Most students will be aware of and may have read reviews of films, books and music, but they might not have seen reviews of places to visit, or of exhibitions/concerts etc. Try to show them examples of different types of review, some positive, and some slightly more critical.

1   Ask students to read the question, and underline the two things they need to do when answering it.

2   Emphasise the importance of answering the whole of the question. Write the following items on the board: Organisation, Use of language, Full answer to the question. Ask students to comment on these areas when looking at the sample answer.

Sentence development

The aim of this Spotlight is to draw students' attention to the need to vary their language and style when writing. Advise them that use of the passive can help them achieve a more formal style, but they should avoid overdoing it!

3   Tell your students to look at the sentences marked in green in the sample. Ask them to rewrite these using suitable passive structures. For weaker classes, provide them with the first one as an example.

4   Tell students they must choose the most suitable conclusion for the sample review. Elicit from them what the conclusion should include, such as a recommendation.

In other words

5   Ask your students to make the review from exercise 2 more descriptive, by varying the language presented in brackets [ ]. Students don't need to use all the words and phrases in the box, but should aim to use some of them effectively.

Answers will vary. Suggested answer:

My family and I recently visited a toy museum. It has been dedicated to a local family who were among the earliest toy makers in my country, and has been built on the site of the family's factory. Their toys were constructed mainly out of wood or metal, but the museum exhibits reflect developments in toy making, from then until now.

The Bryant Toy Museum is an innovative, interactive playground for children. When we arrived, we were presented with a notebook called 'My Toy Scrapbook.' The cover shows a photograph of the original factory. As we wandered through the museum, we were encouraged to fill it with pictures, stamps and notes, if we wanted. Each room is cleverly designed to look like scenes from particular periods in history. For example, one room has been created to look like a scene from a Charles Dickens novel, another from around the time of the Second World War, and then suddenly, you're in a room filled with all kinds of electronic games. My brother and I found this room fascinating. In every room, children are encouraged to play creatively with some of the toys, and when they come to the final room, they are shown how to construct their own toys, if they want.

Word limit reminder

Remind students of the word limit for this task. Note that if you add paragraph c from exercise 4 to the suggested answer above, you have a total of 249 words, which is well within the word limit. If your students are experiencing difficulties, you may like to present this as a model answer.

6   Check that your students know the meaning of the words provided. Elicit their response to the brochures illustrated down the right-hand side of the page.

7   Set this exercise as homework, but perhaps ask the students to underline the points they need to include in their answer before they go away to tackle the task.

Photocopiable activity instructions

1 **Activity 2.1 Find the accomplice**

Aim: To practise use of the passive structures for speculation – *he is thought to be ...* etc.

Instructions:

1 Divide the class into pairs. Give each pair a copy of the photocopy.

2 Tell them to read the information about the theft, and look at the 'photofit' of one of the suspects.

3 The students must give a description of the man's accomplice. They should choose someone else in the class, without that person knowing, and create a description of them, using structures like '*It is believed the suspect had an accomplice. This person is thought to be ... etc.*'

4 When each pair is ready, choose one to stand in front of the class and give a description of the accomplice. The rest of the class has to guess who is being described. Then the next pair does the same, and so on.

FIND THE ACCOMPLICE

This man is believed to have broken into the local school last night. Items of sports equipment were stolen, and several classrooms were vandalised. The suspect is believed to be of average height, approximately 1.65m, and is thought to have been wearing jeans and a black sweater. It is believed the suspect had an accomplice. Not much is known about this person, and witnesses did not get a clear view of them, but this person is thought to be ...

_____
_____
_____
_____
_____

2 **Activity 2.2 Do you see what I see?**

Aim: To practise speaking skills of description and comparison and to practise using the verbs of movement learnt in this unit.

Instructions:

1 Divide class into pairs and give each student in each pair, one part of the photocopy – either A or B. They shouldn't see each other's page.

2 Tell the students that there are eight differences between the two sets of pictures. Students should take turns describing what they can see in each picture, for example: *I can see a little boy climbing a tree*, there are two boys arm wrestling.

3 They continue until they have identified eight differences in the two sets of pictures.

4 They should aim to use as many of the verbs from the unit as they can. (You have the option of not including them when you cut the photocopy.)

DO YOU SEE WHAT I SEE?

A

Verbs to use: bound clamber climb heave hop jump leap march paddle skip
slide stride stroll swing tiptoe wade wander wrestle

B

Verbs to use: bound clamber climb heave hop jump leap march paddle skip
slide stride stroll swing tiptoe wade wander wrestle

Tapescript 2

Listening 2.1

Man: I remember the time we went to the seaside for the day. Er, I must have been about eight. We had to <u>clamber</u> over rocks to get to the beach, with Father <u>heaving</u> this huge picnic basket all the way. Mother was worried he would fall, <u>slide</u> down into the sea and get the sandwiches wet, so she kept shouting instructions to him. The funny thing was that when we eventually sat down to eat, a huge, wet dog <u>bounded</u> up to us and sprayed sand and water all over the sandwiches, so they were spoiled anyway!

We kids didn't care, though, and had a great time. My brother and I <u>wrestled</u> with each other on the sand, and played football with Father, while the girls went <u>skipping</u> off down to the water's edge to look for shells. Mother – not much of a swimmer – <u>paddled</u> in the shallows, while Father boldly <u>waded</u> out into deep water and showed off his swimming skills. Then both of them returned to our spot on the beach, and lay down for a peaceful nap. Not for long with my brother around! He couldn't resist such a golden opportunity. So, filling a bucket with water, he <u>tiptoed</u> over to our dozing parents, and poured ice-cold sea water all over them! He paid for it, though, because, as he ran away, he trod on a piece of broken glass, and cut his foot! So he was forced to <u>hop</u> on one leg all the way back to the car, and, not only face Father's anger, but his brother and sisters' too, at having their glorious day cut short!

Listening 2.2

Anthropologist: We still don't fully understand how or why human language came about, although there are certainly a good number of theories. One main theory suggests that when men became hunters, they needed to develop a language in order to share hunting tactics with one another during the chase, despite the fact that most carnivorous animals – even those that hunt in packs – find <u>silence</u> to be a distinct advantage. And yet historians are agreed that the first spoken languages must have been very crude. How then could they have been of any <u>practical use</u>?

There is, however, one theory that proposes that it wasn't men who first used language. It wasn't even women. It was in fact children who invented it, and taught it to their parents. The truth is that fully grown adults actually lack the ability to learn to speak. Only children can do it. People that have never been exposed to any kind of spoken language before the age of five (and there are a handful of documented cases) have never been able to learn to speak at all, despite concerted efforts to teach them. Similarly, children that are born deaf may have difficulty learning to make verbal sounds because <u>they've never heard them</u>.

Children's natural propensity for learning languages is taken as read. They don't have to be taught their first language – they only have to hear it spoken around them. During the first four or <u>five</u> <u>years</u> of life a child can learn several languages simultaneously, without being taught, without any apparent effort.

Newborn babies all over the world have their own repertoire of involuntary sounds which are useful for <u>communicating to the mother</u> their most basic needs – hunger, pain or the need for attention. This is true of the young of most mammals. However, between three and four months of age the human baby begins to emit new sounds and before long, will start to 'babble'. This baby talk varies from <u>country to country</u>, suggesting that the baby is responding to, and trying to imitate, the sounds around him. Before long, he learns to control the sounds. He gets a response. He says 'ma' and mother responds. This could be the reason why the word for mother is so similar in almost every language. It's one of the <u>first syllables</u> a human child can voluntarily produce. Can we be so sure that baby is really imitating mum or could it be the other way round? Next, he is inventing his own words for objects and his mother is using them too. Language is born. Perhaps this is why girls often learn to speak sooner and more fluently than boys, because at one time the ability to develop language was essential to the <u>mother-infant relationship</u>?

Listening 2.3

Interlocutor: Student one, here are your pictures. They show children doing different activities. I'd like you to compare two of them, and say whether you think these activities are suitable for young children, and how they might be feeling about doing them.
Interlocutor: Thank you.
Interlocutor: Student two, at what age do you think children should be allowed to do these activities?

Interlocutor: Thank you.

Listening 2.4

Interlocutor: Student one, here are your pictures. They show children doing different activities. I'd like you to compare two of them, and say how the children might be feeling.
Interlocutor: Student two, when do you think a young person is mature enough to do these activities?

Answer key 2

Getting started p11

2 clamber; heaving; slide; bounded; wrestled; skipping; paddled; waded; tiptoed; hop

Reading pp12–13

1 The article is about an innovative new kind of nursery that looks after children in an out of doors environment, in all kinds of weather conditions.

2 The middle paragraph would probably contain more information about the two boys, Freddie and Alastair, and the reasons why they are playing outside.

3 a Freddie and Alastair; b the pair; c their childminder

4 a Cathy Bache; b their; c the children; d nursery or kindergarten

5 They both talk about the boys and doing physical activities out of doors.

6 Option B. It is the correct paragraph because it focuses on the two boys, what they are wearing, and introduces the nursery experiment that is also mentioned in the next paragraph. Also the descriptive style of writing seems to fit.

7 1b; 2a; 3b; 4a; 5a; 6a

8 aF; bT; cF; dT; eF; fT; gF; hF; iF; jT

9 G – Monimail Tower: Monimail (first word of the paragraph)

10 2D; 3C; 4A; 5E; 6B

Language development p14

1 [The bad weather] doesn't bother the children at all.

2 a2; b3; c1

3 a see eye to eye; b all fingers and thumbs; c pain in the neck; d tongue in cheek; e bat an eyelid; f wet behind the ears

4 4 catch an illness

5 a2; b4; c8; d1; e7; f6; g5; h3

6 The following words cannot *run* or *be run*: an idea, a party, politics, a message, a conversation

7 a run an errand; b run counter to; c run a story; d run for office; e run a risk

Grammar p15

1 '[the children] will be taught and entertained'; '[their curriculum] will be devoted to'.

2 c

3 1d; 2b; 3a; 4c

4 a Children have been reported stealing from the school cafeteria; It has been reported that children have been stealing from the school cafeteria.
b A dolphin is believed to have rescued the baby; It is believed that a dolphin rescued the baby.

5 a is considered to be too young
b has been rumoured that the children's playground is going
c against underage drinking are thought to be
d is suspected of breaking into
e is estimated to have increased
f is said that the missing boy was a loner and didn't have
g is believed that she went missing somewhere between the bus stop

6 1b; 2a

7 I am allowed to have friends to stay at the weekend; I was made to do my homework before I could go out.

Listening p16

1 For example: temperature, weather, conditions, light etc.

2 a adjective, positive (suitable, safe, reliable, interesting etc)
b adverb/adverbial phrase (temporarily, at the moment etc)
c noun (pollution, radiation, chemicals etc)

3 1 silence
2 (practical) use
3 exposed to
4 four to five; five years
5 communicate
6 countries
7 first
8 relationship

Use of English p17

1 a Not aware or conscious of something, having no knowledge, oblivious to.
b D cannot be used in the sentence. A, B and C can all be followed by 'of'
c D can be used as it is usually followed by a noun.

2 a B 'Perception' means point of view, way of seeing something.

3 1D; 2C; 3A; 4B

4 A, B and C. D could not be used as it requires a singular verb.

5 1B; 2A; 3D; 4B; 5B; 6C; 7B; 8B; 9A; 10C; 11B; 12A

Writing pp18–19

1 Students should underline the following: '*describing what there is to see and do there; you recommend it to other people and why.*'

2 *Organisation* – the student has organised his writing into paragraphs, and describes the museum, and what you can do there in a clear manner.
Use of language – the language is correct, but the structures lack variety, and are rather simplistic, with no use of the passive.
Does it answer the question fully? No, because the student fails to include a recommendation in his answer.

3 They have dedicated it = it has been dedicated to; they have built the museum = the museum has been built; They made toys mainly out of wood or metal = Toys were made mainly out of wood or metal; they gave us = we were given; people encouraged us to fill it = we were encouraged to fill it; They designed each room = Each room was designed; they have created one room = one room has been created; they encourage children to play = children are encouraged to play; some people show the children = the children are shown …

4 c – It is the only one which actually recommends the museum to others.

Vocabulary organiser 2

2.1 1 clambered; 2 bounded; 3 wrestling; 4 waded; 5 hopped; 6 slide; 7 paddled; 8 heaved;

2.2 1 seafarers; 2 squally; 3 pioneers; 4 disinclination; 5 oblivious to; 6 thrive; 7 toxin; 8 sedentary

2.3 1 neck; 2 foot; 3mouth; 4 head; 5 shoulder

2.4 a a pain in the neck; b wet behind the ears; c tongue in cheek; d see eye to eye; e (don't) bat an eyelid

2.6 1 Pick up the pieces: do what you can to recover from a bad situation; 2 Pick somebody's brain: ask for help with a problem; 3 Take your pick: choose from a group; 4 Pick holes in something: criticise something; 5 Pick your way: walk very carefully to avoid obstacles; 6 Pick-me-up: something someone does or has when they are feeling tired/unwell; 7 Pickpocket: a thief who steals from your person; 8 Picky: someone who is difficult to please; 9 Pick through: examine something closely; 10 Pick over: look through something.

Bank of English

1 fair play: when everyone plays by the rules without cheating; foul play: when someone breaks the rules or cheats; horseplay: when someone plays boisterously. Add: *airplay, playback, play off, playtime* (uncountable nouns)

2 playboy: someone who likes to flirt with lots of women; playmate: someone that you can play with; playwright: someone who writes plays

3 downplay: to underemphasise the importance of something; outplay: to try to do better than a competitor. Add: *play down* (phrasal verb)

4 play on words: a pun or joke with language; plug-and-play: an electronic game. Add: *play act* (phrase)

FIND THE ACCOMPLICE

This man is believed to have broken into the local school last night. Items of sports equipment were stolen, and several classrooms were vandalised. The suspect is believed to be of average height, approximately 1.65m, and is thought to have been wearing jeans and a black sweater. It is believed the suspect had an accomplice. Not much is known about this person, and witnesses did not get a clear view of them, but this person is thought to be ...

_____

_____

_____

_____

_____

PHOTOCOPIABLE 2.1

DO YOU SEE WHAT I SEE?

A

Verbs to use: bound clamber climb heave hop jump leap march paddle skip
slide stride stroll swing tiptoe wade wander wrestle

- ✂ - -

B

Verbs to use: bound clamber climb heave hop jump leap march paddle skip
slide stride stroll swing tiptoe wade wander wrestle

20 | UNIT **2**   PHOTOCOPIABLE 2.2   © 2010 Heinle, a part of Cengage Learning

3 Are you game?

Lesson planner

Fast lane: 3 x 1.5 hour lessons = 4.5 hours per unit
(total course = 72–76 hours)

Lesson	Time	Classwork	Exam Booster (EB) homework
7	1.5 hours	Getting started, Reading + Vocab. Organiser (VO)	Getting started + Reading
8	1.5 hours	Check homework, Lang. develop., Grammar, Listening + VO	Lang. develop., Grammar + Listening
9	1.5 hours	Check homework, Speaking, Use of English, Writing + VO	Use of English, Speaking, Writing + Coursebook Writing task

Slow lane: 4 x 1.5 hour lessons = 6 hours per unit
(total course = 96–100 hours)

Lesson	Time	Classwork	EB homework
9	1.5 hours	Getting started, Reading, VO + photocopiable 1	Getting started + Reading
10	1.5 hours	Check homework, Lang. develop., Grammar + VO	Lang. develop. + Grammar
11	1.5 hours	Check homework, Listening, Speaking + VO	Listening + Speaking
12	1.5 hours	Check homework, Use of English, Writing + photocopiable 2	Use of English, Writing + Coursebook Writing task

Before you begin

Write the following list of activities on the board:

cycling, sailing, kayaking, horse riding, aerobics, dancing, jogging, motor racing, swimming, football, tennis, mountaineering, hiking

Ask your students to place them in order, from the most dangerous to the least. Then elicit from them which activities they already do, and which they would be willing to try. Discuss how daring they think they are.

Draw their attention to the first page of the unit. Elicit the meaning of the title, 'Are you game?' If students find this difficult, use one of the activities above, which some students consider risky, but some are willing to try, and go round the class, asking if they are game.

Topic: endurance sports, taking risks

In recent years, there has been a rapid increase in fascination for endurance sports and extreme sports. Some of your students may do such activities, but others may not like them at all. This unit endeavours to take both groups into account, by focusing on the question of risk taking in general.

Unit 3 Wordlist

adrenalin	exhilarating	noncommittal
bodyboarding	extricate	petrified
culminate	gruelling	precariously
daft	guts	prostrate
din	hang gliding	reassuring
dismissive	kite landboarding	stake
dissident	masochist	triathlon
endurance	nauseated	white water rafting

Getting started

1   Ask students to look at the activities listed in the box. Elicit the meanings of any unknown ones. Then, ask them to match the activities with each photograph. Make sure they include the strip across the top of the page.

2   ∩ 3.1 Tell students they are going to hear three people describing how they felt doing some of the activities. Ask them to look at the words in the box. Tell them to listen to each speaker, and circle the words they hear. Play the recording.

3   ∩ 3.1 Ask students to listen again, and match what each speaker says with one of the photographed activities. Play the recording again before checking answers.

→   Vocabulary Organiser 3.1, page 30

Motivating students to respond to visual stimuli

This section aims to encourage students to respond to images. Explain to them that although they may not know some of the key vocabulary for certain images, this need not prevent them from responding to them. They can speculate how the people in the pictures feel, what it might be like to do such activities etc. You may find it useful to have some extra pictures/photographs of funny or strange situations to encourage them to use a variety of language to speculate on the people's feelings in each situation.

4   Ask students to share their stories of experiences they found either exhilarating or frightening. Explain that it doesn't have to be an experience doing one of the activities depicted. It could be their first day at school, for example, or an experience they had while on a school trip.

5   The quiz is located in the Information Files at the back of the book. Have students complete individually if time.

Reading: multiple choice

BACKGROUND

The extract used as the main text in this section is taken from Pete Goss' amazing book, *Close To The Wind*. In 1996, while competing in the Vendee Globe single-handed, round-the-world yacht race, he turned back into hurricane-force winds in order to rescue fellow competitor, Raphael Dinelli, ruining his own chances of success in the race by doing so. Dinelli was almost dead when Goss found him, but he nursed him back to health, and the two men became firm friends, subsequently racing together as a team.

1   Ask students to read through the extract quickly, and identify the victim and the rescuer. Then ask them what they think it would be like to be in this situation. If necessary, allow them time to read the extract again.

SPOTLIGHT ON READING

Understanding the writer's/narrator's attitude
2   Elicit students' views on the writer's feelings, and ask them to underline key words and phrases that help them reach their conclusions.

3   Explain to the students that this exercise is simply a multiple choice version of exercise 2. Ask them to answer the question without looking at the text, then allow them to check.

   →   Vocabulary Organiser 3.2, page 30

4   Ask students to read the first paragraph of the text on page 23, and decide what *Aqua Quorum* is. Notice that

they may decide it is a submarine, or a boat. If students are in disagreement, ask them to explain their choice before you explain which one is correct.

5   Ask the students to read through the multiple choice questions. Allow students time to complete the task. Then ask students to justify their choices, and say why the distractors are wrong.

Vocabulary extension

Explain that sometimes when we read we encounter words which are technical or very specific to the topic. It doesn't matter if we don't understand every word as we can usually get a sense of meaning from the context. Students should not be put off by technical terminology in a text. Questions do not usually focus on knowledge of these, so students should not fear them.

Write the following technical sailing terms from the text on the board:

satcom system	deck	winched in
to windward	downwind	storm jib
make headway	guardrail	helm
gybe	spreaders	rigging

Ask your students to place them in one of the following categories: Part of the boat or Sailing terminology.

Ask them if it was necessary to understand all of them in order to complete the task in exercise 5.

Answers

Part of the boat: satcom system, deck, guardrail, spreaders, storm jib, helm, rigging

Sailing terminology: to windward, make headway, gybe, downwind, winched in

   →   Vocabulary Organiser 3.3, page 30

Language development:
phrases with *up* and *down*

1   Ask students to pinpoint the target phrase in the short text on page 22. Then, elicit ideas about its meaning. Advise them to use the context of the paragraph to help them.

2   Students do this in pairs. Suggest they write their initial answers down in a separate notebook, rather than on the page, in case they make any mistakes. Set a time limit for the task.

   →   Vocabulary Organiser 3.4 + 3.5, page 30

Phrasal verbs with *take*

3   Ask your students to locate the target phrase in the text on page 23 and share their ideas about its meaning.

4   Ask students if they know any other phrasal verbs with *take*. Discuss the meaning of each phrasal verb in turn.

take on (responsibility)	agree to do a task or duty
take over (from someone)	take someone else's position when they leave
take back (something you've said)	apologise for something you've said, and admit you were wrong
take out (a subscription)	order and pay for a number of magazine issues to be sent to your home
take (something) apart	separate an object such as a machine into pieces
take to (someone)	immediately like someone when you meet them
take down (notes)	write information in a notebook
take (someone) for (someone else)	mistakenly believe that a person is someone else
take after (someone)	look or be very similar to someone else in your family
take up (an activity)	start a new activity on a regular basis

Phrases with *take*

5   Ask students to find the phrases in the page 23 text. Tell them to use the context to help them choose the meaning. Note that the phrase 'Take no prisoners' needs more explanation, as it really means 'be ruthless, and show no mercy'. The explanation on page 24 is a contextual one. You may find it useful to give a further example sentence of each: *He glanced briefly at his sister, and then did a double take. She looked so different with her new haircut!*

He wasn't sure he'd be able to beat the world record, but he decided to take no prisoners, and train six hours a day.

→   Vocabulary Organiser 3.6, page 30

Key word: *game*

6   Students do this exercise in pairs. Give feedback to their answers and explain any phrases if necessary.

7   Ask students to complete this exercise and then check their answers as a class.

Grammar: modal auxiliaries in discussion

1   This task is intended to be a warmer, and a bit of fun. Ask your students to look at the picture and speculate what it shows. They should use the modals indicated. The possibilities are quite limited, so encourage them to create negative ideas as well, such as 'It can't be a cat, because it's got long ears.' Some debate may begin between those who see a rabbit, and those who see a duck (depending on how you tilt the page).

GRAMMAR SPOTLIGHT

Speculation and suggestion

Direct students to look at the Grammar Spotlight. Read through the information with them, and provide an example sentence for each type of modal. Suggestions:

Perhaps that awful noise could be George playing his violin. (speculation)

If you don't know what to do, you could try talking to him. (suggestion)

Jane's arrived. It must be 6 o'clock! (deduction)

The phone's ringing! That will be Dad! (assumption)

→ Grammar Reference 3.1, page 171

2   Ask your students to read the rubric and the sentences. Allow them time to consider their answers. Elicit answers.

3   🎧 3.2 Tell your students they are going to hear a couple talking about why their daughter is late. Read the questions with them. They will hear some speculation, assumptions and a deduction. Play the recording twice if necessary.

Grammar extension

Ask your students to speculate what might have happened to Jane. Ask them to use the following structures: She might have been involved in … She could have had … She may not have been looking …

---

4   Before attempting exercise 4, write the following sentence from the cliff top rescue passage on page 22 on the board.

'I might be terrified, but I wasn't going to abandon another human being in need.'

Ask your students to rewrite it in their own words. Expect to hear something to the effect of 'Although I was very frightened, I was determined to help someone when they needed it'.

Direct students to the Grammar Reference section on page 171, and read through it with them. Make sure they understand what *refute* and *qualify* mean. Drill them with further examples.

Now direct your students to read the rubric for exercise 4. Allow them time to read the sentences and choose their answer.

5   Direct your students to read the rubric. Tell them that while this reflects an exam task type, the target structures are all modals. This would not happen in an actual examination.

Listening: multiple choice

EXAM SPOTLIGHT

PAPER 4, PART 3 Understanding the speaker's attitude
Direct your students to read the Exam Spotlight. Explain that multiple choice questions sometimes focus on the speaker's attitude towards the subject they are talking about.

1   Ask them to look at the rubric and tell them you are going to say the phrase in the different tones of voice indicated. They must identify your tone of voice. Do so, using a random order. Students should then try this in pairs. Ask them to practise saying the phrase to each other using the different tones. Observe from a distance, and correct only when the intonation is placed wrongly.

2   🎧 3.3 Direct your students to read the rubric. Check they understand the meaning of each attitude option (A–E). Play the recording. Allow students time to consider their answers before replaying the recording.

3   🎧 3.4 Tell your students to look at the pictures at the top of the page. Find out what they think is happening in the pictures, and why the man is holding a flag. Tell them they are going to listen to an interview with the man in the photographs. Direct them to read through the questions and elicit any unknown words.

4   Discuss as a group.

TEACHING IN PRACTICE

Listening strategies
Advise your students to try and answer as many questions as possible on the first listening. They should listen carefully the second time round, and check every question again, in case they misheard something. It is not a good idea to only concentrate on items they didn't catch first time round.

Speaking: interactive

EXAM SPOTLIGHT

PAPER 5, PART 3 Interactive task
Direct your students to read the rubric in the Spotlight. Tell them that they need to use a variety of language, and avoid simply repeating words and phrases that their partner uses.

1   Ask them to read the rubric and look at the photographs above. This could be done as an open pair task, to give students an idea of what is expected. Encourage students to express their own feelings about doing such activities.

TEACHING IN PRACTICE

Classroom management for speaking activities
Closed pairwork for speaking tasks can often be difficult to both monitor and control. It is a good idea to introduce the target task using open pairs, but warn all your students that you will invite them to respond to what has been said at random, to ensure that they listen to each other, and don't drift off into a daydream!

2   The seven drawings show various ways to improve a sports centre. Your students should use the language in the note provided to discuss whether the tactics of adding a swimming pool, bringing in loyalty cards which reward frequent visitors, introducing a cafe, adding new exercise machines, building a larger gymnasium,

extending opening hours, or adding a rock-climbing wall would be worthwhile.

Use of English: open cloze

2 This exercise allows students to practise using the different structures mentioned in the Spotlight. Ask them to read through the rubric and complete the task.

Degree of difficulty

Decrease the level: for weaker groups, allow students to work on exercise 2 in pairs.

Increase the level: for stronger students see who can find the answers first.

3 Direct students to read the passage through quickly, ignoring the gaps. Elicit what the passage is about and what 'beyond the pain barrier' means. Explain any unknown words. This task should be done individually.

Writing: a formal letter

Aim: To make students aware of the importance of using the input material in a part 1 question effectively, by identifying the target reader, the reason for writing, the information to include and the expected outcome of the letter.

1 Direct them to read the exercise rubric, and elicit their views. If necessary, prompt by asking questions such as:

'What are the dangers involved in taking students on school trips?'

'What is the value of taking students on activity holidays?'

'Should school trips be strictly educational?'

2 Direct students to read the rubric for the sample task. Ask them to decide whether the task requires a formal or informal answer.

4 Direct your students to read the sample answer to the question on page 29. They should consider register/language and organisation: has all the necessary information been included? Students should do this task individually.

5 Direct your students to read the rubric, and the 'In other words' box. For weaker students, you might find it useful to elicit the inappropriate phrases first, and then ask students to rewrite them. Elicit answers, and give feedback.

7 The aim here is to elicit the fact that the student does not support her points in any way, so they read like a list of notes. Ask students to read through the sample answer again, and decide what is missing.

8 Direct your students to read through the rubric and input material. Ask them to explain the points that they need to include in their answer. Set the task for homework.

Degree of difficulty

Decrease the level: ask a weaker class to repeat the task from exercise 3 in exercise 8 to make sure they know what is expected of them.

Increase the level: for stronger students ask them to simply prepare their answer for homework.

Photocopiable activity instructions

1 **Activity 3.1 Take it or leave it!**

Aim: To revise the different uses of phrasal verbs with *take*.

Instructions:

1   Photocopy page 30 and cut out each of the phrasal verbs and the contexts.

2   Divide the class into two teams and share the phrasal verbs between them, making sure that *take to* goes to one team, and *take down* goes to the other. Keep the contexts for you to read out.

3   Tell the teams that the phrasal verbs they are holding can be used in more than one context. They must listen to each context as you read it out, and decide, in their team, whether the context fits one of their verbs or not. If they think it does, they shout 'take it'. If they think it does not, then they shout 'leave it'. Whichever team shouts correctly first, receives two points. Record their points on the board.

4   Read out a context. If a team shouts 'take it' correctly, then give them the context, and write up the points on the board.

5   If a team shouts 'leave it' first, then place the context on your desk.

6   Each phrasal verb has three contexts, except for *take to* and *take down*, which have only two. The winners will be the team that gains the highest number of points, or the first one to find all the contexts for their phrasal verbs.

2 **Activity 3.2 Intrepid explorers**

Aim: To practise using modals for speculation and suggestion.

Instructions:

1   Separate your students into three groups (or two, if your class is small).

2   Give each group a photocopy of one of the situations and its accompanying picture.

3   Direct your students to read the information for their situation. Then, using the picture to help them, as a group, they should speculate and suggest possible solutions to their problem.

4   When they have discussed various possibilities, they should reach a decision about what to do next.

5   Each group reads out its situation, then reports its decision to the rest of the class, giving reasons for its choice.

Tapescript 3

Listening 3.1

Speaker 1: So, I said, well, I'm game, if you are. But I wish I hadn't. It was <u>terrifying</u>! The water flows so fast, with rocks appearing out of nowhere ... There's no time to think. I was <u>petrified</u>! Never again!

Speaker 2: Well, the long hours without sleep were <u>exhausting</u>, and the <u>loneliness</u> got me down occasionally, but I was <u>determined</u> not to give up, and would keep myself busy, by repairing sails and ropes, or sending faxes to folks back on dry land. Also, listening to music had a way of <u>relaxing</u> me, and was quite <u>reassuring</u>.

Speaker 3: That was <u>awesome</u>! Absolutely <u>incredible</u>! A real <u>adrenalin rush</u>! Everything happens so fast, you've got to be on your toes, and, like, keep control of both the board and the kite, otherwise you'll overturn ... and ... Man, it was so <u>exhilarating</u>!

Listening 3.2

Man: ... Right! That's everything. Are we ready to go?
Woman: Jane still hasn't arrived. It's not like her to be so late.
Man: <u>She might have missed the bus.</u>
Woman: I don't think so. She would have phoned to say she'd be late.

Man: She may have forgotten to take her mobile phone with her. You do that all the time!

Woman: Yeah, much to your annoyance! No, Jane's so organised. She wouldn't have forgotten her mobile, and even if she had, she would still be able to use a payphone! No. Something must have happened.

Man: Oh, come on, love. Don't worry so much. There's always a first time for forgetting things, you know. I'm sure it's ...There! That'll be her now!

Woman: Hello, Jane, is that you? ... Oh, sorry ... Yes ... Oh no! When? How did it happen? Yes, I'm on my way.

Listening 3.3

Speaker 1: Well, naturally, I was disappointed, but ... nothing I could do about it. Just one of those things, I suppose.

Speaker 2: Honestly, you could have told me about it beforehand. Then I wouldn't have gone to all that trouble, not to mention the expense!

Speaker 3: Who? James? Well, I wouldn't like to say, really. I mean, I don't know him all that well ... Why are you asking?

Speaker 4: Oh, don't let him worry you! He's just a nobody. Don't take any notice of him, dear.

Listening 3.4

Interviewer: ... Right! My next guest is someone who I personally admire very much. Nikos Magitsis has done it all! Whether it be climbing the highest peaks, such as Everest, trekking to the South Pole or kayaking along the coast from Alexandroupolis, on the Greek-Turkish border, to his home town of Agria in Central Greece ... a mere 505 kilometres ... You name it, he's probably done it! Niko, welcome. Tell me, how did all this start?

Nikos: Well, Tracy ... um ... I started rock climbing in 1984, near my home town. Agria is at the foot of Pelion mountain, so there are lots of places to climb there. I trained as a .... how do you say ... P.E. teacher, and I'm not only a climbing instructor for the town council, but I also teach handball, skiing, and watersports such as kayaking and swimming in the summer months. Two summers ago, we took a group of nine teenagers and kayaked down the coast from Alexandroupolis to Agria. That was an amazing experience for all of us.

Interviewer: Wasn't it a little dangerous, being on the open sea in a canoe?

Nikos: Well, um, I suppose it was a little risky, but we were all experienced, and the kids did really well.

Interviewer: Did you see any interesting sea life on your voyage?

Nikos: We saw lots of dolphins. They liked swimming alongside us, but from a distance. Then one day, the leader thought he saw what looked like a sunken ship floating under the surface, but as we approached for a closer look, we realised it was a huge sea turtle. The guys in front were so surprised by the size of it they nearly overturned! It was an amazing feeling.

Interviewer: So, is the sea your true love?

Nikos: I enjoy being on the water, certainly ... but climbing is what I really love. The feeling when you're hanging from a rope, 300 metres from the ground ... There's nothing like it. It's the closest we can get to being a bird.

Interviewer: Is it easy being a member of an international team, Nikos?

Nikos: Not always. At Everest, I was the only Greek, together with an Indian woman, an American guy, two Belgians and two Japanese. That often caused misunderstandings, obviously, some amusing, some frustrating. But on the whole, we got on well and became good friends. You're in close proximity with each other 24 hours a day, under extreme conditions ... There's going to be friction, but also you form strong bonds. Climbing is about teamwork – you have to rely on the next person holding the rope. Every mountaineer understands that, and everyone is working towards a common goal.

Interviewer: Did you experience any difficulties during the climb?

Nikos: Well, the worst thing that happened was that two of the team got very bad ... er, um ... in English it is called, er ... frostbite, and had to have the ends of two of their fingers chopped off. That meant returning to base camp for a while. But they recovered and carried on. It's one of the recognised hazards of mountaineering. Experienced climbers accept it as a risk they take.

Interviewer: I wouldn't like to have been in their shoes, though! Now, the trip to Everest was just part of a bigger project, wasn't it?

Nikos: Yes. We've just managed to complete the ascent of the 'Seven Summits', as it's known. These are the highest peaks in each continent – Everest, in Asia; Aconcagua, in South America; Denali, in North America; ... um ... Kilimanjaro, Africa; Elbros ... in Europe; Vinson, Antarctica; and Carstensz Pyramid, Papua New Guinea. The last of these proved the most difficult to climb, due to problems beyond our control, such as helicopter failure, and before that we were stopped by rebel activity in the area. However, we finally succeeded in March of this year, and it was a special achievement for me, as only 84 people worldwide have ever climbed all seven, none of them Greek. This time, we had a tough climb in a snowstorm, but when myself and the Belgian climber, Robert Huygh, reached the top, it was a moment neither of us will ever forget. The culmination of a lifetime dream ...

Interviewer: The Seven Summits isn't the only 'first' you've achieved for your country, though, is it?

Nikos: I was the first Greek to reach the South Pole – on skis – and I had the honour of setting up my country's flag there. That felt really good!

Interviewer: Very impressive! And I believe you've written a book ...

Answer key 3

Getting started p21

1 1 white water rafting; 2 mountaineering; 3 yacht racing; 4 kite landboarding; 5 bodyboarding; 6 ice skating; picture at top of page shows skiing

2 awesome; terrifying; exhausting; petrified; determined; reassuring; relaxing; incredible; exhilarating; adrenalin rush; loneliness

3 Speaker 1: white water rafting
Speaker 2: single-handed yacht racing
Speaker 3: kite landboarding

Reading p22

2 The narrator appears to feel terrified, sick with fear ('nauseated at the thought'), he doubts his ability to rescue the victim ('what if I wasn't up to it?'), then determined/resolved ('I might be afraid, but I wasn't about to ...')

3 A Incorrect. The narrator is worried he might not be strong enough, not the belt.
B Incorrect. He isn't annoyed, but rather sick with fear.
C Correct. His fear of failing renders him temporarily immobile.
D Incorrect. He is more worried that he won't be able to hold onto the belt with the boy's weight on the end of it.

4 boat/yacht

5 1D; 2C; 3D; 4A; 5B; 6C; 7B

Language development p 24

1 The writer is wondering if he's physically (and perhaps mentally) capable of rescuing the boy.

2 a What are you doing nowadays?
b We must concentrate on working.
c It's your choice what you do.
d The cancellation is Brian's fault.

e I've only got a few pennies left.
f The children do a lot of naughty things at their Grandmother's.
g What's wrong?
h I'm not very happy at the moment.
i Five (letters) completed, and four still to do.
j That film wasn't very good.

3 He automatically remembered the skills he'd learned in his training ...

4 a on; b over; c back; d out; e apart; f to; g down; h for; i after; j up

5 a i; b ii

6 1c; 2h; 3j; 4f; 5g; 6i; 7b; 8d; 9a; 10e

7 a the name of the game; b gave the game away; c Are you game?; d The game's up; e play games with me

Grammar p25

2 aSU; bSU; cD; dA; eSP; fD; gD

3 a She might have missed the bus; b She wouldn't have forgotten her mobile; c Something must have happened.

4 a Answers will vary, but the sentence will probably refute (R); b Answers will vary, but the sentence will probably qualify (Q)

5 1 so it must be
2 may/might have forgotten my birthday
3 can't have written that note
4 will have phoned April to tell
5 I must have dropped them
6 would have called (me) to say
7 might not have won
8 may be good with animals.

Listening p26

2 Speaker 1: E; Speaker 2: C; Speaker 3: D; Speaker 4: B

3 1B; 2A; 3D; 4A; 5C; 6A

Use of English p27

1 Since

2 a After/Once; b Before; c which; d dancing/listening; e this/it; f Nevertheless/However; g on; h into

3 1 Since; 2 being; 3 of; 4 in; 5 involves/includes; 6 known; 7 themselves; 8 few; 9 find; 10 according; 11 also; 12 with/among; 13 this; 14 away/out/free; 15 to

Writing pp28–9

2 formal

3 Who you are writing to = the editor of the newspaper; why you are writing = to respond to criticism which appeared in an article; what information you need to include = that the students were catered for, there was one teacher per ten students, that skiing holidays are more fun than trips to museums; what outcome you expect from your letter = you want it printed to show your view of the situation.

4 The register is inconsistent, and sometimes informal language is used, which is inappropriate. Several phrases have been lifted from the question, and the letter reads like a list of points. She doesn't use examples to support her points. Also, the answer is too short.

5 Inappropriate phrases: Dear Newspaper; ... and I want to give my view of what happened; Something like this had never happened before!; ... but this is often boring; So, I think you are wrong to suggest that ...; Please print my letter ...
In other words: Dear Sir/Madam; ... and I would like to present my own account of the occurrence; This event was unprecedented, and occurred as a result of ...; Unfortunately, this kind of activity does not always interest students;

Therefore, I feel it would be a mistake to suggest that ...; I would be grateful if my letter could be published in the next issue ...

6 Answers may vary. Suggestions: First, the students in question were under proper supervision ...; Five teachers were each responsible for ten students ...; After all, can parents be vigilant all the time?; Activity holidays like this one provide students and teachers with the opportunity to have some fun together ...

7 The answer does not contain any examples to support the points made.

Vocabulary organiser 3

3.1 a awesome; b terrifying; c reassuring; d exhilarating; e exhausting

3.2 1 extracted; 2 stakes; 3 strengthen his resolve; 4 out of your mind; 5 put on the line; 6 atrocious

3.3 1 din; 2 distress call; 3 extricated; 4 daft; 5 atrocious; 6 grabbed at my guts; 7 put on the line; 8 the stakes; 9 strengthen my resolve; 10 (was) game

3.4 1 I'm down to; 2 get up to something; 3 get down to (work); 4 I'm feeling down; 5 not up to much; 6 be down to

3.5 we've been having our problems

3.6 1 take for; 2 take back; 3 take after; 4 take down; 5 take on; 6 take up; 7 take over; 8 take out; 9 take to; 10 take apart; 11 take back; 12 take out; 13 take down; 14 take up

Bank of English

Odd ones out: the bright side; a mountain out of a molehill; or break it

Take it or leave it!

take up	take out
take back	take in
take off	take to
take down	take on

a	start doing a new activity regularly
b	If someone's career does this, it suddenly becomes very successful
c	accept responsibility for something
d	If you do this to someone, you fool them or trick them
e	make notes (during a lesson, perhaps)
f	you like someone the first time you meet them
g	you regret saying something, and apologise
h	remove something from a shelf
i	allow someone who is in trouble to stay in your house
j	accept a new challenge or offer
k	invite someone to go with you to a restaurant, the cinema etc
l	an aeroplane leaves the ground
m	pay attention to something you hear and understand it
n	begin doing something as a habit
o	employ someone to do a job
p	obtain something by applying for it and paying the necessary fee
q	return something you have borrowed
r	use a particular amount of time or effort to do something
s	develop a new appearance
t	go away suddenly and unexpectedly
u	remove something, like a tooth, permanently
v	If something does this to you, it reminds you of the past

Intrepid explorers

SCENE 1

Situation 1:

You are a team of mountaineers taking part in an international competition to climb Everest. You were caught in a snowstorm, and have lost contact with base camp. Your tents have been almost completely covered by snow. One of your members has broken her ankle and needs medical attention. Discuss your options and decide upon the best course of action.

Situation 2:

You are a group of survivors from a plane crash. You have landed on an island, but don't know where you are. One of your group is badly injured and needs medical attention. It is mid-afternoon, and you need to decide what to do before nightfall, to make yourselves safe. Discuss your options and decide upon the best course of action.

SCENE 2

SCENE 3

Situation 3:

You are part of an environmental expedition team exploring the Amazon jungle. Your small group became interested in a particular kind of plant, and were collecting samples, when you got left behind by the rest of the team. The density of the jungle means that mobile phones cannot pick up a signal, and you have no compass with you. Your supplies of food and water are limited. Discuss your options and decide upon the best course of action.

  PHOTOCOPIABLE 3.2

4 Eureka!

Lesson planner

Fast lane: 3 x 1.5 hour lessons = 4.5 hours per unit
(total course = 72–76 hours)

Lesson	Time	Classwork	Exam Booster (EB) homework
10	1.5 hours	Getting started, Reading + Vocab. Organiser (VO)	Getting started + Reading
11	1.5 hours	Check homework, Lang. develop., Grammar, Speaking + VO	Lang. develop., Grammar + Speaking
12	1.5 hours	Check homework, Listening, Use of English, Writing + VO	Listening, Use of English + Writing
Extra	__ hour	Review 1	Can be either set as homework or completed in class

Slow lane: 4 x 1.5 hour lessons = 6 hours per unit
(total course = 96–100 hours)

Lesson	Time	Classwork	EB homework
13	1.5 hours	Getting started, Reading + VO	Getting started + Reading
14	1.5 hours	Check homework, Lang. develop., Grammar, VO + Photocopiable 1	Lang. develop. + Grammar
15	1.5 hours	Check homework, Speaking, Listening, Use of English + VO	Speaking, Listening + Use of English
16	1.5 hours	Check homework, Writing + photocopiable 2	Writing + Coursebook Writing task
Extra	__ hour	Review 1	Can be either set as homework or completed in class

Before you begin

Ask students to think of one important scientific invention or discovery that is very important in their lives. Have a class vote as to which is the most important and discuss the reasons.

Topic: Science and discovery

This topic involves anything to do with scientific discovery, technology, the past, the future, inventions, predictions, robots and dinosaurs. Most students are interested in some aspects of discovery and will probably enjoy using their imaginations.

Unit 4 Wordlist

advance	duration	inscribe
anatomical	eclipse	intervention
android	efficient	legislation
aristocracy	emit	palaeontology
astound	eradicate	phenomenon
concisely	erode	predator
detect	genetics	rational
device	geology	rigorous
disintegrate	impact	salvage
dissolve	inhabitant	visually
diversity		

Getting started

Aim: To generate interest in the subject, to see how much students already know and to introduce some important vocabulary for the unit.

1   Elicit answers from the class. Most students will probably have some idea about where the expression comes from.

> **BACKGROUND: EUREKA!**
>
> 'Eureka' is an exclamation used as an interjection to celebrate a discovery. It is most famously attributed to Archimedes who is said to have uttered the word when, while bathing, he suddenly realised that the volume of an irregular object could be calculated by finding the volume of water displaced when the object was submerged in water. After making this discovery, it is said that he leapt out of his bathtub and ran naked through the streets of Syracuse.

2 Students attempt the quiz in pairs or teams.

3 Look at the photographs and elicit descriptions of what they show. Elicit that the title strip depicts futuristic buildings (although that is not one of the categories provided). Ask students to choose a category from the box for each of the remaining pictures. You could also ask students to describe photographs that could be used to represent each one. For example, archaeology = some people excavating ancient ruins.

→ Vocabulary Organiser 4.1, page 40

Reading: multiple matching texts

Aim: The purpose of this section is to teach students how to approach part 4 of the Reading Paper, where they have to scan a number of texts for specific information.

1 Discuss the topic with the class. Ask questions such as: 'What films can you think of with robots or androids in them?' Possible answers could include *Star Wars* films (R2 D2 and C3PO), *AI, Robocop, I Robot, Wall-E* etc.

SPOTLIGHT ON READING

Scanning texts for information

Emphasise that scanning is a useful technique, especially for part 4 of the Reading Paper, and when you need to find something quickly.

2 Go through the rubric with the class and ask students to read Text A individually to scan for the information requested. Tell them to raise their hands as soon as they have finished, in order to encourage them to do the task quickly.

TEACHING IN PRACTICE

Skills practice in text reading

The reading texts provided are meant to be used in such a way that they develop the skills needed for students to pass the relevant part of the exam. By following the instructions and doing the tasks, students will learn how to handle any text in the exam, not just these ones. Therefore, it is not so important to analyse other aspects of the text, such as vocabulary, although this can be done later after the main tasks have been finished.

3 Point out that in the actual part 4 of the Paper, there are between four and six texts that students have to read, and they may have to read each text several times to find a particular piece of information. It would therefore be useful for students if they learnt to summarise the gist of each separate text in their heads, or to assign a mental tag of some sort to each one. Ask them to attempt the task individually. Check answers with the group.

4 Students should attempt the following exercise alone or in pairs. Point out that by this stage they should have a good understanding of what each text is about, without needing to refer to dictionaries or analyse the text in detail.

5 Before students read the texts on page 33, elicit as much information as possible. It doesn't matter if the students don't know the answers. Some students may know quite a lot; other students may not have any idea, in which case focus more on the last question and elicit guesses. Ask them to scan the texts to find the answers and raise their hands when they find them.

Degree of difficulty

Decrease the level: for weaker groups, allow students to work in pairs.

Increase the level: for stronger students see who can find the answers first.

BACKGROUND: DINOSAURS

Dinosaurs were the dominant animals on land for over 160 million years, from the late Triassic period (about 230 million years ago) until the end of the Cretaceous period (65 million years ago), when most of them became extinct in the Cretaceous-Tertiary extinction event. Most paleontologists today regard birds as the only surviving dinosaurs. The term 'dinosaur' was coined in 1842 by Sir Richard Owen and means 'terrible, powerful, wondrous lizard'.

6 Students should now attempt the exam task individually. Check answers with the group and ask students to quote from the text directly to justify their answers.

→ Vocabulary Organiser 4.2 + 4.3, page 40

7 Elicit various answers from the group. Students should give their reasons.

Language development: colourful language

1 Elicit answers from the group. Encourage them to refer back to the text if necessary.

2 Encourage students to use their dictionaries for the next exercise. They should work alone or in pairs.

→ Vocabulary Organiser 4.4, page 40

Key word: *tell*

If you *tell* someone something, you give them information.	*In the evening I returned to tell Phyllis our relationship was over ...*

If you *tell* something such as a joke, a story, or your personal experiences, you communicate it to other people using speech.	*His friends say he was always quick to tell a joke …*
If you *tell* someone *to* do something, you order or advise them to do it.	*A passer-by told the driver to move his car so that it was not causing an obstruction …*
If you *tell yourself* something, you put it into words in your own mind to persuade yourself about something.	*'Come on', she told herself …*
If you can *tell* what is happening, you're able to judge correctly what is happening or what is true.	*It was already impossible to tell where the bullet had entered …*
If you can *tell* one thing *from* another, you are able to recognise the differences between them.	*I can't really tell the difference between their policies and ours …*
If you *tell*, you reveal or give away a secret. (INFORMAL)	*Many of the children know who they are but are not telling.*
If facts or events *tell* you *something*, they reveal certain information to you through ways other than speech.	*The facts tell us that this is not true …*
If an unpleasant or tiring experience begins to *tell*, it begins to have a serious effect.	*The pressure began to tell as rain closed in after 20 laps …*

Phrases

As far as I *can tell* or *so far as* I *could tell* indicates that what you are saying is based only on the information you have.	*As far as I can tell, Jason is basically a nice guy …*
I tell you, I can tell you, or *I can't tell you* adds emphasis to what you are saying. (INFORMAL)	*I tell you this, I will not rest until that day has come …*
You never can tell means that the future is always uncertain.	*You never can tell what life is going to bring you.*
If someone disagrees with you or refuses to do what you suggest and you are eventually proved to be right, you can say *I told you so.* (INFORMAL)	*Her parents did not approve of her decision and, if she failed, her mother would say, 'I told you so.'*
I'll tell you what or *I tell you what* introduces a new topic of conversation. (SPOKEN)	*I tell you what, I'll bring the water in a separate glass.*

3 Ask the group to suggest words or phrases that can follow 'tell'.

4 Students should do this exercise individually or in pairs.

5 🎧 4.1 Students should read the dialogue before they listen. Ask if they can predict any of the phrases that may fill the gaps. After they listen, check their answers.

→ Vocabulary Organiser 4.5, page 40

Grammar: the future

1 Discuss the statement with the class. Brainstorm the different ways we can talk about the future in English by writing ideas on the board. Afterwards students should underline the future forms in the sentences individually. Check answers with the group and ask students to name the future forms.

2 This task can be done together with the class to iron out any problems, or students can attempt it first individually or in pairs.

→ Grammar Reference 4.1, pages 171–2

3 Write further examples of any unfamiliar structures on the board and drill further examples from students.

GRAMMAR SPOTLIGHT

Future time in subordinate clauses
Read the rubric with the students. Ask them to identify which is the main clause and which is the subordinate clause in each sentence. Point out that the main clause is not always the first clause, but is usually the one that contains the subject and the main verb (for example, in question 3 the second clause is the main clause).

4 Students should do this individually.

5 Students should do this individually.

→ Grammar Reference 4.2, page 172

6 Students should attempt the task alone or in pairs. Then make sure everyone has understood the grammar here.

7 Students can do this alone or in pairs. Check the answers with the whole group.

8 Discuss the point with the class.

9 Brainstorm ideas and discuss with the whole class to finish the lesson.

Speaking: three-way task

Aim: The aim of this section is to encourage students to talk at length about a subject and to build their confidence so that they can talk about unfamiliar topics or topics about which they may not have a clear view.

1 Discuss this point with the whole class. Notice that there will usually be more fluent speakers who will offer their views. Other students may be more reticent. The teacher should ask the students who have not spoken why they did not raise their hands. With gentle prompting, all students can be made to see that they have an opinion.

PAPER 5, PART 4 Developing topics for discussion

2 🎧 4.2 Read the exercise rubric and then play the recording. Elicit students' answers to the question before reading the follow-on rubric.

3 Divide the class into pairs. Wherever possible try to have one confident speaker with one less confident speaker. Tell the class that you want each student to try to speak an equal amount and that they should try to help each other if necessary.

TEACHING IN PRACTICE

Helping reticent speakers
It is tempting sometimes, especially if a teacher wants to finish a section quickly and move on, to elicit answers from the more confident speakers and to praise them for their linguistic skills. However, less confident students need to be constantly encouraged to speak and praised for what they do right, even if this means the class has to wait longer for them. As a teacher, you may have to instruct certain students to refrain from answering all the questions!

4 Students remain in their pairs and discuss the topic as instructed. The student who started second last time should now begin first. Go round the class listening to each group and give encouragement. After they have all practised discussing the point, ask for volunteer pairs to demonstrate to the rest of the class.

Listening: getting the gist

1 Discuss the topic with the class. The purpose is to lead in to the listening subject matter, that is, scientific inventions.

SPOTLIGHT ON LISTENING

PAPER 4, PART 4 Listening for gist
Read the rubric with the students so they understand what they have to do.

2 🎧 4.3 Play the recording. Students complete the task individually. Check the answers with the group. Point out that not all of the key words will accurately describe the invention. Some words will probably be red herrings.

3 🎧 4.4 Tell students to read the rubric. Ask them what they should do next and elicit that they should read the questions, underline key words and predict what they

think each person may talk about. Then play the recording. Students should work individually and try to complete both tasks. After the second listening check the answers with the class. Tell students to turn to the tapescript on page 208 and underline the correct answers.

TEACHING IN PRACTICE

Listening again
After one listening ask the class to raise their hands if they managed to complete all the questions. Ask how many students feel they don't need to listen again. Some students may well raise their hands, confident that one listening is enough. However, very often students do not check their work and they do make mistakes. Tell the class that you are going to play the recording a second time anyway and that they should all check their answers. Afterwards, ask if anyone changed any of their answers during the second listening.

Use of English: prefixes

Prefixes
Ask the class if they know what a prefix is and then draw their attention to the definition and examples in the Spotlight.

1 Students can work in pairs or individually.

PAPER 3, PART 3 Forming words from stems
2 Do this as a class activity and check the answers with the group.

3 Tell the class to read the text once through before they attempt the exam task. Elicit that the text is about a mysterious ancient Greek computer that was discovered in a shipwreck.

→ Vocabulary Organiser 4.6, page 40

Writing: a newspaper or magazine article

1 Elicit that articles in magazines usually have a lively and engaging style. They may have a catchy title that grabs your attention, and the first few sentences may be rhetorical questions or short catchy sentences that make the reader want to read on. They can have an informal or semi-formal style and may use direct address between the writer and the reader.

PAPER 2, PART 1 Analysing and organising input material
Read the rubric with the students. Make sure they understand why it is important to use the input material wisely.

2 Students should attempt this task on their own or in pairs.

3 Students work in pairs. They should select topics from the main key word categories they have underlined and think about what they would say for each topic.

4 Instruct your students to spend a few minutes reading each article. Ask for a class vote as to which article they think is best. Students should give reasons for their choice.

5 Students need to refer back to the text to answer the question.

Writing extension

Write the following paragraph plan on the board. Ask the class: Which article is it for?

Paragraph one: introduction about the future, climate change, species extinction

Paragraph two: medical advances (eradicating diseases, ageing population, infertility, designer babies)

Paragraph three: technological advances (robots in the home, transport, having less use of car)

Paragraph four: conclusion and summary of how I see the future.

6 Students can do this alone, in pairs or you can do it with the class as a whole if they don't have any problems with the grammar. Check the answers with the class.

In other words

Draw students attention to the 'In other words' box and read the rubric. Ask them to point out statistics the first article used.

7 Elicit answers from the group. You can add a few more percentages of your own on the board to practise further.

PAPER 2, PART 1 Editing your work
Read the rubric with the class.

8 Students work individually and in pairs. Check answers with the group.

→ Vocabulary Organiser 4.7, page 40

9 Preparation of the topic can be done in class and the writing task can be set as homework.

Photocopiable activity instructions

1 Activity 4.1 The Time Machine

Aim: to use the future tenses and forms as much as possible.

Instructions:

1 Divide the class into pairs and give each pair a copy of the photocopiable activity.

2 Tell them that they have to take turns imagining that they could travel forward in time to the dates in the pictures but before they go, they should tell their partner what they expect to find when they get there. One partner should be pessimistic, and expect only the worst, while the other is full of optimism about what he/she will find there.

3 Student 1 uses future forms to discuss the future concerning the points shown. For example: *'Fifty years from now I think the Earth's climate will …'*

4 Student 2 should ask questions to establish as much as possible about what his/her partner expects to find. Student 2 should also express disagreement: *'I don't agree with you. In 200 years I think …'*

2 Activity 4.2 The Nutty Professor

Instructions:

1 Divide the class into two teams. Explain that a Nutty Professor wants to tell the world about his work, but he can never remember the right words to use.

2 Photocopy the activity and cut out each list of words. Select one person from each team to be 'speaker' and give them one list of words. Keep a copy of the lists yourself and have a stopwatch to time them.

3 The first speaker begins. He or she has one minute to communicate as many of the words on the list as he or she can, using synonyms or definitions only.

4 As soon as someone on the team shouts out the right word the speaker moves on to another word on the list. He or she can choose any word in any order. If they do not know what a word means or how to communicate it, they should say 'pass' and move on.

5 Keep score of the number of words correctly communicated and cross them off your list.

6 When a minute is up, the other team repeats the game, with another list.

Tapescript 4

Listening 4.1

Kate: Hi Sally. I wanted to tell you about what happened to me yesterday, but I don't want you to think I'm being a <u>tell tale.</u>

Sally: <u>Tell you what,</u> why don't you tell me about it and I promise I won't <u>kiss and tell.</u>

Kate: I'll try. But I don't want you to say <u>'I told you so'</u>!

Sally: Well, <u>you can never tell …</u>

Kate: I can't tell you how much it means to me that you're my friend.

Sally: <u>As far as I can tell</u> you're my friend too!

Kate: Yes, but <u>only time will tell!</u>

Listening 4.2

Interlocutor: In the future, do you think it will be essential to know how to use a computer to get a job in your country, Fernando?

Student A: No, I think there will always be a need for people who don't know how to use a computer. Computers cannot do everything – for example, we still need bus drivers, and shop assistants, farmers, erm … craftsmen, and, although technology may help them, it's not an essential aspect of those jobs.

Interlocutor: What do you think, Maria?

Student B: I agree with that point. Er …

Student A: And … erm, I also think that at some point, technology will have given us all it has to offer, and after that, people will be looking for alternatives. I mean, even today, you see that more and more people actually want to cycle to work instead of driving, or go to the gym more instead of watching TV. Technology has taken over our lives so much, we are almost fed up with it. What do you think?

Student B: Yes, er … that sounds like an interesting point. Erm …

Interlocutor: Thank you. That is the end of the test.

Listening 4.3

Speaker 1: Well, I don't know where I'd be without it, to tell the truth. There's just no other way <u>to get around</u> these days, unless you want the <u>stress</u> and <u>pollution</u> brought on by <u>driving</u> in the <u>city</u>.

Speaker 2: At first, I hated them. Only the <u>rich</u> and <u>pretentious</u> seemed to have them – do you remember what they were like then? Uh, <u>great big unwieldy things,</u> almost the <u>size of a briefcase.</u> Now of course <u>they fit in the palm of your hand</u> and I'd be lost without one.

Speaker 3: It's probably <u>the greatest invention of all time</u> because just imagine where we'd be without it. I mean, <u>there wouldn't be vehicles of any kind – except trains</u> perhaps, but even they would have to be redesigned.

Speaker 4: It's <u>amazing – and great fun</u> too. First time I've actually enjoyed doing <u>domestic chores.</u> Marjory can get on with her writing and I just <u>blaze round the house</u> with my new <u>toy!</u>

Speaker 5: I would have to say it's the best invention till now because it offers so many <u>opportunities for research,</u> plus it's great for <u>communication,</u> and the <u>kids</u> can do their <u>homework</u> without having to go to the <u>library</u>.

Listening 4.4

Speaker 1: Well, I don't know where I'd be without it, to tell the truth. There's just no other way to get around these days, unless you want the stress and pollution brought on by driving in the city. I live out in the suburbs, so <u>it's good exercise</u>. And of course, ecologically speaking, I know I'm doing my bit to save the planet. <u>I'm setting an example for the kids to follow as well although you do occasionally get some bright spark shouting out something clever as 'sir' goes by.</u> Just because they're stuck on a double-decker bus in rush hour traffic.

Speaker 2: At first I hated them. Only the rich and pretentious seemed to have them – do you remember what they were like then? Uh, great big unwieldy things, almost the size of a briefcase. <u>Now of course they fit in the palm of your hand and I'd be lost without one. I have to spend so much of my day visiting sites, negotiating with clients, co-ordinating workers and then back to the office to go over designs, or tweak a plan.</u> I use it to check the time, do quick calculations, store reminders. And then of course wherever I am, Harry or the kids can find me if they need to tell me something or to find out what time I'll be home for dinner. In the old days they would just have to leave messages all over the place.

Speaker 3: It's probably the greatest invention of all time because just imagine where we'd be without it. I mean, <u>there wouldn't be vehicles of any kind – except trains perhaps, but even they would have to be redesigned. Boats would be OK, but planes wouldn't be able to take off. We had to do a project on its role in world history and it's quite obvious that we'd still be stuck in the dark ages if some clever sod hadn't come up with it.</u> I know most people would probably say the most important invention was television, or the computer, or something, but I don't think they we would even have them if this hadn't come first.

Speaker 4: It's amazing – and great fun too. First time I've actually enjoyed doing <u>domestic chores.</u> Marjory can get on with her writing and I just blaze round the house with my new toy. Compared to our old one, this has loads of advantages. First, you don't have to carry a heavy load around the house with you; two: there are no bags to change – you just empty the bin every now and then; three: it doesn't smell out the house because the actual engine is down in the basement; and four: it's quieter too. <u>There are several outlets in the house that automatically switch on when you plug in, but the hose is nine metres long anyway, so it reaches every corner.</u>

Speaker 5: I would have to say it's the best invention till now because it offers so many opportunities for research, plus it's great for <u>communication,</u> and <u>the kids can do their homework without having to go to the library. It provides entertainment as well as knowledge, and they enjoy it too. It keeps them off the streets, off the TV and I think they learn a lot.</u> OK, granted, there is a downside because the doors are open to all kinds of dodgy places, but <u>if you trust your children</u> to know what's good for them, and they use it wisely, there's so much potential for their own development.

Answer key 4

Getting started p31

1 See Background box on page 31.

2 1c; 2a; 3b; 4c; 5c; 6b; 7c; 8a

3 Picture of robots: IT (information technology), inventions, electronics. Landscape picture: prehistory, geology, palaeontology, chemistry/physics. Astronaut picture: astronomy.

Reading p32

2 a titanium; b Creatures; c for his work on artificial life

3 Text A suggested answers: building an android, a man who wanted to build an android, the difficulties of building an android etc.
Text B suggested answers: building robots/intelligent machines in order to understand how the human brain works etc.

4 a BOTH; bA; cA; dB

5 Sixty-five million years ago [text B]; birds are thought to be direct descendents of dinosaurs [text C].

6 1E; 2C; 3F; 4B; 5B; 6F; 7D; 8C; 9A; 10D; 11B; 12C; 13A; 14E; 15D

Language development p34

1 A bolt from the blue means something that is very sudden and unexpected.

2 1B; 2C; 3A; 4A; 5B

3 you can tell: a joke, a story, a tale, a lie, the time; you can tell yourself something, tell the difference, tell one thing from another, tell what is happening or what is true, tell someone to do something.

4 1b; 2f; 3a; 4g; 5c; 6d; 7e

5 1 a tell tale; 2 Tell you what; 3 kiss and tell; 4 I told you so; 5 you can never tell; 6 can't tell you; 7 As far as I can tell; 8 only time will tell

Grammar pp34–5

1 1 The icebergs will melt within the next forty years. (future simple/will)

2 By the end of this week I will have been working here for ten years. (future perfect continuous)

3 This time next week we'll be flying to Mexico. (future continuous)

4 The match starts at two so you'd better hurry. (present simple)

5 I'm going to visit Julie after I've picked up my dry cleaning. (future – be going to + inf)

6 James will be here for another hour. (future simple/will)

7 I won't forget to write to you. (future simple/will + not)

8 By the time you're ready everyone else will have left. (future perfect)

9 It looks like it's going to be one of those days! (future – be going to + inf)

10 I'm meeting Jim outside the cinema. (present continuous)

2 a4; b6; c1; d7; e10; f5; g9; i8; j2

3 a about to pick/the point of picking; b bound to pass/certain to pass; c should be/time he was; d chance that everyone will/doubt that anyone won't

4 1 while; 2 By the time; 3 As soon as; 4 until; Main clause tenses:
1 future will; 2 future perfect; 3 future will; 4 future will

5 Subordinate clause tenses:
1 simple present (b); 2 simple present (d); 3 simple present (c); 4 present perfect (a)

6 a is (has been)/will move; b will not leave/tell; c decide/will stop; d will phone/arrive; e get/will have left

7 1 There will have been = There will be; are wanting = will want (will be wanting)

2 will be disappearing = will have disappeared; spelling will have been = will be; Russian will have come = will come second

3 Automobiles are = will be cheaper; are going to be becoming = will become (will have become)

4 are to be used = will be used

5 Cameras will have been = will be connected; telephones are going to provide = will provide

6 Strawberries will be being as large = will be as large; it won't not = it will not (it won't).

Speaking p36

2 Student B did not say enough. She merely expressed her agreement but didn't try to add any further points

Listening p36

2 Speaker 2: rich had them, big things, size of briefcase, now fit in palm/hand; Speaker 3: greatest invention ever, no vehicles without it, except trains perhaps; Speaker 4: amazing, fun, domestic chores, blaze round the house, toy; Speaker 5: opportunities for research, communication, kids, homework, library.

3 1B; 2G; 3E; 4A; 5C; 6B; 7E; 8C; 9A; 10F

Use of English p37

1 a il; b im; c en; d in; e ir; f multi; g un; h re; i ultra; j sub; k pre; l dis

2 1 imprisonment; 2 resurfaced; 3 unhappily

3 1 shipwreck; 2 reconstruct; 3 astronomical; 4 precision; 5 inscriptions; 6 enabling; 7 irregular; 8 Remarkably; 9 comparable; 10 disappear

Writing pp38–9

2 Key words to underline: science magazine; young people; articles; the future; refer to the points raised; describe your own vision of the future; Climate change; medical advance; an ageing population; Robots; transport problems

4 The second article is more likely to be published because it does what it is asked and gives the writer's view of the future.

5 Both articles have covered all the points, but the first article just lists them whereas the second tries more successfully to link the points.

6 The first article uses mainly hypothetical forms 'would' and 'should' while the second article uses future simple, future perfect and future continuous.

7 1 a few/very few/not many/a small number, a minority
2 one in ten, a tenth
3 just over half
4 everyone, unanimous (agreement/vote/decision) etc

8 remove the following: Paragraph 1: 'in my own – somewhat pessimistic – view of the future', 'a world with polluted skies and seas'; Paragraph 2: 'And the population will continue to increase.' 'and select the qualities they would like them to have'; Paragraph 3: 'and only the very rich will be able to afford private transport.'

9 Students should mention the following: the role of schools, the role of the teacher, the role of computers/the Internet in future education.

Vocabulary organiser 4 p40

4.1 1 paleontology; 2 android; 3 astronomy; 4 prehistory

4.2 1 legitimate; 2 vague; 3 avian; 4 swift; 5 predators; 6 eroding; 7 serpents; 8 gestating; 9 gentry; 10 fertile

4.3 1 produce an image in someone's mind; 2 an unpleasant death; 3 to show that they were big and heavy and made a loud noise when they moved; 4 to show that birds are small and light unlike the dinosaurs; 5 ducks, geese or even small children; 6 beneath their physical appearance

4.4 1 black and blue; 2 the black; 3 red-handed; 4 green with envy

4.5 1b off; 2c apart; 3a on

4.6 1e; 2f; 3h; 4a; 5d; 6c; 7g (b is also correct); 8b

4.7 1 astounding; 2 eradicate; 3 restrictions; 4 flora and fauna; 5 menial; 6 pessimistic; 7 soaring; 8 residents

Answer key 4

Bank of English

1 technophobe; 2 technique;
3 technology; 4 techno;
5 technical support; 6 technician;
7 Technicolor ™; 8 technicality

Review 1 pp41–2

1 1 undisciplined; 2 inhumane;
3 inadequate; 4 disobedient;
5 unprotected; 6 reconsider;
7 disagreement; 8 inflexible;
9 unacceptable; 10 disorderly

2 1B; 2D; 3B; 4A; 5C; 6D; 7B; 8C; 9A;
10C

3 1 down to; 2 an eyelid; 3 the slate
clean; 4 rein; 5 the biscuit; 6 down
to; 7 wild; 8 scratch

4 1 skipped; 2 provoked;
3 instigating; 4 strolling; 5 hop;
6 prompted; 7 marches; 8 embarking
on; 9 wades; 10 initiated

5 1 have moved; went; hadn't been;
decided; have opened/opened; is
doing

2 am going; was coming; forgot; will
have to; are going to; really liked;
made

3 did it happen; was riding; was; was
shining; could; came; crashed

6 1 can be criticised for; 2 has been
able to dance; 3 might have been
friends for; 4 has been rumoured
that; 5 they had been living together
for; 6 may be regarded/met/viewed
with; 7 can't have seen Paul with;
8 is going to visit

7 1 ago; 2 with; 3 Instead; 4 had;
5 possible; 6 in; 7 might; 8 that;
9 cannot; 10 these; 11 could/might;
12 has; 13 However/Nevertheless;
14 would; 15 which

8 1 get, will have finished; 2 will be
conducted; 3 has finished/finishes,
will be able; 4 am going to tell, will
believe/believes; 5 will be trekking;
6 will no longer use/be using; 7 am
seeing, are thinking; 8 is taking, is
bound to

The Time Machine (part 1)

50 years from now

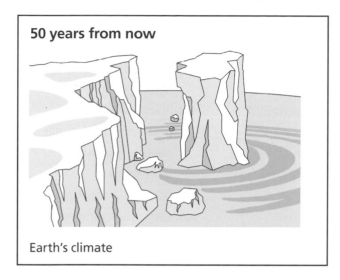

Earth's climate

200 years from now

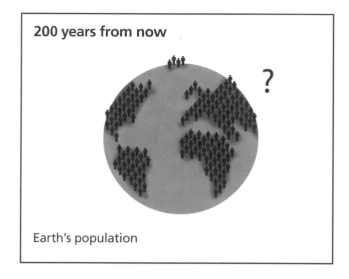

Earth's population

500 years from now

Earth's resources

1000 years from now

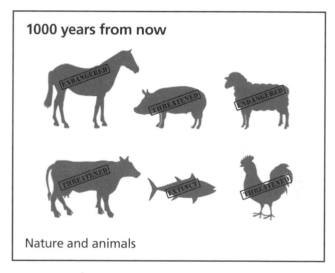

Nature and animals

5000 years from now

Technology

10,000 years from now

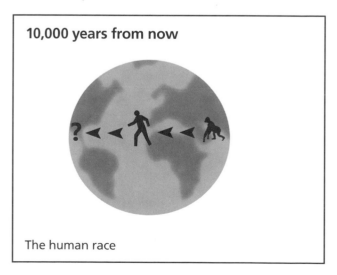

The human race

The Nutty Professor

Nouns	Verbs and phrasal verbs	Adjectives	Expressions
android	astound	aerial	a bolt from the blue
archaeology	construct	anatomical	black card
aristocracy	detect	avian	black list
artificial life	disintegrate	bureaucratic	black mark
astronomy	dissolve	compelling	blue around the gills
automobile	emit	concise	blue in the face
complexity	envision	contrasting	blue moon
device	eradicate	cyber	bring to an abrupt end
diversity	erode	extensive	catch someone red handed
eclipse	expose	fertile	eureka
evolution	flutter	kinetic	green fingers
extinction	inscribe	legendary	green with envy
flora and fauna	meditate	legible	in the red
forensic science	observe	legitimate	playful spirit
fossil	preoccupy	literate	red herring
galaxy	preserve	marine	red tape
genetics	resemble	medieval	seeing red
geology	salvage	mobile	sticky end
graphite	scan	mutable	the grass always looks greener on the other side
impact	seek	obscure	to take something lightly
inhabitant	span	pessimistic	under the skin
intervention	thunder	polluted	
inventions	unpick	profound	
mammal	unravel	provincial	
mercury	conjure up	radioactive	
meteorite	date back to	rational	
Milky Way	get on with	redundant	
mollusc	get through	resolute	
natural selection	give rise to	rigorous	
orbit	gloss over	sane	
organism	jot down	simultaneous	
palaeontology	put back together	soaring	
phenomenon	section off	superfluous	
philosopher	tell apart	swift	
predator	tell off	vague	
prediction	wipe out	vast	
prehistory		viral	

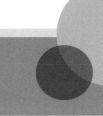

5 Safe and sound?

Lesson planner

Fast lane: 3 x 1.5 hour lessons = 4.5 hours per unit
(total course = 72–76 hours)

Lesson	Time	Classwork	Exam Booster (EB) homework
13	1.5 hours	Getting started, Reading + Vocab. Organiser (VO)	Getting started + Reading
14	1.5 hours	Check homework, Lang. develop., Grammar, Listening + VO	Lang. develop., Grammar + Listening
15	1.5 hours	Check homework, Use of English, Speaking, Writing + VO	Use of English, Speaking, Writing + Coursebook Writing task

Slow lane: 4 x 1.5 hour lessons = 6 hours per unit
(total course = 96–100 hours)

Lesson	Time	Classwork	EB homework
17	1.5 hours	Getting started, Reading, VO + photocopiable 1	Getting started + Reading
18	1.5 hours	Check homework, Lang. develop., Grammar + VO	Lang. develop. + Speaking
19	1.5 hours	Check homework, Listening, Speaking + VO	Listening + Speaking
20	1.5 hours	Check homework, Use of English, Writing + photocopiable 2	Use of English, Writing + Coursebook Writing task

Before you begin

Aim: to revise vocabulary connected with crime. Students should be familiar with these items.

1   Write the following list of crimes on the board: *arson; burglary; fraud; hacking; kidnapping; manslaughter; mugging; murder; shoplifting.*

2   Separate the class into two groups. Tell them you are going to describe several different crimes that have taken place recently.

> On Thursday evening, someone set fire to the local secondary school. It is believed to have been a student.
>
> Is that arson?

In their groups, they have to identify each crime. The first team to identify the crime gets a point. If a team identifies a crime incorrectly, they lose a point. The winning team is the one with the most points at the end of the game.

Topic: Internet crime, DNA profiling, road and fire safety

Internet crime is the fastest growing type of crime in modern society. As more and more students have access to and make regular use of the Internet, we decided to focus on this aspect of crime. Similarly, DNA profiling is a very fashionable theme in many TV detective series, so we've included this as a topic.

Unit 5 Wordlist

anti-virus	crimeware	infamous
arson	cyber-crime	kidnapping
backup	decode	law-abiding
benign	drug trafficking	lawsuit
broadband	fraud	malicious
confess	hacker	murder
confide	hitman	solicit
convict	hoax	undercover
crack	incite	

Getting started

1   Ask your students to look at the two photographs. Elicit what is happening in them, and a possible connection between them. Hope to hear some of the following words: *hacking, cybercrime, Internet crime, viruses.*

2   Ask students to read the 'Strange but true' box. Then, in pairs, they should discuss what kind of punishment to give crimes 1–5. You may wish to allocate one item per pair. Note that item 3 is not actually a crime, but students need to decide what should be done about

the convict. Should he be punished in some way for having escaped in the first place?

3 Discussion point. Elicit views and comments on Brighton Police Force's decision.

4 Discussion point. Make sure students understand that the question does not ask them to say which is the most serious crime, but to consider which one is the most difficult for the police to combat.

Reading: gapped texts

BACKGROUND: ANTI-VIRUS SOFTWARE

There are competing claims for the innovator of the first anti-virus product. Perhaps the first publicly-known neutralisation of a wild PC virus was performed by Bernt Fix (also Bernd) in early 1987. Three short years later, by December 1990, the market had matured to the point of 19 separate anti-virus products being on sale. As broadband connections became the norm and more viruses were released, it became essential to update virus checkers more and more frequently; even then, a new virus could spread widely before it was detected, identified, a checker update released, and virus checkers round the world updated.

1 Tell your students to read the rubric and the headline. Make sure they know the literal meaning of 'worm' and 'woodpecker'. Elicit ideas about the subject of the article. Do not give a definite answer yet.

2 Tell students to read through the first paragraph fairly quickly, and find out who the 'woodpeckers' are. Now ask students who or what 'worms' might be.

EXAM SPOTLIGHT

PAPER 1, PART 2 Following a line of argument in a text
Explain that in the gapped text task more than one option sometimes appears to be suitable for a particular gap.

3 Two choices are possible here. This is intentional. The aim is to highlight the fact that students must also look at the paragraph which follows the gap, and not make rash judgements when making their choices. Allow your students time to make their choices before giving feedback.

4 Tell your students to read the paragraph in the text which follows the gap, and decide which of the two options is the correct answer.

SPOTLIGHT ON READING

Supporting points in an argument
5 Tell them to read the rubric for exercise 5 and choose which type of supporting information they would expect to follow such a paragraph.

6 Direct the students to the main text, and ask them to predict which of the supporting information types mentioned in the Spotlight could fit into each gap. Give them time to do this. Elicit answers and give feedback.

TEACHING IN PRACTICE

Explaining their choices
The aim of exercises 3–6 is to encourage students to consider the options for each gap carefully, and to highlight the importance of checking their choices. You should expect some disagreement among your students, and allow them to discuss their choices and ask questions. Encourage them to give reasons for their choices, in order to help them check.

SPOTLIGHT ON READING

Text organisation features
Comparison:

7 Direct your students to the Spotlight on page 45. Tell them to read the first point, and answer question 7. Give them time for this, then listen to their answers and give feedback.

Reference:

8 Tell students to read the second point in the Spotlight, and explain that an article often includes references to experts' opinions, in order to strengthen a point the writer is making. The full name and title will be given the first time they are mentioned.

9 Direct your students to the exam task rubric and ask them to complete the task. Allow them time to do this. They should not need longer, as they have already studied the text quite closely now. [Note that in question 4 of the task, paragraph E also appears possible. This is intentional. Students' attention needs to be drawn to the fact that the paragraph which follows doesn't really tie in with it, and that paragraph F is the correct one.]

→ Vocabulary Organiser 5.1, page 52

p/c 5.1

Language development: verbs followed by particles

1   Remind students of the warm-up activity they did. Elicit a list of crimes, and then elicit another to do with punishment (for example, *arrest s/o for*, *charge s/o with*, *sentence s/o to* etc). Take no more than five minutes for this, and do not expect a complete list, as this exercise aims to simply get them thinking of the target language.

2   Tell students to quickly read through the text individually. Elicit what it is about. Students work in pairs. Allow three minutes for this.

→   Vocabulary Organiser 5.2, page 52

Language development extension

You may wish to give your students more thorough practice in using verbs which are followed by particles. The questions below give examples of verbs and particles which are often confused. Write them on the board, or prepare photocopies for each student, and ask them to complete the task.

Choose the best answer to complete the following sentences, and explain your choice.

1   'Please _____ from standing on your seats.'

    a deter   b refrain   c resist   d avoid

2   The evidence _____ Kevin in the crime.

    a implicated b involved c incriminated d incorporated

3   Helen _____ Paul of cheating on her, but decided to get proof before saying anything.

    a suspected   b accused   c blamed   d charged

4   It is believed that the fire resulted _____ a leaking gas pipe.

    a in   b from   c of   d as

5   Ann finished college last year and now works _____ advertising.

    a on   b in   c for   d at

Key: *1b, 2a, 3a, 4b, 5b*

Phrasal verbs with *turn*

3   This exercise revises structures your students should already know. Tell them to read the rubric. They should be able to answer without referring back to the text. Elicit answers and give feedback.

4   Ask your students to read through the sentences. Tell them they may not know all the phrasal verbs, but they should try to complete the task. Allow them time to do so.

→   Vocabulary Organiser 5.3, page 52

Key word: *law*

5   This task can be done as pairwork in class, if dictionaries are available, or as homework.

Above the law = believing yourself to be too important to obey the law	*One opposition member of parliament accuses the government of wanting to be above the law ...*
Against the law = illegal	*It is against the law to park your car on double yellow lines in Britain.*
Break the law = disobey a law	*You have broken the law by speeding.*
By law = the law states what you can or can't do	*By law all restaurants must display their prices outside ...*
Enforce a law = ensure it is obeyed	*It is the responsibility of the police to enforce the law in this country.*
Lay down the law = insist upon the law	*... traditional parents, who believed in laying down the law for their offspring.*
Obey the law = follow the rules	*As a police officer, you should set an example, and obey the law at all times.*
Take the law into your own hands = refuse to wait for the legal system to work	*The speeding motorist was pinned to the ground by angry locals who took the law into their own hands until police arrived.*
A law-abiding person = someone who obeys the law rightfully	*The Prime Minister said: 'I am anxious that the law should protect decent law-abiding citizens and their property ...'*
Law and order = generally accepted laws	*If there were a breakdown of law and order, the army might be tempted to intervene.*
Law-enforcement agencies = officials responsible for catching criminals	*We need to restore respect for the law-enforcement agencies.*
Lawsuit = a case in court concerning a dispute	*The dispute culminated last week in a lawsuit against the government.*
Within the law = not doing anything unacceptable to authorities	*But officer, I've kept within the law, and only drunk one glass of wine ...*

6   This exercise offers practice using items from exercise 5, so you may wish to set it as homework together with that.

→   Vocabulary Organiser 5.4, page 52

Grammar: verbs followed by infinitive or -ing

1   Direct students to read the verbs in the box. You may wish to do this exercise as an open class exercise, eliciting the structures in turn, to ensure that students complete the table correctly.

2   Tell students to complete the sentences with a verb from exercise 1. Make sure they realise that more than one verb may be possible.

4   This exercise aims to consolidate the contextual use of some of the sentences from exercise 3, while also being a bit of fun. Allow students time to look at the cartoons, and perhaps react to them before matching sentences to each drawing.

5   Direct students to read the exam-style rubric. Ask them to complete the exercise, and remind them to check the context in order to ensure that they use the correct structure in each case. Allow them five minutes for this.

→   Grammar Reference 5.1, pages 172–3

Listing: sentence completion

Please note that the tapescript for the exam task is quite demanding, and for this reason, there is an introductory task to highlight some abbreviations used.

1   Tell students to look at the photographs. What can they see? Ask them to read the rubric to exercise 1. Elicit answers and explanations, if necessary.

2   Students do this in pairs. Ask them to read the rubric and complete the exercise before giving feedback to their answers.

3   🎧 5.1 Tell students to read the rubric. The talk they are going to hear describes the different methods forensic scientists use to analyse DNA samples, and contains quite a lot of technical information. Tell them they only need to extract the information relevant to the task. They should not worry about understanding everything. Play the recording.

4   Direct students to read the rubric. Play the recording again. Allow students time to consider their answer.

7   Direct students to read the question sentences in exercise 8. Elicit the type of word needed for each gap, such as a noun, verb, adjectival phrase, or a statistic.

8   🎧 5.3 Direct students to look at the question sentences again. Play the recording. Pause for ten seconds, then play the recording again. Allow the students time at the end to finish writing in the gaps.

9   Separate the class into four groups and ask them to brainstorm arguments in favour of the DNA database, and arguments against it. Explain that, in a discussion, one way of winning an argument is to anticipate the opposing argument.

10 Divide the class into two groups, and allocate the arguments in favour of the database to one group, and those against to the other. After each team has spoken, ask everyone to take a vote for or against the database.

Use of English: gapped sentences

3   This exercise requires dictionaries. Students work in pairs. Ask them to complete the task. They won't need to look up all the phrases.

4   Direct students to read the rubric for the exam-style task. They should do this individually. Elicit answers and give feedback.

→   Vocabulary Organiser 5.5, page 52

Speaking: giving personal information

1   🎧 5.4 Direct your students to read the rubric. Tell them to listen carefully to how the two candidates answer each question, and comment on them.

3   Tell your students to listen to the recording again and make notes on Beret's answers.

4   Students should use their imagination to expand on Juan's answers. Elicit answers and give feedback.

Writing: a report

1   Direct your students to read the questions. Elicit answers, and allow some discussion.

write down four paragraph headings as a plan. They should note that paragraph 1 will be the Introduction, and paragraph 4 the Conclusion and recommendations.

3   Direct students to read the three opening paragraphs presented, and decide which one is the most suitable, and why. They should think about the purpose of an introduction, as well as register and appropriateness of the language.

4   Elicit what is wrong with the other two options and give feedback.

In other words

5   Make sure you have dictionaries available, preferably one for every two students. Allow students time to complete this task and write questions a, b and c out in their notebooks. When students have completed a and b, elicit answers. Then allow them to do question c.

6   Direct students to the rest of the sample answer. Ask them to read it and comment on how well it answers the question.

7   Elicit suitable headings for each paragraph of the sample answer. Give feedback.

8   Students do this in pairs. Read through the instructions with them. Allow them to read through the exam task, and discuss a plan for the answer.

9   🎧 5.5 Direct students to read the rubric, and elicit what they have to do. Make sure they have their notebooks ready. Play the recording through twice if necessary.

10 Set this exercise as homework. Emphasise the fact that this is a part 2 question, and remind students that they must write 220–260 words.

Photocopiable activity instructions

1   **Activity 5.1 How to avoid catching a virus**

Aim: To consolidate and develop awareness and use of language connected with safety on the Internet.

Instructions:

1   Make sure you have one photocopy per student. Hand these out.

2   Explain that there is no real right or wrong order for the advice items. The aim is to make sure you get the correct items under the 'Do' column, and the correct ones under the 'Don't' column.

Key: A Do; B Don't; C Do; D Do; E Don't; F Don't ; G Do

2 **Activity 5.2 Verb noughts and crosses**

Aim: To revise and consolidate use of some of the verb structures covered in this unit.

Instructions:

1 Separate the class into two teams: a noughts team and a crosses team. Make sure each student has a copy of the game image. Toss a coin to see which team will have the first go.

2 The team chooses a word in a suitable square, and makes a sentence with the word. If the word is used correctly, then the team places its mark – O or X – in the square.

3 Tell the students that they have a time limit of one minute to choose their square and make a sentence. If the team creates a sentence that is incorrect, then the square will be left open, and the other team can try. The winning team is the one which creates a line of its marks, horizontally, vertically or diagonally.

Tapescript 5

Listening 5.1

... The three main types of forensic DNA testing, then, are all extremely useful, but each has its own limitations. The first type, RFLP testing, requires large amounts of DNA from a recent sample. Therefore, old evidence from a crime scene is quite unlikely to be suitable for RFLP testing. Furthermore, warm and moist conditions usually cause DNA to become degraded quicker, so samples from crime scenes near water are unsuitable. The second type, STR testing, can be used on smaller amounts of DNA, but is still subject to the same limitations as the first type.

The third type, PCR-based testing, has certain advantages over the other two, in that it requires smaller amounts of DNA, and the sample may be partially degraded. However, it still has limitations which must not be ignored. PCR testing can easily become contaminated, both at the crime scene and in the lab. This can affect the test results, particularly if laboratory regulations are not strict.

Listening 5.2

Personally, I see the idea of a national DNA database with everyone's DNA on record as a necessary evil. Yes, it has its risks, and there would need to be strict legislation to protect people, but if it were universal, surely it would eliminate the possibility of suspects being picked out at will.

More importantly, the risk of almost certain detection would act as a powerful deterrent to first-time offenders, and so reduce the risk of innocent people becoming the victims of a violent crime.

Listening 5.3

Daniel: Since the mid-1980s, when Sir Alec Jeffreys first discovered that every human being has his or her own unique genetic makeup, DNA profiling has replaced fingerprinting as the chief forensic tool in criminal investigations. Technological advances enable new techniques for testing DNA to be developed all the time, and forensic scientists are now able to solve cases from years ago. The recent conviction of John Lloyd, who attacked a number of women between 1983 and 1986, is a case in point.

As a result of all the media attention, the discipline has come to be seen as glamorous, with forensic scientists now occupying centre stage in TV detective series, rather than detective inspectors. Many people assume that DNA testing provides unquestionable proof of a person's guilt or innocence, leaving no room for error. Yet the controversy now surrounding the case of Barry George, convicted in 2001 for the murder of TV presenter Jill Dando, brings to light a number of problems with this idealistic point of view. One of the jurors expressed doubt about the conviction, and gained support from several forensic experts who believe the forensic evidence presented in the case should be regarded as 'unreliable' and therefore inconclusive. And this is not the only example where forensic evidence has led specialists to the wrong conclusion.

Don't get me wrong, I'm not trying to suggest that DNA profiling has no place in criminal investigations! But what we need to clarify from the outset is not simply the merits of DNA profiling – and they are indeed many – but also, its limitations. We must dispense with the idealised, glamorous view presented on TV, and rather examine in an objective manner exactly what DNA testing can and cannot do. The processes involved in DNA testing are complex.

The most effective DNA testing procedure to date is STR analysis. It has a greater ability to distinguish differences than the earlier type of testing, RFLP analysis, yet can be used on a smaller sample. This method analyses a DNA sample in greater detail, so there is less chance of two individuals giving the same results.

STR analysis is now used together with the 'polymerase chain reaction', or PCR, as it is commonly known, a process which enables DNA contained in a degraded sample to be analysed. The present technology allows scientists to find DNA matches with odds estimated at 1 in 37 million, but this does not mean that it is not possible for individuals to have similar matches.

For this reason, strict rules must be maintained within the laboratory, and while technology has enhanced the level of accuracy, it is not perfect, nor should we rule out the possibility of human error during the process. Forensic scientists are often under pressure to produce results quickly, and this can lead to errors in judgement.

Speaking 5.4

Interlocutor: Hello. My name is Jill Simpson, and this is my colleague, Helen Jones. And your names are …?

Juan: Juan.

Beret: Beret.

Interlocutor: OK. First of all, we'd like to know something about you. Where are you from, Juan?

Juan: Spain.

Interlocutor: And you, Beret?

Beret: I'm from a small village on the edge of the Norwegian fjords.

Interlocutor: And what are you doing here in England, Beret?

Beret: I'm studying Accountancy at the London School of Economics, and generally having a good time!

Interlocutor: And you, Juan?

Juan: Er, I'm working, and trying to improve my English.

Interlocutor: So, how important is sport and exercise to you, Juan?

Juan: I play football every Saturday, and I train twice a week.

Interlocutor: And how about you, Beret? Is sport and exercise important to you?

Beret: Oh yes, very important. I think we all need to do some form of exercise to stay healthy. Personally, I do aerobics at a gym three times a week, and also I cycle to my lessons every day … I wear, um a … how do you say, scarf over my nose and mouth, to stop breathing the smoke from the cars.

Interlocutor: If you had the opportunity to take up a new activity, what would you like to do … er, Beret?

Beret: Well, there are lots of things I'd like to do if I had more time … and money, of course! … But, I think I'd really love to go

horse riding. I love horses, and I like being out in the fresh air. It's difficult here in London, though, and very expensive.

Interlocutor: Yes, indeed. How about you, Juan? What would you choose to do?

Juan: Er … Can you repeat the question, please?

Interlocutor: What new activity would you like to do, if you had the chance?

Juan: I'd like to play water polo.

Interlocutor: That's interesting. Why?

Juan: Er … because I like swimming.

Interlocutor: … OK. Now, in this next part of the test, I'm going to show you …

Listening 5.5

Now, I think we'd all agree that prevention is better than cure, particularly in the case of fire. So, it is vital to establish a fire safety plan in your school. Teaching staff must be instructed on what to do in case of fire. Fire alarms and fire exits must be clearly marked, and all teachers should be aware of their location. Teachers must know where the nearest fire exit is at all times, and must be able to evacuate students efficiently. Therefore, it is advisable to hold regular fire drills for the whole school, so that students can also be made aware of procedures.

In case a fire does break out, teachers should always sound the alarm at the first sign of smoke or flames. Even if it turns out to be nothing, you will have ensured the safety of everyone in the building. Instruct your students to leave the room in an orderly fashion, and move towards the nearest fire exit. If you are able to, use the nearest fire extinguisher to put out the fire. If you are unable to control the fire, leave immediately, and close all doors behind you, to prevent smoke from spreading. Once outside the building, teachers must check that all students are accounted for. Students must stay in their classroom groups, to avoid confusion.

Teachers should learn how to use the fire extinguishers in the school, and all equipment should be checked regularly by the local fire department. Doorways and fire exits must be clearly marked, and kept clear at all times. This last point is most important. Now, I'd just like to demonstrate how …

Answer key 5

Getting started p43

1 Internet crime (hacking) → someone being arrested.

Reading pp44–5

2 Woodpeckers are members of an anti-virus team of experts; worms are self-replicating computer

programs, which use a network to send copies of themselves to other nodes (computers on the network) and they may do so without any user intervention.

3 a possible: 'they' refers to the 'team of young computer programmers'

b not possible: 'Inspired by such impressive surroundings' does not follow on naturally

c possible: 'It' can be the 'gloomy tower block'; also corresponds with 'this dark skyscraper'.

4 c. The paragraph which follows defines the new kind of 'power struggle' they face.

5 Answers may vary, but c is most likely. An expert will want to comment on how the task 'is proving increasingly difficult'.

6 Answers will vary, but expect the following: 1c; 2c (it follows on from 'with good reason, say experts'); 3a (it follows on from 'research published last year'); 4b or c (historical information about 'Brain', or an expert commenting on the effects of the Brain virus); 5a or c (more statistics could follow, or another expert could respond to Cluley's comments); 6c (it follows on from 'some experts say').

7 After missing paragraph 3: 'It is all a far cry from the earliest days of hacking'.

8 F (Sal Viveros: likely to be first, as the full name is given); A ('Mr. Viveros agrees').

9 1D; 2B; 3G; 4F; 5A; 6C

Language development p46

1 arrest sb for/in connection with …; convict sb of -*ing*; charge sb with -*ing*/sth; admit to -*ing* sth; deny -*ing* sth; confess to -*ing* sth; sentence sb to __ years' imprisonment.

2 1 of; 2 with; 3 to; 4 of; 5 in; 6 of; 7 with; 8 for; 9 to; 10 to; 11 of; 12 to

3 a turned out to be; b turned (them) into

4 1 in; 2 to; 3 over; 4 in; 5 down; 6 on; 7 off; 8 out

6 1 law enforcement; 2 breaking the law; 3 are above the law; 4 lawsuit; 5 by law; 6 law and order; 7 is against the law; 8 laying down the law

Grammar p47

1 Followed by infinitive with *to*: advise someone; dare someone; agree; decide; order someone; persuade someone; arrange; encourage someone; ask (someone); attempt; expect (someone); refuse; threaten; choose; fail; invite someone; remind someone.
Followed by infinitive without *to*: dare (= modal) '*Don't you dare do that!*' and '*How dare you say that?*'; let someone do.
Followed by -*ing*: appreciate doing; deny doing; practise doing; enjoy doing; avoid doing; face doing; involve doing.

2 1 practise; 2 threatened; 3 decided/arranged/agreed/refused; 4 contemplated; 5 denied

3 1 '*I don't like doing*' is a general truth about a like/dislike; '*I don't like to* …' means I don't think it is right to do something in this way.

2 '*I remember doing*' means I have a memory of something I did; I can recall it; '*I remembered to do*' means that I didn't forget to do something I had arranged to do.
3 '*I go on doing* …' means that I continue doing something for a long time, and sometimes implies criticism, that I do it for too long; '*I go on to do…*' means that I continue something perhaps after a break, or move on to another activity.
4 '*I mean to do* …' means that I intend to do something. Used in the past tense, it usually means I intended to do something but I forgot; '*It means doing* …' means an activity involves doing something, or requires you to do something.
5 '*I stop to do something*' means I interrupt the activity I'm doing in order to do something else; '*I stop doing something*' means that I stop the activity I'm doing at the moment.

4 1 Helen stopped to talk to her neighbour. 2 'Will you stop talking for five minutes!' 3 'Oliver went on talking for an hour, and some people fell asleep!' 4 Trixie went on to thank her teacher for all his help.

5 1 threatened to shoot the old lady 2 denied taking/having taken the wallet 3 Mrs Smith remembered noticing anything unusual 4 don't like to phone her 5 didn't mean to set

Listening p48

1 Forensic science is the study of physical evidence found at the scene of a crime in order to help the police in their investigation. DNA analysis is the study of human tissue to see if a person is connected with a crime.

2 1b; 2b

3 a PCR testing; b STR testing; c RFLP Testing

4 There are limitations to DNA testing and it is open to error.

5 + 6 (DNA) database or (strong) deterrent.

7 1 noun (kind of investigation technique); 2 date (statistic); 3 noun (an institution, group of people); 4 adjective (possibly negative idea); 5 adjective (possibly negative idea); 6 adjective or phrase; 7 noun (statistic); 8 adjective.

8 1 fingerprinting; 2 1983; 3 media; 4 idealistic; 5 unreliable; 6 degraded; 7 37 million; 8 perfect

Use of English p49

1 aim
2 goal
3 a your eye; b factor; c out; d mannered; e work; f lose
4 1 proof; 2 charges; 3 turn; 4 light; 5 cry

Speaking p49

1 Beret is fluent, and gives full answers, whereas Juan doesn't say very much, and gives very short answers.

3 1 Beret gives information about the location of her village, not just the country she's from; 2 She doesn't just give the reason for being in Britain, but also includes personal information; 3 She expresses an opinion about the importance of exercise, and then says what she does to keep fit; 4 She not only says what she would like to do, but also why.

Writing pp50–1

2 Suggested paragraph headings: 1 Introduction; 2 Traffic in the area; 3 Existing safety measures (or Signals, Crossings and Cycle lanes); 4 Recommendations

3 c

4 a (an introduction more suitable for an essay); b doesn't give the reason for writing the report.

5 a look at (examine, study, scrutinise, investigate), consider (assess, evaluate, analyse), suggest (recommend, propose, put forward) b evaluation; provision; consideration; effect/ effectiveness; scarcity; recommendation; improvement c Suggested answer: The purpose of this report is to assess the level of road safety in this area, by examining the amount of traffic, and the effectiveness of existing traffic signals, pedestrian crossings and cycle lanes. It will also make recommendations for improvements.

6 Yes

7 1 Problems caused by traffic; 2 Present level of road safety; 3 Recommendations/Conclusion

8 Suggested answers: 1 Introduction, 2 Existing safety measures; 3 Foreseeable/Potential problems; 4 Recommendations
9 See underlined tapescript on page 47.

Vocabulary organiser 5 p52

5.1 a a person who creates and develops computer programmes.
b a computer program that introduces itself into a system, and alters or destroys information
c a solution to the problem of a computer virus
d computer software which introduces viruses into a system.
e crime connected with the Internet
f a person who perpetrates crime on the Internet
g the act of illegally breaking into computer systems in order to gain secret information
5.2 1 suspected Larry Jones of committing
2 accused Wayne of stealing
3 arrested Jones
4 confessed to robbing
5 denied helping
6 charged the couple with committing
7 convicted Larry of
8 sentenced him to three years imprisonment.
5.3 1 to; 2 in; 3 off; 4 over; 5 over
5.4 1B; 2C; 3A; 4A; 5B
5.5 1F; 2T; 3T; 4F; 5T

Bank of English

battle cry = phrase used to encourage support for a protest or campaign; cry out for = need something desperately; a far cry from = something very different from something else; for crying out loud = spoken phrase showing annoyance or impatience; a shoulder to cry on = someone to listen sympathetically; cry off = say you cannot do something you have agreed to do; cry wolf = ask for help when you don't need it; cry foul = protest that something is unfair; a crying shame = say that something is upsetting; it's no use crying over spilt milk = don't waste time feeling sorry about a mistake.

How to avoid catching a virus

You are a representative from an anti-virus company. You have been asked to create a leaflet giving advice to PC users on how to protect their computer from viruses. You must complete the table below, by adding the notes A–G to the appropriate boxes.

Do ...	Don't ...
delete any mail you suspect may be infected, and empty your 'Deleted items' folder regularly.	open any attachment you are not sure about, even if you have a virus scanner.
1	2
3	send an email about a 'new virus' without checking it out. Visit sites to check for hoaxes.
send any email you think is infected to an anti-virus company (you may have to own a copy of their virus software). They can tell you if it is a virus or not.	4
5	6
7	relax, even if you have a virus scanner. You will still need to keep your eyes open for any new viruses.

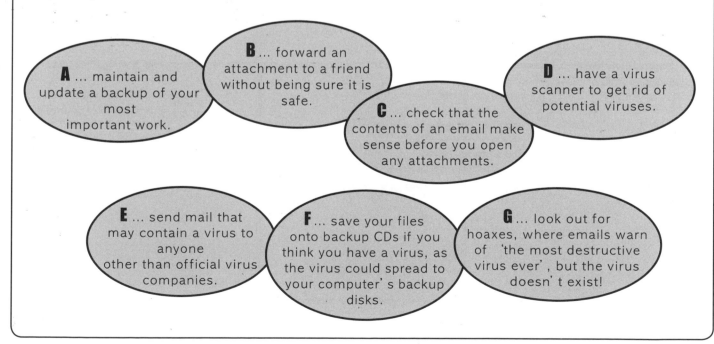

A ... maintain and update a backup of your most important work.

B ... forward an attachment to a friend without being sure it is safe.

C ... check that the contents of an email make sense before you open any attachments.

D ... have a virus scanner to get rid of potential viruses.

E ... send mail that may contain a virus to anyone other than official virus companies.

F ... save your files onto backup CDs if you think you have a virus, as the virus could spread to your computer's backup disks.

G ... look out for hoaxes, where emails warn of 'the most destructive virus ever', but the virus doesn't exist!

PHOTOCOPIABLE 5.1

Verb noughts and crosses

o   *x*

advise	CONVICT	dare
deny	**confess**	**contemplate**
appreciate	remember	**threaten**

       PHOTOCOPIABLE 5.2

6 Hale and hearty

Lesson planner

Fast lane: 3 x 1.5 hour lessons = 4.5 hours per unit
(total course = 72–76 hours)

Lesson	Time	Classwork	Exam Booster (EB) homework
16	1.5 hours	Getting started, Reading + Vocab. Organiser (VO)	Getting started + Reading
17	1.5 hours	Check homework, Lang. develop., VO, Grammar + Listening	Lang. develop., Grammar + Listening
18	1.5 hours	Check homework, Speaking, Use of English, Writing + VO	Speaking, Use of English + Writing

Slow lane: 4 x 1.5 hour lessons = 6 hours per unit
(total course = 96–100 hours)

Lesson	Time	Classwork	EB homework
21	1.5 hours	Getting started, Reading + VO	Getting started + Reading
22	1.5 hours	Check homework, Lang. develop., photocopiable 1, Grammar + VO	Lang. develop. + Grammar
23	1.5 hours	Check homework, photocopiable 2, Listening, Speaking, Use of English + VO	Listening, Speaking + Use of English
24	1.5 hours	Check homework + Writing	Writing + Coursebook Writing task

Before you begin

Decide who the healthiest person in the class is. Ask questions and write down the name of the person who gives the 'healthiest' answer for each question:

> What did you have for breakfast this morning?

> When was the last time you exercised?

> How often do you eat vegetables or fresh fruit?

Topic: good health and nutrition

One of the most important aspects of our lives is good health. More and more these days we are told how important diet is to good health, that prevention is better than cure and that different kinds of medical practice can bring different results.

Unit 6 Wordlist

abundant	eliminate	nutritive
boost	endorse	obesity
complementary	enhance	optimism
component	external	organic
confection	harmonious	prescribe
consume	immune system	processed
consumption	impairment	raw
conventional	invasive	renovate
derive	medication	resistance
digest	moderation	restore
discretion	morality	stimulating
duplicate	nourishing	subsequent
efficacy	nutrient	

Getting started

Aim: To generate interest in the subject of good health and healthy eating; to introduce topic vocabulary.

1 Discuss the topic with the students. Brainstorm various ideas about what constitutes a healthy lifestyle. Students can then work in pairs or alone.

2 🎧 6.1 Play the recording. Students should be able to match certain key words they hear to exercise 1. They can check their answers in the tapescript on page 210.

3 Discuss the point with the class. Point out that conventional western medicine tends to prescribe medication and therapies that will alleviate or dispel the symptoms of an illness whereas alternative medicine often tries to find a way of defeating the cause of the problem.

For and against points in discussion

Try to use this technique in class whenever discussing a subject that may be new, unfamiliar or controversial to students. Get students to make a list of both the advantages and disadvantages of a topic. This will give students a much bigger choice of things to say and will help them think up ideas in similar situations in both the Speaking and Writing Papers.

4 Students discuss this point in pairs. Afterwards brainstorm ideas on the board.

Conventional medicine: *For:* scientifically proven; highly trained doctors; years of research. *Against:* unpleasant side effects; only treats the symptoms; illnesses often return.

Alternative medicine: *For:* treats the whole person/illness; less intrusive; boosts immune system. *Against:* not always clinically proven; results unpredictable; doesn't always work

→ Vocabulary Organiser 6.1, page 62

Reading: text analysis

1 Discuss this point with the class unless you have already discussed it in the Getting started section.

Understanding written texts

2 Students should do this individually. Check answers with the class. Point out that there is no correct order. Each of the points is important and will be useful to students to different degrees. Students should be able to justify their reasons.

3 Students should read the text individually and attempt to use techniques a and b according to their own particular requirements. When they have finished reading, ask students to raise their hands for each point. Point c they are asked to do in exercise 5 and point d is covered in exercise 6.

Justifying answers by reference to the text

Students should get into the habit of justifying all their answers by reference to the text itself. Ask students to underline the parts of the text that give an answer or refute an incorrect option. Some students think they know the answer after just one reading but most of the time these are the students who are caught out by tricky questions.

4 Students have deliberately been given the correct answers because this focuses the task on locating the key information in the text and underlining it.

5 Students work in pairs to find the parts of the text that can refute the incorrect option stems. They should be able to explain why each option is wrong with reference to the text.

PAPER 1, PART 1 Text analysis

6 The aim of this exercise is to train students to pay better attention to the texts they read and to recognise the different devices that writers use, so that they will have a better understanding of the text overall. Students should work individually. Check answers with the whole class.

7 Tell your students they are now going to have further practice understanding the meaning of unknown vocabulary in a text. Ask them to read the text briefly and underline any unknown words.

Analysing unknown words

Go through the rubric with your students. Then elicit some of the unknown words that students underlined in exercise 7 and write them on the board. Ask a student who doesn't know the meaning of a word to make use of the techniques listed in the Spotlight to identify the meaning of the unknown word as much as possible.

8 Students attempt the task on their own. Check answers with the group.

9 Students should attempt to answer this without reference to the text in order to see how much of the text they have properly understood. Then tell students to justify their answers by reference to the text.

10 Students should do the exercise individually. Check answers with the class and ask students to justify their answers.

11 Students should read the text and answer the questions by themselves, without any analysis of the text or class discussion, in order for them to get a feeling of the exam situation. When everyone has finished, check answers with the class. You can then analyse the text in the same ways that have been seen in this section: working out the meaning of new words from context, asking comprehension questions, analysing the writer's style and justifying answers with reference to the text.

→ Vocabulary Organiser 6.2, page 62

Language development:
expressions with food

> **SPOTLIGHT ON VOCABULARY**
>
> **Using idioms in speech**
>
> 1 🎧 6.2 Students listen to the recording and do the task. Afterwards they should work in pairs, turn to the tapescript, locate the idioms and discuss their meaning.

2 Students should read the questions and choose the answer they think is right. If they have never seen or heard these idioms before ask the class which answers they think would be right, and to then check their answers in their dictionaries.

3 The point of this task is to show students that very often it is possible to work out what an idiom means by thinking about it. Elicit various suggestions from the class.

4 Students can work in pairs. They should use a dictionary to find as many idioms as they can.

→ Vocabulary Organiser 6.3, page 62

p/c 6.1

Key word: *life*

Phrases using *life*

If you *bring something to life* or if it *comes to life*, it becomes interesting or exciting.	*The cold, hard cruelty of two young men is vividly brought to life in this true story ...*
If you say that someone is *fighting for their life*, you mean they may die as a result of an accident or illness.	*He was in a critical condition, fighting for his life in hospital.*
For life means for the rest of a person's life.	*He was jailed for life in 1966 for the murder of three policemen ...*
If you tell someone *to get a life*, you are expressing frustration with them.	*'Really Natalie, why don't you just go and get a life?'*
If you say that someone or something is *larger than life*, you mean that they appear more exaggerated than usual.	*Throughout his career he's always been a larger than life character.*
If someone *lays down their life* for another person, they die so that the other person can live. (LITERARY)	*Man can have no greater love than to lay down his life for his friends.*
If someone *risks life and limb*, they do something very dangerous that may cause them to die or be seriously injured.	*Viewers will remember the dashing hero, Dirk, risking life and limb to rescue Daphne from the dragons.*

If you refer to someone as *the life and soul of the party*, you mean that they are very lively and entertaining.	*Lilla was in such a good mood – she really was the life and soul of the party!*
Expressions such as to *come to life*, to *spring to life*, and to *roar into life* to indicate that a machine or vehicle suddenly starts working or moving. (LITERARY)	*To his great relief, the engine came to life ...*

5+6 This section can be handled in a number of ways, according to the abilities of the class. For advanced classes you could do the exercises with the whole class, eliciting their answers and explanations. For mixed level classes it might be better to ask students to do this as pair-work and check the answers with the group. For weaker classes, encourage students to work individually and to use their dictionaries. Check answers with the class.

Grammar: conditionals

Aim: The aim of this section is to revise conditional structures and conditional type sentences, and perhaps introduce students to some more unfamiliar kinds of conditional structures.

1 Students should turn to the tapescript and underline the conditional sentences. Check with the class that they can identify which one is used for which purpose.

2 Students work individually or in pairs. The aim is to make sure that students know the appropriate situation for each conditional type and understand its meaning.

> **TEACHING IN PRACTICE**
>
> **Checking conditionals**
>
> In order to check that students have understood the function and meaning of a conditional sentence ask questions about the sentence. For example, for the sentence:
>
> *'If it rained we took the bus, but if the sun came out we always walked.'*
>
> Ask:
>
> 'Did it rain?' 'Yes.'
>
> 'How often?' 'Sometimes.'
>
> 'What did we do when it rained?' 'We took the bus.'
>
> 'What did we do the other times?' 'We walked (when it was sunny).'
>
> 'Did we do this more than once?' 'Yes.'
>
> 'When?' 'In the past.'
>
> Therefore elicit that we use this structure to talk about past habits.

3   Students work individually or in pairs. The aim is to refresh their memories of the different conditional types. They should already know 1st, 2nd and 3rd type conditional quite well, but this is a good time to introduce them to mixed conditionals, zero conditionals and false conditionals which they may not be so familiar with. Refer to the Grammar Reference section if required.

→   Grammar Reference 6.1, page 173

4   Students work individually or in pairs, but check the answers with the class to make sure they have understood what they should do.

5   Students attempt the task individually as this is an exam type question. Time them and give them no more than ten minutes.

Listening: multiple choice questions

p/c 6.2

SPOTLIGHT ON LISTENING

PAPER 4, PART 3 Understanding a speaker's main points

1   Students should underline key words to show that they can recognise the important words in a question that may reveal part of the answer.

2   🎧 6.3 Play the recording. Elicit from the class the speaker's main point.

3   🎧 6.4 Make sure students spend about a minute reading the questions and underlining key words before you play the recording. Students should listen to the recording twice, as they would in the exam. Remind them they should check their answers even if they think they are correct.

Degree of difficulty

Decrease the level: For weaker groups pause the tape after each part of the listening that provides the answer to each question.

Increase the level: For stronger groups, tell students to read the questions and options once and then to close their books while they listen.

Speaking: comparing pictures

EXAM SPOTLIGHT

PAPER 5, PART 2 Comparing pictures

1   Tell students to look at the pictures and think of things they would say. Ask individual students to demonstrate their answers in front of the class. Time them for one minute.

TEACHING IN PRACTICE

Helping your students talk for a minute

Tell your students not to waste time explaining which pictures they are going to talk about as this will become obvious when they begin the task. It also will make it harder for them to change their minds about which picture they are going to talk about once they have started. Advise your students against using 'closure' techniques such as, 'I've finished!' They should keep talking until the interlocutor says, 'Thank you'.

2   Arrange the class into groups of three and if you have any groups of two you can also use an 'interlocutor' from another group to help, or one of the students can read their own 'interlocutor' parts. Students should time each other to speak for one minute. Student B should also get used to speaking for up to 30 seconds on the same topic.

Speaking extension

Comparing pictures from magazines

Ask your students to collect pictures from newspapers and magazines and use these in class to practise comparing them. Students should group pictures into sets and imagine what they might be asked to talk about in a Part 2 task in the exam.

Use of English: identifying collocations

SPOTLIGHT ON VOCABULARY

PAPER 3, PART 1 Identifying collocations

Elicit from the class what a collocation is. Get them to give you examples of some and write them on the board.

1   Students can work in pairs or individually. They should use their dictionaries. Tell them they have two minutes to note down as many collocations as they can find.

2   Students attempt exercise 2. They may be familiar with some of the collocations. Tell them to underline or tick the ones they know to be correct. For any they are unsure of, they should use a dictionary.

3 Remind students that before attempting to answer any of the questions they should read through the whole text first in order to gain a general understanding of it. You could ask some general comprehension questions to check this. Tell students to then try to answer the questions by looking at each option individually and checking the sentence, both before and after the gap, for evidence of collocations. Students should spend no more than eight minutes on this. Check the answers with the class.

→ Vocabulary Organiser 6.4, page 62

Writing: developing an argument in an essay

Aim: The purpose of this section is to introduce students to the techniques needed to write and plan an essay, especially in this case, the development of an argument. (Issues that surround a topic will be dealt with in unit 14.)

1 Discuss the topic with the class. Try to give everybody a chance to put forward ideas and to warm up to the subject.

EXAM SPOTLIGHT

PAPER 2, PART 2 What is an essay?
Read the rubric with the class. If you like refer students to the model essay on page 187.

2 Students can do this individually or in pairs. Or, you might like to ask one student to read the essay out loud. This would highlight the problems with it.

SPOTLIGHT ON WRITING

Doing an essay plan
Read the Spotlight with the students, or ask them to read it to themselves. Afterwards ask them to close their books and ask students to tell you the order of the essay plan from memory.

3 Students work alone or in pairs. Check answers with the group.

4 Students read the introductory paragraphs, either individually or select three students to read a paragraph each to the class. Elicit the class's choices and their reasons for selecting them.

5 Tell students they now have to write the main body paragraphs for the essay. They should use the words in the boxes to help them. Remind students to look back at exercise 3 and to use the paragraph summaries as topic sentences.

6 Tell your students that this task highlights the way that they could develop their points and strengthen their argument. Read through the box with the students and then tell them to attempt the second task on their own. Elicit the best answers from the group and write them on the board.

In other words

7 Students attempt the task individually or in pairs. Check the answers with the class.

You are what you eat in that if you eat good food then you feel good whereas if you eat bad food, you feel awful. If you eat lots of junk food you will get fat for which reason you won't be able to go out to exercise, which is why you'll feel heavy. Furthermore, you'll be tired all the time. Subsequently, you'll just sit on the couch watching even more TV. Moreover, you'll eat lots of pizzas and drink fizzy drinks as a result of which you'll get even fatter. However, if you eat lots of healthy food like fruit, vegetables, beans or rice then you will have lots of energy. In view of this your food won't all turn into fat so you'll have more energy to do the things you want to do. Consequently, you'll feel really great.

8 Ask a student to read the conclusion out loud. This will highlight how bad it sounds. Students should attempt to rewrite the sentence as two or three sentences. They can make any structural changes they need to.

9 Students choose one of the essay titles and write it for homework. If time allows, elicit a brief discussion about each one, just to brainstorm a few pertinent points.

→ Writing Reference, page 187

Photocopiable activity instructions

1 **Activity 6.1 Food idioms**

The Gossips: Vera and Betty

Aim: To learn some new food idioms and use them in an appropriate context, while emphasising the absurdity of using too many idioms at once!

Instructions:

1   Divide the class into pairs and give each pair a copy of the worksheet.

2   Tell them they are going to do a little role play activity, and they will each play one of the female gossips.

3   Students rehearse the script. At each gap they have to insert the correct food idiom, but they shouldn't write it down.

4   Give them a few minutes to practise rehearsing their characters and learning their script as much as possible.

5   Afterwards students should take turns to stand in front of the class and act out their plays. They can refer to their scripts as much as necessary. Finally, the class votes for the best act.

2 **Activity 6.2 The time machine (part 2)**

Aim: To practise using the second and third conditional.

Instructions:

1   Divide the class into pairs and give each pair a copy of the photocopiable activity.

2   Tell each pair that they have to take turns imagining that they could travel back in time to the situations in the pictures and that their aim is to change history.

3   Student 1 has to tell their partner which time they would go back to and what they would have done there in order to change history. Student 2 should ask questions to establish how their partner would have changed history.

Tapescript 6

Listening 6.1

Speaker 1: Well, my old man was always going to the doctor for this, that or the other reason, but never for any life-threatening cause. Whatever the doctor said was gospel. No questions asked. Didn't have a clue what he was putting into his system, poor man. <u>If the doc said it was the thing to take, you can bet he believed it.</u> Sometimes it worked, but more often than not the problem just got worse. I've read up quite a bit about conventional medicine since then and discovered that prescription meds, more often than not, just tend to treat the symptoms, never the root cause. 'Course, that's what made me interested in holistic medicine and the like, right.

Speaker 2: We live in an age where synthetic compounds surround us on a daily basis, from the solvents in our woodwork, to the ingredients in our shampoo. I read somewhere that we are exposed to over 70 000 different chemicals every single day. Did you know the same ingredients in our toothpaste can be found in car engine oil? Some of these have of course been classified as carcinogens, so it's hardly surprising that the more domestic products we use in the home, the more we see an increase in cancer rates. <u>If you're worried about your health there are alternatives to chlorines and bleaches.</u> In pre-industrial eras, our grandmothers used vinegar and lemon juice, salt and bicarbonate of soda to clean the house! You can do the same.

Speaker 3: <u>I first started doing it</u> about three years ago when I heard about how it can reduce stress and therefore decrease heart rate and blood pressure. I also read about how in some cases <u>simple visualisation exercises</u> have caused the regression of cancer. It is said to boost the immune system and is often used in hospitals with patients who are terminally ill. The medical community tends to agree that if mental factors such as stress were significantly reduced, a person's physical health would be much better. There's a growing movement in mainstream science to fund research into this kind of exercise. Personally, <u>I do it because I find it so relaxing on both my mind and body, and because it keeps me fit and healthy. I don't need any equipment, just a quiet room or a spot in the garden where no-one will disturb me.</u>

Listening 6.2

One

Man: I found a box of abandoned kittens by the side of the road the other day.

Woman: Oh no! That's terrible! What did you do?

Man: Well, I took them to the cat rescue centre of course. They were a bit hungry, but basically OK.

Woman: Well that was good of you. Anyone worth their salt would have tried to give them a chance. But what heartless person could have left them there in the first place?

Two

Young woman: Did Sally tell you that she's been having a hard time at work?

Older woman: No, why? What's been happening?

Young woman: She's been putting in all this overtime and is just fed up of being taken for granted. Everyone expects her to run around for them all the time.

Older woman: Why doesn't she complain to her supervisor?

Young woman: She'd never do that. She's the next in line for promotion so she knows which side her bread is buttered!

Older woman: Yeah, I suppose you're right.

Three

Man: Emily got into trouble at school yesterday.

Woman: No! You're joking? Whatever for?

Man: Well, apparently, she was accused of breaking a window.

Woman: No! I don't believe it. What did she say?

Man: She denied it of course and I think the headmaster believed her story.

Woman: Well, of course he did. How could anyone suspect Emily of lying? She looks as if butter wouldn't melt in her mouth! And it's true. It wouldn't.

Four

Woman: Hello Bob! How's business?

Man: Not so bad. Pretty good in fact.

Woman: Really? That's fabulous. I always knew you'd make a good salesman.

Man: It's not me – it's the book. Everyone just wants a copy. The first 1000 sold like hotcakes. I'm already half way through the second shipment. How about you? Why don't I try and interest you in …

Woman: … Oh no, you don't! I certainly don't need any more books, thank you!

Listening 6.3

Maureen: Raw foods, such as fresh fruit and vegetables, nuts and seeds, are foods which contain enzymes, the living energy of plants. Enzymes are of vital importance to our health because without them we would get sick and many of our bodily systems would not be able to function properly. We need enzymes to digest our food, to strengthen our immune systems, to flush out toxins and to regenerate our cells. In fact, clinical tests have shown that enzyme-rich diets can even help people suffering from some serious illnesses.

Listening 6.4

Interviewer: Today we are in the studio with Dr Maureen Cunningham whose latest book, *Raw Power*, has raised a few eyebrows. Dr Cunningham, your book advocates that a diet rich in raw fruit and vegetables is the healthiest diet of all. Can you tell us a little bit more about it?

Maureen: Raw foods, such as fresh fruit and vegetables, nuts and seeds, are foods which contain enzymes, the living energy of plants. Enzymes are of vital importance to our health because without them we would get sick and many of our bodily systems wouldn't be able to function properly. We need enzymes to digest our food, to strengthen our immune systems, to flush out toxins and to regenerate our cells. In fact, clinical tests have shown that enzyme-rich diets can even help people suffering from some serious illnesses.

Interviewer: I think most people are aware that fresh fruit and vegetables are good for us. But in your book you mention that eating too much cooked food can actually be bad for us and this has caused some strong reactions. Can you tell us why you advocate reducing our intake of cooked food?

Maureen: I'm certainly not suggesting that anyone should suddenly switch to a strictly raw food diet, but most of us do rely far too heavily on cooked meals to fulfil most of our nutritional requirements, which it simply can't do because cooking destroys so many of the nutrients. Obviously, if we're always eating cooked food, then we can't be eating enough raw plant food.

Interviewer: In your book, you cite a famous experiment involving about 900 cats I think.

Maureen: Yes, that's right. Half of the cats, which were studied over four generations, were fed a diet of raw meat (which is of course the natural diet of cats), while the other half were fed cooked processed meat (tinned cat food). Within only one generation this second group had started to develop a variety of pathological problems, similar to the health problems that so often afflict even humans today. The second generation of cats suffered even more and with each subsequent generation, the problems increased so that by the fourth generation the cats were displaying all kinds of problems. Conversely the majority of cats in the first group lived healthy long lives in each generation, with very few of them developing serious illnesses.

Interviewer: But surely humans are not cats – and our bodies react differently to cooked foods?

Maureen: Yes, but we all need enzymes to digest our food, which unfortunately suffer complete and total destruction by cooking. This means we have to draw on our own limited reserve of enzymes, which puts enormous strain on our bodies. Similarly, as most people are aware, much of the vitamin content of foods is destroyed by cooking. But that's not all; a great deal of protein is damaged or destroyed when we cook our food, so that it becomes either completely useless or worse still, toxic to us.

Interviewer: Well, how are we supposed to get enough protein then?

Maureen: Well – fortunately most raw foods contain protein in easily digestible form. All nuts and beans are rich in protein, and in fact the richest source of protein is found in sprouted seeds and beans.

Interviewer: So does that mean that we don't need to worry about eating two square, home-cooked meals every day, as long as we eat a salad or some fruit?

Maureen: Well, basically, I would recommend eating plenty of raw food salads and vegetables with every meal. Further evidence is showing that the majority of our health problems are related to an ineffective immune system that has been weakened by a bad diet: too much junk food, not enough raw plant food. In fact, it is has been shown that the body's response to cooked food is to suddenly increase the number of white blood cells in our blood, something that usually happens when our bodies are attacked by alien invaders. By mixing our cooked food with at least 50 per cent raw, we can reverse this reaction and keep our immune system on standby for when it's needed.

Interviewer: So your advice to anyone who hates boiled carrots, as I do, would be …?

Maureen: That's simple. Eat them raw!

Answer key 6

Getting started p53
2 1h; 2f; 3g
3 1b; 2a

Reading pp54–5
4 1 'flavanoids are also present in onions, grapes, red wine and tea, among other plant-derived foods'
2 'focus on foods proven to help enhance heart health and prevent disease – fruits, vegetables and whole grains for example.'
6 a 'Will any chocolate do?'/'So what are you to do?' They make it less formal in style and give the writer a chance to focus on the topic quickly; b 'And milk chocolate has fewer of these beneficial chemicals than does dark chocolate'./'But, allow yourself to enjoy a small piece of dark chocolate'. The use of conjunctions makes the register less formal and establishes a more direct connection to the reader; c 'Remember, most chocolate products …' Using an imperative makes a direct point to the reader more emphatic; d 'have our cake and eat it too'. It means to make the best of a situation in two conflicting ways. The writer chose it for its double meaning and association with cakes (not being very healthy) but being able to enjoy them.
8 1 components; 2 consumption; 3 efficacy
9 aT; bF; cF; dT; eT
10 1A; 2B
11 3D; 4B

Language development p56
1 1 anyone worth their salt; 2 she knows which way her bread is buttered; 3 butter wouldn't melt in her mouth; 4 selling like hotcakes
2 1D; 2D; 3A

3 This means that in order to achieve something it is necessary to do something first, nothing can be gained without sacrifice.
4 bacon: bring home the bacon
butter: butter wouldn't melt in one's mouth, know which way one's bread is buttered
cake: you can't have your cake and eat it, piece of cake, selling like hotcakes
egg: to have egg on one's face, to put all of one's eggs in one basket, a chicken and egg situation, you can't make an omelette without breaking eggs, a nest egg, a bad egg, an egghead
salt: salt of the earth, anyone worth their salt
5 1d; 2a; 3a; 4b; 5d; 6d; 7c
8 dream, killer, vision

Grammar p57
1 1 Speaker 1: 'If the doc said it was the thing to take, you can bet he believed it.' (c); 2 Speaker 2: 'If you are worried about your health there are alternatives to chlorines and bleaches' (a); 3 Speaker 3: '… if mental factors such as stress were significantly reduced, a person's physical health would be much better.' (b)
2 1D; 2C; 3B; 4A; 5F; 6E
3 a4; b3; c2; d5; e6; f1
4a 1 Unless; 2 If I should; 3 Provided; 4 As long as; 5 Even if; 6 If you were to; 7 Had it not been for; 8 Supposing; 9 But for
4b 1c; 2b; 3d; 4g; 5f; 6i; 7a; 8e; 9h
5 1 goes down/drops/falls/ decreases I intend to call
2 had had time I would have
3 for William's advice
4 happen to come to
5 had been taller I would have
6 you to cut down on
7 to taking antibiotics even if
8 younger I would have beaten

Listening p58
1 'According to the speaker, why are enzymes essential in our diet?'
2 She says enzymes are essential because they keep us healthy. Her main point is that they strengthen our immune systems and protect us even from serious diseases.
3 1C; 2A; 3D; 4A; 5D; 6C

Use of English p59
2 a fault; b luck; c a process; d justice; e fortune; f off power
3 1B; 2D; 3B; 4A; 5A; 6D; 7B; 8C; 9C; 10D; 11A; 12D

Writing p60
2 No, it is not well organised: it has no introduction or clear development, and the writer doesn't give reasons for their views.
3 1d; 2a (or b); 3b (or a); 4c
4 a is OK, but quite simple, while b is a good introduction to the topic but c is repetitive.
6 Eating too much junk food can make you feel bad about yourself. For example, someone who eats too much junk food is likely to be overweight, and therefore less likely to exercise. Exercise releases endorphins which promote a sense of well-being and happiness.
7 Suggested answer:
You are what you eat in that if you eat good food then you feel good whereas if you eat bad food, you feel awful. If you eat lots of junk food you will get fat for which reason you won't be able to go out to exercise, which is why you'll feel heavy. Furthermore, you'll be tired all the time. Subsequently, you'll just sit on the couch watching even more TV. Moreover, you'll eat lots of pizzas and drink fizzy drinks as a result of which

you'll get even fatter. However, if you eat lots of healthy food like fruit, vegetables, beans or rice then you will have lots of energy. In view of this your food won't all turn into fat so you'll have more energy to do the things you want to do. Consequently, you'll feel really great.
8 Therefore, if we want to live long healthy lives we should follow a number of general guidelines, like for example not smoking and exercising more, but also we must be aware of the food we eat and aim to eat more of the right foods. Good health is fundamental to our sense of well-being and feelings of happiness and, as good food equals good health, we should make every effort to eat well.

Vocabulary organiser 6 p62
6.1 1 plenty of fresh fruit
2 foods high in fats or sugar
3 your immune system
4 much healthier for you
5 fighting off any viruses or bacteria
6 if you have a cold
7 exercise and meditation
8 cause of the problem.
6.2 1T; 2F; 3T; 4F; 5F; 6T; 7F; 8T
6.3 1 ia; iib; iiic; 2d; 3a; 4b; 5 salt; 6a fact, b matter, c lay down
6.4 1 take; 2 do; 3 run; 4 make; 5 give; 6 fall; 7 fall; 8 let

Bank of English
1 healing, healer, health, healthful, healthy, healthily, healthier, healthiest, unhealthy
2 bus, provider, school
3 a incorrect = get better, improve; b correct; c correct; d incorrect = cure

Food idioms

- he's a hard nut to crack, that one
- it's not my cup of tea I'm afraid
- you're going to turn into a couch potato
- he had to eat humble pie
- that really takes the biscuit
- the apple never falls far from the tree
- he was as cool as a cucumber
- he had his hands in the cookie jar
- it's no use crying over spilt milk
- he gave her some half-baked story about what he'd been up to

The Gossips ... Vera and Betty

Vera: Did you hear about Mrs Rogers and her son Tony? No. Oh, well, if you've got nothing better to do love, why don't I tell you what I heard from Nora in the corner shop. Well, it goes like this ... Mrs Rogers was getting fed up with her Tony being on the dole, lounging around at home, doing nothing. I mean, he is twenty-two and he's finished college and everything. So she says to him: "_____ if you don't get off your behind and go out and get yourself a job!"

Betty: Just like his father. You know what they say: _____!

Vera: That's right. Anyway, Nora – that's Mrs Rogers – sends him off without another word to get a job, although months go by and he still can't find anything he likes.

Betty: _____! He never was satisfied about anything, even when he was little.

Vera: In the end, Nora's going to throw him out on his ear unless he gets himself a job, so he finally accepts a job in a sports shop, stocking shelves.

Betty: _____!

Vera: No, mine neither, but what can you do? Anyway, before long, guess what happens? Tony's given the sack, isn't he? And do you want to know why? According to his boss, he'd been helping himself to free stuff! Not that it could be proved mind you, but that's what the rumour is.

Betty: What, you mean _____?

Vera: That's right.

Betty: Well, I'm shocked! Of all the things he could've done, _____. What did he tell his mother?

Vera: Oh, you know, _____. He told her he'd been made redundant due to a shortage of work, that kind of thing.

Betty: Did she believe him?

Vera: Of course she did. After all _____ when he told her. She was very upset. Not that it would've done any good. You know what they say: _____!

Betty: That's right Vera. But what happened in the end?

Vera: Well, she found out the truth eventually didn't she? She went ballistic at him! Of course _____ after that, didn't he? He apologised to her, and he's been a good boy ever since. Got himself a good job in a lawyer's office.

Betty: I say!

PHOTOCOPIABLE 6.1

THE TIME MACHINE

1

'The town of Pompeii, beneath Mount Vesuvius, a few days before the eruption, AD 79.'

2

'Extinction of the dodo, mid 17th century.'

3

'A bakery on Pudding Lane, source of the Great Fire of London, 2nd September 1666.'

4

'SS Titanic, 14th April 1912, shortly before hitting an iceberg in the North Atlantic.'

5

'The assassination of Archduke Ferdinand of Austro-Hungary, one of the key events leading to the start of World War I, 28th June 1914.'

6

'Mr and Mrs Hitler (Adolf's parents) marry, 7th January 1885'.

7 Wish you were there ...

Lesson planner

Fast lane: 3 x 1.5 hour lessons = 4.5 hours per unit
(total course = 72–76 hours)

Lesson	Time	Classwork	Exam Booster (EB) homework
19	1.5 hours	Getting started, Reading + Vocab. Organiser (VO)	Getting started + Reading
20	1.5 hours	Check homework, Lang. develop., Grammar, Listening + VO	Lang. develop., Grammar + Listening
21	1.5 hours	Check homework, Speaking, Use of English, Writing + VO	Use of English, Speaking; Writing + Coursebook: Writing task

Slow lane: 4 x 1.5 hour lessons = 6 hours per unit
(total course = 96–100 hours)

Lesson	Time	Classwork	EB homework
25	1.5 hours	Getting started, Reading, VO + photocopiable 1	Getting started + Reading
26	1.5 hours	Check homework, Lang. develop., Grammar + VO	Lang. develop. + Grammar
27	1.5 hours	Check homework, Listening, Speaking + VO	Listening + Speaking
28	1.5 hours	Check homework, Use of English, Writing + photocopiable 2	Use of English; Writing + Coursebook: Writing task

Before you begin

Write the following quiz on the board or photocopy it. Students can do this in pairs or groups of three, and allow them time to do the quiz.

Quiz: Know your geography

1   The world's highest waterfall is in ...

   a Brazil   b Venezuela

   c Colombia   d Canada

2   What is the world's longest river?

   a The Danube   b The Amazon

   c The Nile   d Yangtze

3   If I have just entered the city of Cuenca, which country am I in?

   a Argentina   b Italy

   c Spain   d Ireland

4   I am walking down the Spanish Steps. Which city am I in?

   a Rome   b Madrid

   c Lisbon   d Argentina

5   I visited Ayers Rock yesterday, and I'm going to the Taronga Zoo next week. Which country am I in?

   a Canada   b South Africa

   c Australia   d New Zealand

Key: *1b; 2c; 3c; 4a; 5c*

Topic: travel, cities, virtual worlds, tourism

Travel is a very broad subject, and due to the Internet, opportunities for new kinds of travel experiences are becoming increasingly available.

Unit 7 Wordlist

autonomy	extortionate	roadshow
avatar	grandeur	roadside
beckon	industrious	roadworks
board up	overlook	run down
breathless	persona	shoddy
crumbling	pragmatic	simulated
distorted	roadblock	slum
dome	roadhog	surreal
eerie	roadhouse	triumphal
essence	roadie	virtual

Getting started

1 Elicit the different types of travel depicted in the photographs. Make sure students include the strip at the top of the page. Give feedback.

2 🎧 7.1 Direct your students to read the rubric. Play the recording. Elicit answers, and if necessary, play the recording again.

3 Ask for students' views on what the tour operator says.

4 Direct students to read the poem and work out the meaning of some of the key vocabulary it features.

TEACHING IN PRACTICE

Reading poetry
Students often find reading poetry in another language daunting. Once they have read the poem once, before asking for their thoughts, write the following on the board:

timeless passage, borne, beckoning

Elicit the meaning of the words above. Prompt with clues where necessary.

Reading: multiple matching texts

Aim: The four short texts in this section have been taken from the travel section of an English newspaper. They are all readers' descriptions of their favourite city. The aim here is to present students with a topic they can realistically relate and respond to in a personal way. The language is of a level which you can encourage your students to emulate in their own writing tasks.

1 Students do this in pairs. Direct them to read the rubric. Elicit the names of some cities from the class as a whole first. Then, allow partners to work together. Monitor from a distance. Then, give general feedback to the class.

2 🎧 7.2 Direct students to read the rubric. Tell them they will hear the recording twice. Play the recording. Then play it again. Allow students time to finish writing in their answers.

Note: F(iona) is not used as an answer at all in exercise 2 above. This is intentional, as some students make the mistake of expecting a question to have a particular answer. They may expect something like N, B, F, for example. Tell them that they should try to avoid such expectations when doing this kind of exercise.

3 Direct students to the rubric. Allow them time to read texts A and B. Elicit one thing each writer likes about their city.

PAPER 1, PART 4 Interpreting the question
Explain that a very important part of reading comprehension lies in understanding what information the question is asking you for. Questions are sometimes phrased in a manner that is confusing. Students should make sure they understand it before answering.

4 Ask them to read the rubric for exercise 4. Allow students to discuss any discrepancies in their answers, by justifying their choice. Give feedback.

5 Tell your students to read the rubric for exercise 5, and consider the wording of each question carefully before answering. Allow them time to complete the exercise.

6 Tell your students that exercise 6 is an exam-style task, and they will need to refer to the four passages, A–D, in order to answer the questions. Direct them to read the rubric of the questions, and elicit any unknown words.

7 Students do this exercise in pairs. Draw their attention to the fact that they are told which text each vocabulary item is taken from.

→ Vocabulary Organiser 7.1, page 72

Reading extension

If relevant, you could ask students whether they have visited any of the cities mentioned in this section. If so, ask them whether their impression of the place was the same as the writer's.

Language development: describing places

1 Direct students to read the rubric for exercise 1. Elicit any unknown words in the box. Suggest that students write the three lists in their notebooks.

→ Vocabulary Organiser 7.2, page 72

2 Direct students to read the rubric for exercise 2, and refer them back to text C on page 65. Check answers as a class.

3 Students do this in pairs before discussing responses as a class.

4 Students should do this exercise individually.

→ Vocabulary Organiser 7.3, page 72

5 Tell students to write out the complete sentences in their notebooks.

6 Students do this exercise and exercise 7 in pairs. Allow them time to complete exercise 6.

7   Tell students to make a list in their notebooks.

→   Vocabulary Organiser 7.4, page 72

8   Direct students to read the rubric on page 67. Explain that this is a word formation exercise, and that Blackpool is a town on the northwest coast of England. Allow them time to read the email and complete the task.

Use of English: open cloze

2   Direct students to read the questions. Allow them time to complete the task before giving feedback.

3   Direct your students to read the rubrics for the exam-style task. This text is quite demanding, so ask them to read it through. Ask if any students have heard of or played this game. If so, get further information from them. If not, refer to the 'Background information' below. Elicit any unknown words: check such words as *concept, simulated* and *persona*.

TEACHING IN PRACTICE

Understanding cloze tests
When you tackle Paper 3, part 2, always ask for ideas from your students about the content of the text before they do the task. This ensures that they understand as much as possible, to help them with the task.

BACKGROUND: 'SECOND LIFE'

Second Life is a virtual world developed by Linden Lab that launched on 23rd June 2003. It is accessible via the Internet. A client program called the Second Life Viewer enables its users, called Residents, to interact with each other through avatars. Residents can explore, meet other residents, socialise, participate in activities, create and trade virtual property and services with one another, or travel throughout the world. Second Life caters for users aged over 18, while its sister site, Teen Second Life, is restricted to users aged between 13 and 18.

Listening: multiple extracts

1   Direct students to read the rubric. Encourage discussion.

2   Tell your students to read the quotation, and decide if the speaker approves or disapproves of space travel, and why.

6   🎧 7.3 Direct your students to read the rubrics for both tasks. Elicit any unknown words. Play the recording, then play the recording again before discussing answers.

7   Direct your students to look at Tapescript 7.3 on page 212. Elicit their views on the value of commercial space travel.

Grammar: inversion

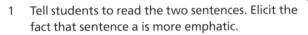

1   Tell students to read the two sentences. Elicit the fact that sentence a is more emphatic.

GRAMMAR SPOTLIGHT

Using inversion
Direct your students to read the rubric. Give an example of each use of inversion, and elicit a further example of each from students.

2 Tell students to read the sentences and invert them. Elicit answers and give feedback.

3   Direct your students to read the sentences. Explain that they are all possible, but that in certain situations, you would be more likely to hear one type or the other. Allow them a few minutes to think about this before asking for answers.

4   Direct your students to the tapescript on page 212, and ask them to underline inverted phrases. Elicit these. Then, ask them which speaker does not use inversion.

5   Students do this in pairs. Tell them to play around with the third speaker's speech, and make it more emphatic and persuasive. Please note that not many changes need to be made to the speech, and there is only one point which can be realistically inverted, but that is intentional. Highlight the fact that inverted phrases are used sparingly, so as to be more effective.

TEACHING IN PRACTICE

Inversion in writing
Make it clear to your students that whenever they wish to use inversion in a piece of persuasive writing, they should avoid using the structure more than once or twice.

You may like to prepare an example of the over-use of inversion in a text, and listen to comments from your students.

6   Students should do this exercise individually before you check their answers.

7   Direct your students to read the text. Tell them or make sure they acknowledge the fact that they should emphasise the idea that this will be a first-time experience (so 'never before ...'). Allow them time to think about it.

→   Grammar Reference 7.1, page 174

→   Vocabulary Organiser 7.5, page 72

Speaking: discussing possible future developments

1   Invite their reactions to each statement. Allow for some disagreement. Don't allow them to go into too much detail, however, as they will be able to do this in exercise 2. While they speak, make a note of frequently used phrases, and repetition of language.

2   Tell your students to look at the Useful Language box. Comment on some phrases you felt were used repetitively in the discussion. Ask students which phrases could replace these. Students do this in pairs. Direct them to the question on page 69. Allow them time to respond to it, using some of the phrases from the Useful Language box. Monitor from a distance. Give feedback.

Writing: a proposal

Tell your students that they are going to look at how to write a proposal in this section. Give a brief introduction, and ask for some ideas about the difference between writing a proposal and writing a report. Make sure they know that while the format is similar (use of headings, suggestions for improvements etc), the main body of a report focuses on the problems with the present situation, and usually makes recommendations in the final paragraph, whereas the main body of a proposal evaluates various suggestions for improvement, and concludes which is the most practical.

1   Direct your students to read the rubric for the sample task on page 70.

TEACHING IN PRACTICE

Making tasks active
Even when a question in a coursebook only appears to ask students to read something passively, always make the task active, by eliciting information about what they have read. Make it clear to them that the task in exercise 1 is a part 1 question type. Elicit what the question is asking for, and ask them to pinpoint key information they would need to include in an answer to this question.

2   Tell your students to read the two sample answers, and compare them. Tell them to consider style, register and effective use of the input material from the question. They should make notes in their notebooks individually. Then, elicit comments from the class as a whole.

SPOTLIGHT ON WRITING

Persuasive language
Emphasise that most questions in the Writing Paper will contain some element of persuasion.

3   Tell them to go through sample answer B on page 70, and underline examples of ways in which the student makes her answer sound more convincing. Students should underline the following: A good idea would be to offer stimulating alternative art forms. For example, we could hold a photographic exhibition, then one of sculpture, followed by fabric design or possibly graphic design. Not only would this cater for a broader range of contemporary specialist tastes, but the variety would also arouse the interest of the general public.

Costs to the gallery could be kept to a minimum by charging participants a nominal fee. The workshop feature could be further developed by the creation of an Art Club for young people. Through this, painting and photography competitions could be held, with sponsorship from local businesses.

Only by developing a broader range of exhibits, more in line with contemporary interests, can we make the gallery successful once more.

4   Tell students to read the sentences and compare them. Elicit which pair sounds more persuasive. Then direct them to read the 'In other words' feature. They must try to improve sample answer A from page 70, using phrases from the box. Encourage them to make any other changes they think are necessary. This could be done in pairs.

5+6   Direct students to read the rubric for the exam style task. Elicit what the question is asking them for, and any key information in the input material that they need to use in their answer. Make sure everyone is clear what they have to do, then set this task for homework.

Photocopiable activity instructions

1 **Activity 7.1 Holiday dilemmas**

Aim: To revise and consolidate grammatical language areas covered in units 1–7.

You will need:
- One photocopy of the game board per four students
- Enough dice for one per group of four
- Buttons or coins as tokens (one for each player)

Instructions:

1   Explain that when they land on a square they must follow the instructions on that square. Many of the squares ask a question, or ask you to say something in a certain way.

2   Each student takes turns throwing the die. They should each throw the die once. The person with the highest number goes first.

3   When they land on a square with a question, they must answer it. If they fail to answer the question successfully, they will miss their next turn.

4   The winner is the person in the class who reaches the 'FINISH' square first.

2 **Activity 7.2 The space escape**

Aim: To revise and consolidate language learned in this unit, and to encourage students to express their views effectively in a persuasive manner.

Instructions:

1   Photocopy activity 7.2 on page 70, and hand one copy to each member of the class.

2   Explain to the students that the Earth is dying, and they have to go and live on a space station. The last space shuttle is about to leave, but there are only five places left on it.

3   Each student must choose to be one of the characters outside the shuttle and try and persuade the pilot to let them on the shuttle. They must use as many of the language items presented on the photocopy as possible to give reasons why they should be allowed on the flight.

4   When everyone has spoken, the class must take votes on who deserves to go on the shuttle, based on how successfully they used the target language.

Tapescript 7

Listening 7.1

Well, I think you're going to see <u>airship hotels.</u> You know, like cruise ships, but in the air. That's likely to be big business, because it'll be affordable for most people. Space hotels are a possibility, but they'll be pricey, so accessible only to the few. What's really taking off are <u>eco-friendly holidays,</u> as people are becoming more concerned about how they affect the environment. They're going to be really big, I reckon. Another thing in the offing is your holiday down under. <u>Hydropolis is being designed for an area off the coast of Dubai, an underwater paradise,</u> but again, this is not going to do your bank balance a lot of good. Also, we shouldn't forget that <u>you're still going to get the traditionalist tourist who wants to see the world as it is at ground level, who still yearns to walk the streets of cities of old.</u> You know what I mean? <u>What I can't see happening is this so called virtual tourism being popular.</u> I mean, you like travel because you want to leave home for a while. That's the whole point, isn't it? I don't think computers will ever be able to really capture that feeling of excitement you get as you climb on board a plane or a ship to go somewhere new, do you?

Listening 7.2

Nick: ... You know, I think of all the places we've been to, Edinburgh was my favourite.

Fiona: Really? It's certainly one of my favourites, but compared to Prague, and Amsterdam ... I don't really think I've got one particular favourite.

Nick: No? Well, for me, Edinburgh's got it all. Amazing architecture, culture, great shops and this warm, friendly air about it.

Fiona: I have to agree with you on that point. You feel safe walking about. Perhaps because it's a small city, and everything's easy to get to. Personally though, <u>I found the architecture rather intimidating. All those tall, stark buildings and dark stone.</u> You can really believe all the ghost stories that come out of Scotland!

Nick: That's exactly what's so amazing about it! <u>The setting and buildings make you feel you've walked onto a Charles Dickens film set, with their medieval and Georgian facades.</u> Then you walk <u>inside, and you're hit with vibrant colours and the innovative designs of modern life.</u>

Fiona: Umm ... I think what I liked about the place most were the coffee shops and art cafes. As you say, they were colourful, but I was struck by <u>the friendliness of the people.</u> Did you notice how chatty everyone was? And the laughter ... I seem to remember lots of animated conversation and laughter. Fantastic!

Nick: Yes, <u>they were very helpful, too,</u> weren't they? And I remember <u>the aroma of fresh coffee and bread in the shops, while outside, the crisp sea breeze left a faint taste of salt in my mouth.</u>

Fiona: Yes ... Definitely worth a return visit, possibly around Festival time ...

Listening 7.3

Speaker 1: I've been fascinated by the universe and our place in it for as long as I can remember! <u>As a property developer I built up a real empire here</u> in sunny California, all the time keeping a close eye on developments in the space program. The current race to create spaceflights for tourists is particularly exciting, <u>but no sooner had NASA announced plans for a space station than I decided I had to have a piece of that pie.</u> Space tourism is just moments away, <u>so why not be the first to build an orbiting space hotel?</u> Wild, huh!? We're almost there, though!

Speaker 2: To be honest, <u>studying the space science modules in my physics course here at university</u> have put me right off the idea of going into orbit in a spacecraft in this day and age. <u>Not only are there risks involved in launching, but there's also the danger of space debris ...</u> surely that's more than enough to make me feel just fine looking at the stars with my feet placed firmly on the ground!

Speaker 3: Astronaut passengers will come to the spaceport three days prior to their flight for pre-flight training. <u>This is to prepare them mentally and physically for the spaceflight experience, and enable astronauts to become acquainted with the spacecraft and their fellow passengers. As we speak, doctors and spaceflight specialists are developing the training programme, which will include g-force training.</u>

Speaker 4: Space tourism, I ask you! No sooner have they made it to the moon than they start talking about commercialising space travel! Has anybody really stopped to consider the effects this is going to have on the environment? Not only on earth, but in space, too! <u>I recently interviewed an astro-environmentalist for an article I was writing,</u> who stressed the need to avoid making the same mistakes in space as we have on earth. What I want to know is, <u>does anybody in authority really care about these issues,</u> or are the potential profits to be made from commercial space travel too great?'

Speaker 5: It's been my dream since I was small, really. I used to look up at the night sky and think about what it must be like to be up there, among the stars ... And the money? Well, I know it's a lot, and I've heard all the ethical arguments about what better use it could be put to, and <u>I agree with them all, but I think it'll be worth it. I've worked hard all my life, and it's my money!</u> Rarely do people of my generation get the chance to fulfill such a dream. <u>At my age, don't I have the right to have this once-in-a-lifetime experience?</u>

Answer key 7

Getting started p63

2 airship hotels; eco-friendly holidays; he believes a certain number of traditionalists will still be touring the world. He doesn't think virtual tourism will be popular.
4 promise of exploration; opportunity to have new experiences, see new things, travel into the unknown

Reading pp64–5

2 a N; b N; c B
3 Text A: Suggested answer: Dublin is walkable, and it is by both the mountains and the sea.
Text B: Suggested answer: St. Petersburg seems timeless, and contains the spirit of its past.
4 1 They have family ties with the place, but were not necessarily born there; 2 They were actually born in that place. Sentence one is true of both texts.
5 1T; 2F; 3F; 4T; 5F
6 1C; 2A + D; 3D; 4 B + C; 5D; 6A, C + D; 7D; 8C; 9B; 10B + D
7 a chains; b rush; c crumbling; d eerie; e funding; f triumphal; g bureaucracy; h cripple; i appealing; j misconception; k industrious; l jolly; m autonomy

Language development p66

1 Note: Some words are used in more than one category.
a buildings: crumbling, grandeur, run down, dusty, shoddy, slums, gothic, old
b atmosphere: sparkling snow, lovely fresh air, the essence of, eerie, industrious, magical, threatening, touristy, remarkable, sober, unique
c personal reaction: amazing, disgusting, like home, open mind, appealing, horrible, passion, shoddy, breathless, threatening, it has it all, remarkable.
2 taking care of; showing consideration for
3 1c; 2e; 3a; 4g; 5b; 6h; 7f; 8d
4 1T; 2F; 3F; 4T; 5T

5 1f; 2g; 3a; 4b; 5c; 6d; 7e
6 1b; 2a; 3a; 4b; 5b
7 block; hog; house; map; rage; side; sign; show; works; worthy
8 1 outing; 2 seaside; 3 touristy; 4 grandeur; 5 investment; 6 lookalike; 7 unforeseen; 8 memorable

Use of English p67

1 1 never; 2 Despite
2 a hardly; b many; c Despite; d without; e However; f with; g hardly; h Few
3 1 However; 2 only; 3 without; 4 themselves; 5 First; 6 begin/start; 7 with; 8 that; 9 can; 10 although/ but; 11 which; 12 has; 13 form/ create/begin; 14 to; 15 becoming

Listening p68

2 disapproves
3 a
4 'anyone who studies outer space for a living as I do …'
5 b
6 Task one: 1G; 2H; 3C; 4D; 5A
Task two: 6E; 7G; 8F; 9H; 10C

Grammar p69

1 a is more emphatic than b.
2 a this tough cleaning gel will clean your kitchen surfaces, but it will also make your pans shine
b had she opened the door than flames swept into the room
c has anything like this happened in this town
d must visitors take photographs inside the museum
e will you have an opportunity to buy our product at this price
3 Note: In some cases, this may be open to question, but you can explain that the alternatives are in no way grammatically wrong, we are simply discussing the contexts in which inversion can be used 'naturally', to add emphasis.
1a (it's more emphatic and persuasive); 2b (a small child is unlikely to use inversion, as it is too sophisticated); 3a (a newsreader

wants to gain the audience's attention, and so may use inversion for emphasis); 4 a/b (depending on age: an older person may use inversion).
4 Speaker 1: 'no sooner had NASA announced plans for a space station than I decided I had to have a piece of that pie'
Speaker 2: 'Not only are there risks involved in launching, but there's also the danger of space debris'
Speaker 3: no inversion
Speaker 4: 'No sooner have they made it to the moon than they start talking about commercialising space travel'
Speaker 5: 'Rarely do people of my generation get the chance to fulfil such a dream.'
5 It is Speaker 3 only that needs changing. Suggested answer: 'Three days prior to their flight, astronaut passengers will come to the spaceport for pre-flight training. This is not only to prepare them mentally and physically for the spaceflight experience, but also to enable them to become acquainted with the spacecraft and their fellow passengers. As we speak, doctors and spaceflight specialists are developing the training programme, which will include g-force training.'
6 a Never before had; b No sooner had; c Under no circumstances must
7 Suggested answer: 'Never before has commercial space travel been available to the public, so book tickets for the first flight. This is a once-in-a-lifetime opportunity for anyone who is interested in space.'

Writing pp70–1

1 proposal: so formal in style. Need to include: suggestions for workshops in order to attract different age groups; give examples; suggestions for a variety of art media to be exhibited (photography, sculpture, textile design, graphic design etc).

2 Answer A answers the question, but the student lifts words and phrases from the input material, and doesn't support her suggestions with reasons or examples. She doesn't 'persuade' the reader in any way. Also, she mentions some negative aspects (that is, the costs) without softening them in some way.
In answer B, the student uses more varied language, and supports her suggestions with positive reasons. Use of noun forms of words and inversion are effective in convincing the reader that her ideas are good ones.

Vocabulary organiser 7 p72

7.1 1 funding; 2 industrious; 3 crippled; 4 triumphal; 5 autonomy; 6 chains; 7 rush; 8 bureaucracy; 9 appealing; 10 misconception
7.2 a Positive description: amazing, appealing, breathless, cosy, grand, industrious, magical, sparkling, passionate, remarkable, unique. Negative description: crumbling, disgusting, dusty, eerie, horrible, run down, shoddy, sober, threatening.
7.4 1F (A road hog is a driver to drives selfishly and doesn't consider other drivers); 2T; 3F (We say a vehicle is roadworthy when it is in a good condition and can be driven); 4T; 5F (A roadshow is a touring TV or radio programme, which broadcasts from a different town each day or week); 6F (A road block is when the police stop cars at a certain point on the road in order to search them); 7T

Bank of English

Verb: travel by train, car, plane etc; travel light; travel widely.
Noun: air travel; on their travels; rail travel; travel agent; travel rug; travel sickness; traveller's cheque; travelogue.
Adjective: travelling expenses; travelling musician; travelling salesman.

Holiday dilemmas

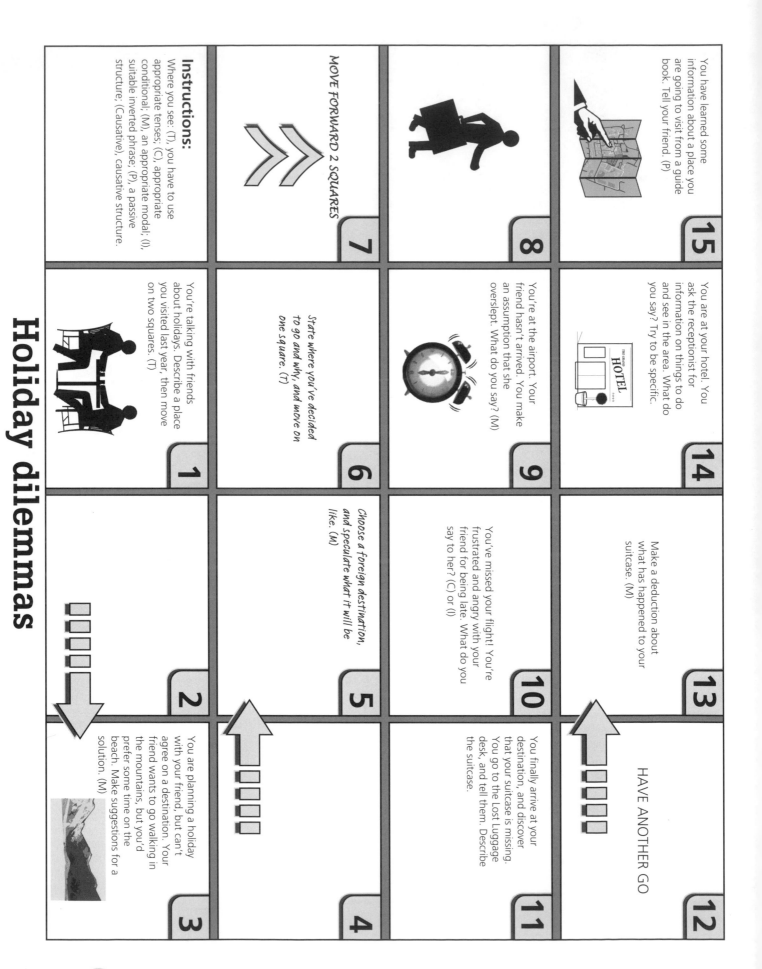

Instructions:

Where you see: (T), you have to use appropriate tenses; (C), appropriate conditional; (M), an appropriate modal; (I), suitable inverted phrase; (P), a passive structure; (Causative), causative structure.

1 — You're talking with friends about holidays. Describe a place you visited last year, then move on two squares. (T)

2 —

3 — You are planning a holiday with your friend, but can't agree on a destination. Your friend wants to go walking in the mountains, but you'd prefer some time on the beach. Make suggestions for a solution. (M)

4 —

5 — Choose a foreign destination, and speculate what it will be like. (M)

6 — State where you've decided to go and why, and move on one square. (T)

7 — MOVE FORWARD 2 SQUARES

8 —

9 — You're at the airport. Your friend hasn't arrived. You make an assumption that she overslept! What do you say? (M)

10 — You've missed your flight! You're frustrated and angry with your friend for being late. What do you say to her? (C) or (I)

11 — You finally arrive at your destination, and discover that your suitcase is missing. You go to the Lost Luggage desk, and tell them. Describe the suitcase.

12 — HAVE ANOTHER GO

13 — Make a deduction about what has happened to your suitcase. (M)

14 — You are at your hotel. You ask the receptionist for information on things to do and see in the area. What do you say? Try to be specific.

15 — You have learned some information about a place you are going to visit from a guide book. Tell your friend. (P)

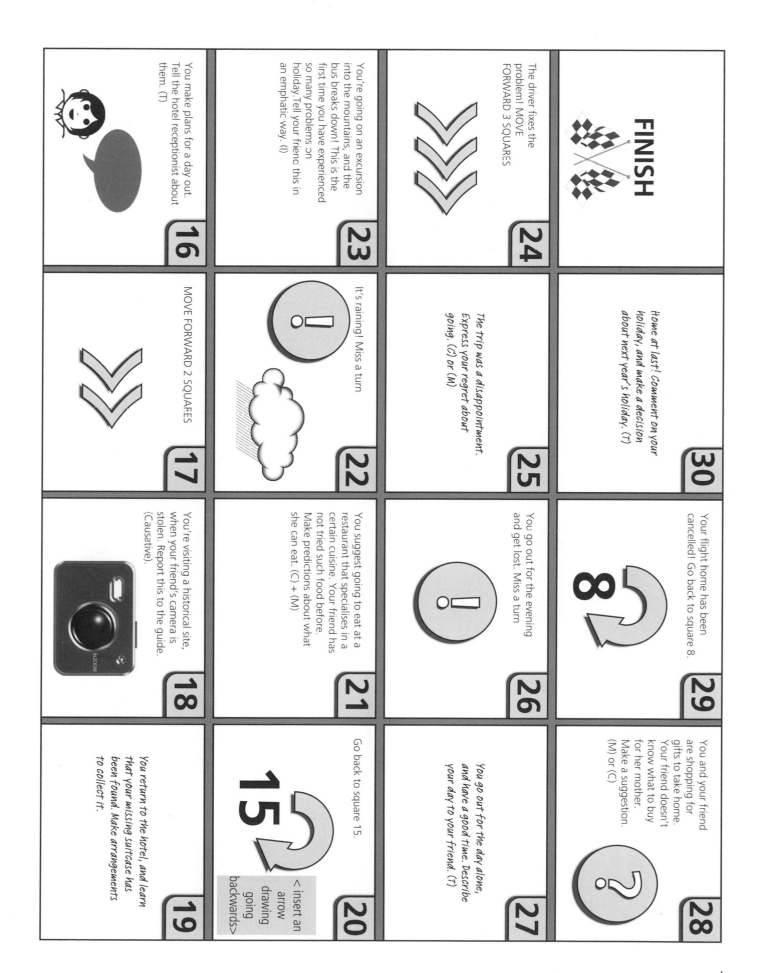

16 — You make plans for a day out. Tell the hotel receptionist about them. (T)

23 — You're going on an excursion into the mountains, and the bus breaks down! This is the first time you have experienced so many problems on holiday. Tell your friend this in an emphatic way. (I)

24 — The driver fixes the problem! MOVE FORWARD 3 SQUARES

FINISH

17 — MOVE FORWARD 2 SQUARES

22 — It's raining! Miss a turn

25 — The trip was a disappointment. Express your regret about going. (C) or (M)

30 — Home at last! Comment on your holiday, and make a decision about next year's holiday. (T)

18 — You're visiting a historical site, when your friend's camera is stolen. Report this to the guide. (Causative).

21 — You suggest going to eat at a restaurant that specialises in a certain cuisine. Your friend has not tried such food before. Make predictions about what she can eat. (C) + (M)

26 — You go out for the evening and get lost. Miss a turn

29 — Your flight home has been cancelled! Go back to square 8.

19 — You return to the hotel, and learn that your missing suitcase has been found. Make arrangements to collect it.

20 — Go back to square 15. < insert an arrow drawing going backwards>

27 — You go out for the day alone, and have a good time. Describe your day to your friend. (T)

28 — You and your friend are shopping for gifts to take home. Your friend doesn't know what to buy for her mother. Make a suggestion. (M) or (C)

The space escape

phrasal verb or phrase with *look*

inverted structure

passive structure

investment

unforeseeable

memorable

ethical

despite

however

without

8 Making our mark

Lesson planner

Fast lane: 3 x 1.5 hour lessons = 4.5 hours per unit
(total course = 72–76 hours)

Lesson	Time	Classwork	Exam Booster (EB) homework
22	1.5 hours	Getting started, Reading + Vocab. Organiser (VO)	Getting started + Reading
23	1.5 hours	Check homework, Lang. develop., Grammar, Speaking + VO	Lang. develop., Grammar + Speaking
24	1.5 hours	Check homework, Listening, Use of English, Writing + VO	Listening, Use of English + Writing
Extra	__hour	Review 2	Can either be set as homework or completed in class

Slow lane: 4 x 1.5 hour lessons = 6 hours per unit
(total course = 96–100 hours)

Lesson	Time	Classwork	EB homework
29	1.5 hours	Getting started, Reading + VO	Getting started + Reading
30	1.5 hours	Check homework, Lang. develop., Grammar, VO + photocopiable 1	Lang. develop. + Grammar
31	1.5 hours	Check homework, Speaking, Listening, Use of English, VO + photocopiable 2	Speaking, Listening + Use of English
32	1.5 hours	Check homework + Writing	Writing (+ write one composition)
Extra	__hour	Review 2	Can either be set as homework or completed in class

Before you begin

Ask your students to tell you what they think is the greatest mark ever made by human beings on this earth: a building, a monument, a piece of art and so on. Write their suggestions on the board and discuss them.

Topic: architecture and archaeology

Since the dawn of civilisation, human beings have been 'making their mark' on the landscape in more ways than one. This unit therefore concentrates on human-made monuments and buildings, artwork and architecture.

Unit 8 Wordlist

abode	excavate	painstakingly
accessible	flexibility	pivotal
awe-inspiring	habitat	precision
commemorate	immigrant	preconception
construction	imposing	protruding
contaminant	imprecise	radically
disarming	installation	remote
dominating	insulate	residence
durability	invariably	resume
dwelling	isolate	stunning
empowering	motivation	topple
erect	novice	vanquish

Getting started

Aim: To generate interest in the subject of landmarks, monuments, historical buildings and architecture, and to introduce vocabulary useful for describing such things.

1   Ask this as an open question and accept students' answers as a way of introducing the title and theme of the unit.

2   Most students should be able to match the monuments to the pictures quite easily.

3   Accept various answers. Try to elicit responses about several of the main buildings or monuments shown on this page, plus any others that students may want to discuss.

4   Students should attempt this task in pairs if they are familiar with the vocabulary, otherwise do it as a large group activity.

→   Vocabulary Organiser 8.1, page 82

Reading: understanding opinion

Aim: Understanding a writer's opinion is a key element of the Reading Paper, so students need to learn how to interpret the writer's own opinion before they attempt to answer multiple choice questions.

1   With climate changes occurring in many parts of the world, and the need to reduce the amount of carbon dioxide in the atmosphere, it is now considered imperative by many scientists, governments, organisations and individuals to encourage architectural designs and building techniques that bear this in mind.

2   Students should do this individually or in pairs. Check answers with the class.

BACKGROUND: STRAW BALE CONSTRUCTION

Straw bale construction is a building method that uses straw bales as structural elements and/or insulation. It is commonly used in natural building. It has advantages over some conventional building systems because of its cost, easy availability, and high insulation value. Although grasses and straw have been used in various ways for thousands of years, their incorporation in machine-manufactured modular bales seems to date back to the early 20th century in the mid-western United States.

3   Direct students to look at the picture and elicit answers from the whole group. Write two lists on the board: 1 Advantages; 2 Disadvantages.

4   Give students a minute to discuss the point in pairs.

BACKGROUND: THE THREE LITTLE PIGS

Once upon a time there were three little pigs. When they grew up their mother told them they would have to go off into the big wide world and find their own homes. Each wandered off looking for something with which to build a house for him or herself. The first little pig came across a bale of straw and decided to build a house with straw. The second little pig found some sticks so he built a house of sticks, and the third managed to acquire some bricks with which to build her house. Unfortunately the big bad wolf came along. He was able to blow down the first and the second houses quite easily and eat the pigs inside, but he was unable to blow down the third house, which was strong and durable. Instead, he decided to climb down the chimney, but the clever third little pig had already anticipated this, and had put a pot of hot water on the fire. The wolf fell into this and was killed. The third little pig lived happily ever after.

5   8.1 Students should listen to the recording and note down the answers. Afterwards check the answers against the advantages and disadvantages lists you have written on the board. You will probably note that many of the 'disadvantages' students originally noted, are in fact 'advantages'.

SPOTLIGHT ON READING

Understanding opinion

The point here is to encourage students to think about what the writer is actually saying before they start looking at the multiple choice options.

6   Students should read the each paragraph carefully and answer the questions in their own words.

TEACHING IN PRACTICE

Paraphrasing texts

One way to make sure students have understood what they are reading is to ask them to paraphrase a text in their own words, one paragraph at a time. They should first read the paragraph, then cover it and say what they have understood.

7   Students should read the text again and answer the multiple choice questions by reference to the text. Check answers with students and ask them to justify their answers.

→   Vocabulary Organiser 8.2, page 82

Language development:
phrases with *bring*

1 + 2 + 3   These questions aim to revise phrases and phrasal verbs with *bring* and to introduce some new ones. Students should attempt exercise 1 individually to see how much they remember. Students should make a note of any new phrasal verbs and expressions in their vocabulary notebooks.

→   Vocabulary Organiser 8.3 + 8.4, page 82

Key word: *that*

4 + 5 + 6   In completing these questions, students should become more aware of the different uses of the word *that* so that they will be able to correctly infer the meaning in a text and use the word more effectively themselves. Students should attempt exercises 4 and 5 individually. Check answers and straighten out any problems. Exercise 6 can be done in pairs or small groups or as a class activity.

Speaking: reaching a decision through negotiation

Aim: The purpose of this section is to help students with part 3 of the Speaking Paper, in which they are awarded marks for their ability to interact and negotiate with their partner in reaching a decision. A common fault in this part of the Speaking Paper is that students may simply take turns answering the examiner's question rather than working together.

SPOTLIGHT ON SPEAKING

Reaching a decision through negotiation

1 Ask students to read the options and then elicit their answers. Ask them to give reasons.

2   Students work in pairs.

TEACHING IN PRACTICE

Mixing pairs

It would probably help your students more here if you mixed pairs so that each student is working with a student they aren't so familiar with. It is generally harder to interact with someone you don't know well than with a close friend, so try to give them practice working with people they don't know as often as possible. Try to listen to each pair as they do the task and give feedback.

Listening: interpreting context

Aim: The purpose here is to help students to listen to indirect clues in a dialogue in order to understand its context. This will help them answer multiple choice questions that may ask for contextual information.

EXAM SPOTLIGHT

PAPER 4, PART 1 Interpreting context

1 🎧 8.2 Play the recording. Students should jot down words or phrases that provide the answer if they can.

2 Play the recording again and tell students to listen out for distractors.

3 Play the recording again and elicit answers to all the questions. If you think they still didn't 'catch' the answers, tell them to turn to the tapescript on pages 212–13 and check their answers there.

4   🎧 8.3 Tell students to utilise the same techniques to answer the remaining questions. Tell them you will play the recording twice to give them the opportunity to identify the context in each case.

Grammar: relative pronouns / defining and non-defining relative clauses

1 + 2 + 3 Students complete the exercises individually and by referring to the Grammar Reference if required. Check answers with the class.

→   Grammar Reference 8.1, page 175

Grammar (exercise 4) extension

Rewrite the following sentences in two different ways using the word in brackets. Which sentence is more formal?

1 Do you know that girl? John is talking to her. (that/whom)

2 The seat which I was sitting on was at the back. (where/which)

3 The film ended and everyone got up and left. (when/at which point)

5 + 6 Students work individually or in pairs. Answers should be checked with the whole class and an opportunity given to all students to clarify any points of confusion.

→   Grammar Reference 8.2, page 175

GRAMMAR SPOTLIGHT

Reduced relative clauses

7 + 8 Go through the exercise and rubric with the students. Elicit the changes that have been made. Ask students to tell you in which situations they think reduced relative clauses might be used more frequently.

Use of English: word building (noun groups)

1   Most students should be able to complete the table with the correct form of the word in most cases, although there may be some words which confuse them. Ask them to have a go at the table first by themselves, but to leave blank any noun formations they are unsure of. Afterwards go through the words one by one. Use the teaching in practice tip on page 74.

Noticing word patterns

Ask a student to tell the class their answer. Ask for a show of hands to see how many people agree; if the class is unanimously correct, move on. If not, ask any students who disagree or are unsure, which words are most likely in their opinion. Narrow the list of possible options by asking if they can think of other words that follow the same formation. In this way you will be able to show the class that many words habitually fall into patterns, and that the more words they learn and record, the easier it will be to form the correct noun from the given word.

Compiling noun groups

2 Point out that very often there is more than one form of a particular word in a particular part of speech (in this case nouns). It is important that students are aware of this so that they do not always automatically choose the first word they think of. They have to also make sure it is the correct word in the given context.

Easter Island is a Polynesian island in the south-eastern Pacific Ocean. Easter Island is famous for its monumental statues, called *moai*, created by the Rapanui people. The history of Easter Island is rich and controversial. Its inhabitants have endured famines, epidemics, civil war, slave raids and colonialism, and the crash of their ecosystem; the population has declined precipitously more than once.

3 Elicit as much information as you can about the statues in the picture, or about Easter Island. If the class has never seen them before or knows nothing about Easter Island, elicit guesses and ideas from the class by asking questions:

> Who do you think made them?

> Why did they make them?

Ask the class to then quickly read the text to see if they had guessed any information correctly. This will also ensure that they read the text once through for understanding before attempting exercise 4.

4 Students should do the exercise individually. Check answers with the whole class.

→ Vocabulary Organiser 8.5, page 82

5 Discuss the topic with the class. Point out that although the text seems to clearly imply that the people of Easter

Island brought about their own destruction, it may in fact not be correct. Elicit further suggestions of what could have happened to them.

Afterwards ask students to read the questions for exercise 6 to see whether they reveal any further information.

6 🎧 8.4 Students should do the listening task individually. Before you play the recording remind students to follow the steps given in previous units:

1 Read the questions to identify key words;

2 Identify the part of speech required in each gap;

3 Try to guess the possible meanings required to complete the sentences.

Writing: contributing to a larger piece

Aim: The purpose of this section is to inform students about this part of the writing task, which is a new feature of the Revised CAE exam introduced in December 2008. The aim is to show that writing a contribution to a longer piece of writing is similar to writing a report in many ways.

1 Try to get a varied response from your students to this question, so after the first student has described their home, ask: 'Who lives somewhere very different from that?'

Writing a contribution to a longer piece

2 Read the rubric with the class. Ask questions to make sure they have understood what this kind of writing requires. If necessary, refer students to the model composition on page 190. For question c, tell students to spend a couple of minutes jotting down heading titles in their notebooks.

3 Students read the model individually. Afterwards ask questions about the writer's description.

4 Ask students to refer back to page 50 in Unit 5 to recall a report. Elicit the differences and similarities from the class.

Brainstorming vocabulary

5 Ask students to read the model again and underline the descriptive vocabulary. Write key words and phrases on the board if you like. Point out that they will have to brainstorm different vocabulary for different tasks.

6 Students can do this exercise individually or in pairs. Check answers with the class.

In other words

7 Students use their dictionaries to complete the sentences. They can also find other meanings for each of the words listed (or other words) that can be used to mean 'house' in some way. Check answers with the class.

→ Vocabulary Organiser 8.6, page 82

8 Students should plan their piece of writing in class. Check heading titles and ideas of descriptive vocabulary. Students should then spend up to half an hour writing their contribution or should finish it for homework.

Photocopiable activity instructions

1 **Activity 8.1 The Seven Wonders of the Ancient and Medieval World**

Aim: To practise using the skills of debate and argument.

Instructions:

1 Divide the class into pairs or groups of three and give each a copy of the photocopiable 8.1.

2 Explain that the 'Great Pyramid at Giza' is the only surviving monument from the original list of the 'Seven Wonders of the Ancient World' and tell your students that it has been selected as number one in a new list of 'Surviving Wonders from the Ancient and Medieval World.'

3 Your students have to choose six more monuments from the list and put them in order of importance.

4 First each group works together for a few minutes to compile their lists. They should agree as much as possible.

5 When they have completed their lists say that you will only accept one finished list. Each group has to argue why their list should be accepted.

2 **Activity 8.2 Party People**

Aim: To practise using relative pronouns and relative clauses.

Instructions:

1 Photocopy the first column of the activity once, cut out the statements and hand them out to the class so that everyone has at least one, and some people may have two or more, depending on the size of the group.

2 Photocopy the second column of the activity and give one copy to everyone in the group.

3 Tell everyone to stand up and 'mingle' in the middle of the room. Tell them they are at a party and they are all strangers. The information they have in their slips of paper says something about them. They must not show these slips to anyone.

4 The questioner should ask questions until they have found out the relevant information to complete one of the boxes on their sheet. At the same time, the person they are talking to can ask them questions to try and fill in their own sheet.

5 Allow your class roughly one minute with each person; five or six minutes in total.

6 The first person to complete all the names and information on their sheet is the winner. They should raise their hands and shout 'Got it!' They should then read their sheets out to the class to check their information is correct. If they make a mistake they lose.

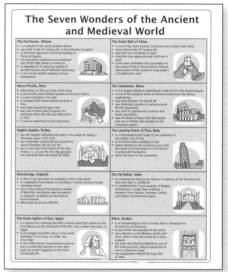

Tapescript

Listening 8.1

Here are seven great reasons why you should consider building your next house with straw bales:

Reason number one: Energy efficiency. A well-built straw bale home can save you up to 75 per cent on heating and cooling costs. In fact, in most climates, we do not even install air conditioning units into our homes as the natural cooling cycles of the planet are enough to keep the house cool all summer long.

Reason number two: Sound proofing. Straw bale walls provide excellent sound insulation and are superior wall systems for home owners looking to block out the sounds of traffic or aircraft in urban environments.

Reason number three: Fire resistance. Straw bale homes have roughly three times the fire resistance of conventional homes. Thick, dense bales mean limited oxygen which, in turn, means no flames.

Reason number four: Environmental responsibility. Building with straw helps the planet in many ways. For example, straw is a waste product that is either burned or composted in standing water. By using the straw instead of eliminating it, we reduce either air pollution or water consumption, both of which impact the environment in general.

Reason number five: Natural materials. The use of straw as insulation means that the usual, standard insulation materials are removed from the home. Standard fibre glass insulation has formaldehyde in it, which is known to cause cancer. Bale walls also eliminate the use of plywood in the walls. Plywood contains unhealthy glues that can off-gas into the house over time.

Reason number six: Aesthetics. There is nothing as calming and beautiful as a straw bale wall in a home. Time and time again I walk people through homes and they are immediately struck by the beauty and the "feeling" of the walls. I really can't explain this one, you'll just have to walk through your own to see what I mean.

Reason number seven: Minimise wood consumption. If built as a 'load bearing assembly', which can support a roof, the wood in the walls can be completely eliminated, except for around the windows. The harvesting of forests is a global concern and any reduction in the use of wood material is a good thing for the long term health of the planet.

Listening 8.2

Interviewer: So what interests you most about your work?

Man: Well, being able to create something that has real value is the main thing. I mean, it's great to be an artist or a sculptor and I'm certainly not belittling the value of fine art in society, but it's a totally different feeling knowing that what you create will have real practical value. I mean, people actually live in your creations! And of course, egotistically speaking, it's a chance to make a real

mark on the landscape, something that can probably be seen for miles around.

Interviewer: Sometimes that's not such a good thing though. There are some undeniable monstrosities in the landscape which somebody must have thought was beautiful.

Man: Well, that's the second main reason I love my work. My philosophy is to design structures that blend into the landscape, using natural materials and organic shapes. My clients come to me for that reason. I am confident that no-one would call any of my designs an eye-sore and that gives me a real feeling of satisfaction.

Listening 8.3

Extract 1

Woman 1: When I first saw it I didn't realise quite how important it would turn out to be, although my first thought was that I was probably looking at something very old indeed.

Woman 2: It must have been very exciting.

Woman 1: I suppose it was, but I didn't know then that it would be a turning point for the project, and for me. I mean, the dig had been turning up very little, and our sponsors were threatening to pull our funds, so it was significant in more ways than one.

Woman 2: When did you realise the significance of the find itself?

Woman 1: Well, more or less at once. I called over Professor Hargreaves, and we carefully brushed out the piece in order to define it more clearly. It appeared to be manmade, but of course we couldn't date it until we submitted it for radio carbon testing, but from the level of the dig, we knew we must have been looking at something pre-Egyptian, possibly ten thousand years old.

Extract 2

Interviewer: So it was ambition that drove you, from an early age?

Angel: Yeah, I suppose you could say that. I knew I wanted to be famous when I was little. I used to tell all my parent's friends and say: 'I'm gonna be dead famous one day!'

Interviewer: And what did they say?

Angel: Well they laughed mostly. They thought I was being cute but that just made me more and more determined, see, so that's all I thought about all through school. I wrote my own songs and got a band together, even though my teachers kept telling me I'd never achieve anything the way I was going.

Interviewer: And do you think that your fame will last? Are you more concerned about being the flavour of the month, or creating a legacy in music that has your name on it?

Angel: Well, I've since realised that being famous isn't all roses. I mean, I love the media attention, and the money ain't bad either, but there comes a point where you think: 'OK, that's enough for today, can you leave me alone now!' and they don't. It just keeps going on and then you start to cherish your privacy and you put dark glasses and hats on and try to achieve anonymity like you had before – well, some of the time anyway.

Interviewer: It must be a tough life!

Listening 8.4

Between 1200 and 1600 AD, the people of Easter Island built and erected around 400 enormous statues, or 'moai' as they are called, and another 400 were left unfinished in the quarries where they were made. Up to ten metres tall and weighing up to 75 tonnes, the enigmatic statues raise a host of questions – not least, why did the islanders build them, how did they move them and why were so many left unfinished? One theory is that different groups <u>competed</u> against each other, striving to build the most impressive *moai*.

Some researchers have suggested that this 'moai mania' was a disaster for the society. Yet others point to mounting evidence that prehistoric occupants made a success of life on the island and state that there is in fact painfully little archaeological <u>evidence</u> for the fundamental claims that underpin the self-destruction theory.

When the Dutch explorer Jacob Roggeveen 'discovered' the island on <u>Easter day</u> in 1722, he was stunned at the sight of monumental stone statues lined along the coast. He could see few trees, and he wondered how this apparently small, primitive society had transported and erected such monoliths without timber or ropes. Later on, pollen and soil analysis revealed that the island had once been home to <u>flourishing palm forests</u> with an estimated <u>16 million</u> trees. <u>Deforestation</u> seems to have begun as soon as the settlers arrived around 1200, and was complete by about 1500. The reason why the islanders wiped out their forest has long nagged at researchers and is still open to dispute. Some palms may indeed have been cut down to assist in moving the statues, though, with their very soft interiors they would not have been ideal for the job. Other trees were used for firewood, and land was cleared for agriculture. Still, the blame for the disappearance of the palms might not rest entirely with people. Recent genetic research suggests <u>rats</u>, which love to eat palm nuts, were introduced to the island in the canoes of the original colonisers.

Most of the evidence for starvation and cannibalism comes from oral histories, which are extremely contradictory and <u>unreliable</u>. Some researchers suspect that stories of cannibalism, in particular, could have been <u>invented by</u> missionaries. Very few of the remains of prehistoric islanders show any signs of personal violence. True, the 17th and 18th centuries saw an increase in artefacts identified by some as spearheads, but many believe the artefacts are <u>agricultural</u> implements.

The story of ecocide may usefully confirm our darkest fears about humanity but, for every society that self-destructs there is another that does the right thing. It is far from clear that the Easter Islanders made their situation much worse for themselves, but only more evidence will resolve the issue.

Answer key 8

Getting started p73

1 All the pictures show human-made monuments or buildings. To 'make one's mark' means to deliberately leave a permanent or long-lasting trace of your existence.
2 Clockwise from the top: Stonehenge, The Eiffel Tower, The Taj Mahal, The Great Pyramid of Giza and the Sphinx, the London Eye, The Statue of Liberty. Background: prehistoric cave paintings, the Nazca Inca lines of Peru.

Reading pp74–5

2 The order of answers may vary. There is no absolute right and wrong, but the most important ones that answer the question are b, f and h. Of secondary importance are: i & j (these points are obviously important, but for other reasons); e (the longer the house lasts, the less need there is to construct new buildings). Finally a, c, d, g (these may be important

to the house owner/builder and need to be considered, but have less environmental significance).
3 Advantages: cosy, cheap to build, good insulation, ecological. Disadvantages: unstable, fire-risk, not durable etc.
4 A bale of straw is usually associated with farms, farming, animal feed. A famous children's tale that many students should have heard of is that of the three little pigs and the big bad wolf.
5 1 energy efficiency; 2 sound proofing; 3 fire resistance; 4 environmental responsibility; 5 natural materials; 6 aesthetics; 7 minimise wood consumption.
6 [Para 1] Because builders are starting to realise that straw bale houses can have more advantages than other kinds of house.
[Para 2] Optimistic, joyful, motivated and it encourages women to join in.

[Para 3] It's flexible, organic and challenging, but it can be alarming to people who prefer complexity and precision.
[Para 4] Cost effectiveness and energy efficiency.
[Para 5] Organic, round shaped houses with deep window seats, thick walls and cosy interiors.
[Para 6] You should be flexible, adaptable and patient. You should try to get a feel for it and not force it into precise measurements or calculations.
[Para 7] People are learning more about the dangers of chemicals and toxins in the atmosphere and environment, which can have a detrimental effect on health.
7 1D; 2B; 3D; 4A; 5B; 6C; 7D

Language development p76

1 a out; b down; c up; d about; e forward; f on
2 1g; 2d; 3f; 4a; 5b; 6c; 7h; 8e

3 bring about = cause to happen; bring down = reduce
4 a4; b2; c5; d1; e3
5 Sentences b + c
6 It has been used 12 times in total: 1 6; 2 0; 3 2; 4 4; 5 0

Speaking p77

1 1 b (a is too repetitive of what student A says); 2 a (b just disagrees without showing that the speaker is listening); 3 b (a is too short and doesn't demonstrate any fluency).

Listening p77

1 A

2 B – 'it's great to be an artist or a sculptor and I'm certainly not belittling the value of fine art in society.'; C –'My philosophy is to design structures that blend into the landscape, using natural materials and organic shapes.'
3 C (A is wrong because he says: 'My clients come to me for that reason'; B is wrong because, although he

says his job gives him the chance to 'make a mark on the landscape', he goes on to say that his main 'philosophy is to design structures that blend into the landscape, using natural materials and organic shapes'. This is also the reason why C is correct).

4 1B; 2A; 3C; 4A

Grammar p78

1 a whose; b when; c which; d where; e who

2 c

3 a by which time; b the person whom; c as a result of which; d in which; e all of whom; f neither of whom; g some of which; h both of whom; i at which point.

4 1a: ND (talking about all the Indians); 1b: D (talking only about the Indians who used to live there); 2a: ND (we're talking about Petra who studied in London. The fact that she is the architect who built the house is extra information); 2b: D (here we are defining that the architect who built the house actually studied in London); 3a: D (only the trees that had been growing for over a century were cut down) 3b: ND (all the trees were cut down).

5 Commas are used in non-defining sentences to separate the additional information inserted into the main clause, to show that this information is not essential to the meaning. In defining clauses there are no commas because all the information is essential to the meaning of the clause. In defining clauses, *that* can be used instead of *who* or *which*.

6 1a The exhibits, which were very old, were in the Egypt section; 1b The exhibits that were very old were in the Egypt section. 2a The students that wanted some extra money got part-time jobs; 2b The students, who wanted some extra money, got part-time jobs. 3a The girl that was waiting for the bus was wearing a school uniform; 3b The girls, who were waiting for the bus, were wearing school uniforms.

4a The house that has a beautiful garden is going to be knocked down; 4b The house, which has a beautiful garden, is going to be knocked down.

7 1 'which are' has been removed; 2 'which was' has been removed; 3 'who walked' has become 'to walk'.

8 1 The tunnel, weakened by years …; 2 Children attending …; 3 Gillian was the only person to volunteer….; 4 Rebecca, embarrassed by what …; 5 Adrian, expecting to be paid …

Use of English p79

1 -ism: racism; -ity: stupidity, sensitivity; -ation: combination; -ness: naughtiness, tiredness; -sion: persuasion, obsession, tension; -ology: cosmology; -ment: development; -cy: redundancy, dependency; -ant: inhabitant; -ry: delivery

2 inhabitant, habitat, habitation

4 1 inhabitants; 2 Ecological; 3 felled; 4 cannibalism; 5 enslaved; 6 chillingly; 7 isolation; 8 illustration; 9 humanity; 10 eagerness

6 1 competed; 2 evidence; 3 Easter day (in 1722); 4 16 million; 5 deforestation; 6 rats; 7 unreliable; 8 invented; 9 agricultural

Writing pp80–1

2 a The research is for a friend so it doesn't have to be very formal. However, it is academic research so it will probably have a neutral, rather than an informal register. b You are being asked to provide a general description of the buildings in your town/city/country, especially houses, churches and other public buildings. c Headings can include any of the following: Personal residences (Houses/Flats); Places of Worship (Churches/Temples/Mosques); Educational Establishment (Schools/ Colleges/Universities); Government buildings; Public Buildings; Architecture in General; Hospitals, etc.

4 It has a subject heading and paragraph headings. However, the

content is more descriptive than a report usually is.

5 Suggested answers include: 'dull, rectangular blocks of grey cement, with protruding balconies on most sides'; 'rounded balconies, circular columns, and more attractive colours'; 'small, white-washed cubic houses built into the island rock'; 'no great diversity of style'; 'round domes and huge vaulted ceilings. Spires and minarets are not common'; 'painstakingly painted with scenes from the Bible, in particular those commemorating the saint after whom the Church has been dedicated.'

7 a housing; b dwellings; c habitat; d residence; e abode; f place

Vocabulary organiser 8 p82

8.1 a massive; b awe-inspiring; c peculiar; d imposing; e unattractive

8.2 a innovative; b sustainable; c accessible; d imprecise; e Organic; f inflexible; g inspirational; h empowering

8.3 a bring off; b bring down; c bring along; d bring out; e bring forward; f bring back; g bring about/on; h bring up; i bring in

8.4 a action; b home; c herself; d knees; e bear; f alive

8.5 a destruction; b obsession; c remoteness; d inevitability; e rivalry/rival; f vanquished/vanquisher

8.6 a housing; b residence; c abode; d dwelling; e lodging; f habitat

Bank of English

a outhouse; b get on like a house on fire; c housekeeper; d Houses of Parliament; e housing benefit

Review 2 pp83-4

1 1 confessed; 2 digest; 3 erected; 4 sustain; 5 overlooked; 6 beckoned; 7 consume; 8 confide; 9 convict; 10 incite

2 1 turning … down; 2 ward off; 3 looked up to; 4 brought back; 5 turned out; 6 look into; 7 turn in; 8 bring up

3 1 spill the beans; 2 look the other way; 3 go down that road; 4 lay down her life; 5 brought it home to me; 6 on the road to recovery; 7 bitten off more than you can chew; 8 is above the law

4 1 take; 2 do; 3 run; 4 make; 5 give; 6 fall

5 1B; 2A; 3D; 4B; 5C

6 1 deter from; 2 accuse of; 3 implicate in; 4 charge with; 5 refrain from; 6 works in

7 1 preconceptions; 2 consumption; 3 destruction; 4 digestive; 5 motivation; 6 restoration; 7 tiredness; 8 maintenance; 9 contaminants; 10 prescription/ prescribed

8 1 law; 2 health; 3 life; 4 take; 5 run

9 1 denied setting the house on; 2 went on [talking] about; 3 [Any/ Much] later I would not have; 4 for Jasper's warning not to; 5 no account must you; 6 before have I seen such; 7 as a result of which; 8 neither of whom has/have

The Seven Wonders of the Ancient and Medieval World

The Parthenon, Athens

- is a temple to the Greek goddess Athena
- was built in the 5th century BC on the Athenian Acropolis
- is the most important surviving building of Classical Greece
- its decorative sculptures are considered one of the high points of Greek art
- is regarded as an enduring symbol of ancient Greece and of Athenian democracy
- is one of the world's greatest cultural monuments.

The Great Wall of China

- is one of the most massive structures ever to have been built
- dates back to the 5th century BC
- was built over hundreds of years
- stretches over approximately 6400 km in total
- it has been estimated that somewhere in the range of two to three million Chinese died as part of the centuries-long project of building the wall.

Maccu Picchu, Peru

- referred to as 'The Lost City of the Incas'
- is one of the most familiar symbols of the Inca Empire
- is a pre-Columbian Inca site
- is located 2430 metres above sea level in Peru
- was built around the year 1460
- was said to have been forgotten for centuries when the site was rediscoverd in 1911
- is now an important tourist attraction.

The Colosseum, Rome

- is the largest elliptical amphitheatre ever built in the Roman Empire
- is one of the greatest works of Roman architecture and Roman engineering
- was built between 70 and 80 AD
- was originally capable of seating around 80 000 spectators
- was used for gladiatorial contests and public spectacles
- saw the death of about 500 000 people and over a million wild animals in the Colosseum games.

Haghia Sophia, Turkey

- was the largest cathedral ever built in the world for nearly a thousand years, until 1520
- was originally constructed as a Byzantine church between AD 532 and 537
- was in fact the third Church of the Holy Wisdom to occupy the site (the previous two had both been destroyed by riots).

The Leaning Tower of Pisa, Italy

- is a freestanding bell tower of the cathedral of the Italian city of Pisa
- is the third oldest building in Pisa
- began leaning to the southeast soon after the onset of construction in 1173 due to a poorly laid foundation
- presently leans to the southwest.

Stonehenge, England

- is one of the most famous prehistoric sites in the world
- is composed of earthworks surrounding a circular setting of large standing stones
- sits at the centre of the densest complex of Neolithic and Bronze Age monuments in England, including several hundred burial mounds
- dates back to around 3000 BC.

The Taj Mahal, India

- is a mausoleum built by an Emperor in memory of his favourite wife after she died in childbirth
- is considered the finest example of Mughal architecture, a style that combines elements from Persian, Ottoman, Indian, and Islamic architectural styles.

The Great Sphinx of Giza, Egypt

- is a statue of a reclining lion with a human head that stands on the Giza Plateau on the west bank of the Nile, near modern-day Cairo, in Egypt
- is the largest monolith statue in the world, standing 73.5 m long, 6 m wide, and 20 m high
- is the oldest known monumental sculpture, and is commonly believed to have been built by ancient Egyptians in the third millennium BC.

Petra, Jordon

- is an archaeological site in Jordan that is renowned for its rock-cut architecture.
- is one of the new wonders of the world
- was unknown to the Western world until 1812, when it was discovered by a Swiss explorer
- has been described by UNESCO as 'one of the most precious cultural properties of man's cultural heritage'
- was designated a World Heritage Site in 1985.

Party People

Your dog just bit someone.	_____ is the person _____ dog just _____ me.
You were born in 1995.	1995 is the year _____ _____ .
You went to the same school as someone.	_____ is the person _____ _____ school as me.
You speak five languages.	_____ is the person _____ _____ languages.
You are a year older than someone.	_____ is the person _____ _____ older than me.
You have green hair.	_____ is the person _____ hair.
You were born in St. Mary's Hospital.	_____ is the name of the hospital _____ .
You have someone's bag.	_____ is the person _____ _____ bag.
You loaned your pen to someone.	_____ is the person _____ _____ you borrowed.
You live in Texas.	Texas is the name of the place _____ _____ .
August is your favourite month.	August is the month which _____ _____ likes best.
Your cat's name is 'Wobbles'.	_____ is the name of the cat _____ belongs to _____ .
You want to go to the moon.	_____ is the person _____ _____ the moon.
Your favourite animal is a tiger.	Tigers are the animal _____ _____ .
Someone likes your shoes.	_____ is the name of the person _____ shoes _____ .
Yesterday morning you realised you would be famous.	Yesterday morning was the moment _____

PHOTOCOPIABLE 8.2

Brushstrokes and blueprints

Lesson planner

Fast lane: 3 x 1.5 hour lessons = 4.5 hours per unit (total course = 72–76 hours)

Lesson	Time	Classwork	Exam Booster (EB) homework
25	1.5 hours	Getting started, Reading + Vocab. Organiser (VO)	Getting started + Reading
26	1.5 hours	Check homework, Lang. develop., Listening, Grammar + VO	Lang. develop., Grammar + Listening
27	1.5 hours	Check homework, Use of English, Speaking, Writing + VO	Use of English, Speaking + Coursebook Writing task

Slow lane: 4 x 1.5 hour lessons = 6 hours per unit (total course = 96–100 hours)

Lesson	Time	Classwork	EB homework
33	1.5 hours	Getting started, Reading, VO + photocopiable 1	Getting started + Reading
34	1.5 hours	Check homework, Lang. develop., Listening, Grammar + VO	Lang. develop. + Grammar
35	1.5 hours	Check homework, Use of English, Speaking + VO	Listening + Speaking
36	1.5 hours	Check homework, Writing + photocopiable 2	Use of English, Writing + Coursebook Writing task

Before you begin

Before the lesson, write the following on the board:

a Picasso, Van Gogh, Degas

b Le Corbusier, Henry Ford, Alessi

c T. S. Eliot, Shakespeare, Homer

d Mozart, Vivaldi, Beethoven

Ask your students to find the connection between the people in each group on the board. Tell them that the team who finishes first wins.

Key: *a painters; b designers; c poets/writers; d composers*

Topic: forms of art and design

This unit tries to incorporate a range of art and design forms to accommodate students' varying tastes. The focus is largely on eliciting students' response to visual stimuli, so you may wish to capitalise on this by bringing in your own examples, or getting your students to bring in examples of their own work, or pieces that they like.

Unit 9 Wordlist

absent-mindedly	gravitate	scrap
adjacent	illuminating	sheer
adornment	indispensable	springy
animated	intricate	squint
apprentice	minimalist	strip
banal	modish	stroke
compile	nominate	synergy
composure	patent	transition
convey	perspective	ubiquitous
eyesore	poignant	versatility
fiddle	reams	wordiness

Getting started

1 Elicit your students' comments on the paintings and designs shown on page 85. Encourage them to justify their views.

2 Direct them to read the extracts in the speech bubbles. The first speech bubble describes marine life; the second informs artistic perspective in drawing a landscape; the third instructs on making a mandolin (musical instrument).

3 Elicit students' personal views and allow for disagreement, but encourage them to justify their choices.

Reading: understanding tone and implication in a text

1   Tell students to try and imagine what life was like before the target objects existed. Someone invented these objects, and designed them to perform a specific task.

Reading topic extension

To stimulate students' interest further, you may like to bring some actual household objects into the classroom for them to examine. This could be done in small groups. Present each group with a gadget to comment on. Elicit the group's views on the design of the gadget.

SPOTLIGHT ON READING

Understanding tone and implication
2 + 3 Students should do exercise 2 individually. Elicit answers, and ask them to answer the questions in exercise 3. Elicit answers and give feedback.

4   Direct the students to read the rubric, and answer the questions.

5   Allow students ten minutes to complete the questions before asking for their answers and justifications.

→   Vocabulary Organiser 9.1 + 9.2, page 94

Note: Items 9–12 of exercise 9.1 in the Vocabulary Organiser do not appear in the text. Either ask students to ignore the items, or suggest they find the words in a dictionary and decide how they may relate to the paperclip.

Language development:
compound words

1   Elicit that 'paperclip' is a compound word. Direct students to read the rubric and answer the question. Elicit answers and invite students to provide more examples of compound words.

2   Direct students to read the information in the Spotlight. Then ask them to complete exercise 2. Check answers with the group.

3   Students could do this individually or in pairs.

Key word: *pay*

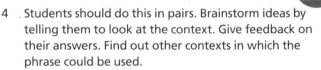

4   Students should do this in pairs. Brainstorm ideas by telling them to look at the context. Give feedback on their answers. Find out other contexts in which the phrase could be used.

TEACHING IN PRACTICE

Eliciting language
If students are struggling, elicit the meaning of phrases they do know, such as 'pay attention to', and 'pay you a compliment', and try to do the exercise with them through a process of elimination. Help them to feel a sense of achievement, and train them to work out the meaning of words and phrases through context.

5   Direct students to read the rubric and sentences. Tell them that all the options can follow the verb *pay*, but only one fits the context in each case. Elicit answers.

Phrases with *pay*

pay attention to	listen carefully to
pay homage to	show great respect towards somebody or something you greatly admire
pay somebody a compliment	say something nice about a person's appearance or character
pay my respects to somebody	go and visit somebody in a formal manner, out of a sense of duty and politeness

pay somebody respect	show somebody consideration
pay the penalty for	experience something unpleasant as a result of a mistake you have made, or something wrong you have done
pay through the nose for	pay a higher price for something than it is really worth
pay tribute to	say or do something to show your admiration and respect for someone
pay my way	pay my share of the expenses of a group outing or a trip

6   Direct students to read the sentences. Elicit the meaning of the italicised phrases.

→   Vocabulary Organiser 9.3, page 94

7   Students should do this individually. Remind them that the same form of the word (noun, verb etc) must fit all three sentences. Allow them time to complete the exercise.

Listening: interview with an artist

BACKGROUND: VASILIS KAPODISTRIAS

Vasilis Kapodistrias lives and works in Volos, Greece. He is a dentist by profession, but has been painting for many years in his spare time. He creates sculptures and three-dimensional paintings using a combination of fibre glass, boat paint and natural substances such as sand, pebbles and spices. Vasilis held his first public exhibition in early 2009, which proved a great success.

1   Find out the students' views on the artwork. They may need some guidance, as the three-dimensional aspect of the works is not clear here.

2   Elicit the difficulty in combining the use of different materials. Accept a variety of views.

3   🎧 9.1 Direct the students to read the rubric. Play the recording. Elicit answers. If there is disagreement or confusion, play the recording again. It is difficult to see the writing on the fourth photo (about which the speaker is referring).

4   Direct the students to read the rubric and the options. If you have not played the recording a second time, do so now.

SPOTLIGHT ON LISTENING

Understanding stated opinion
5   Elicit the opinions of the two speakers in the tapescript. Ask the students whose view they agree with.

6   🎧 9.2 Direct your students to read the rubric and questions. Elicit unknown words. Play the recording. Pause, and play it again.

Grammar: changing sentence structure: a change in emphasis, or a different meaning?

1   Tell your students that you are going to look at how changing the word order in a sentence can affect its meaning. Direct them to read the sentence from the Reading text. Ask them what 'has yet to be' means. Direct them to read the two options. Elicit the sentence which is closest in meaning to the original and then the meaning of the sentence which does not fit.

2   Students work in pairs. Ask them to read and compare the meaning of the two sentences. Let the students know why answers were correct or not.

3   Students work in pairs. Ask them to consider each pair of sentences carefully. Give feedback on each pair separately.

4   🎧 9.3 Direct your students to read through the rubric and sentences. Play the recording. Elicit answers.

5a   🎧 9.4 Direct your students to read the sentence. Play the recording. Pause after the second sentence, to hear how it differs from the first. Then pause after each subsequent one to elicit the change in meaning.

5b   Students work in pairs. Play the recording in the same way again, this time allowing students to write down a suitable question to precede each utterance.

Grammar extension

Ask the students what questions would have preceded these sentences. The students should be able to say:

Who cut off his ear after a quarrel with his good friend Gauguin?

What did Van Gogh do to his ear?

What did Van Gogh cut off?

Why did he cut off his ear?

Who did Van Gogh quarrel with before he cut off his ear?

→   Grammar Reference 9.1, page 176

Use of English: key word transformations

PAPER 3, PART 5 Key word transformations
1 Students work in pairs. Tell them to answer questions a and b together. Ask the class for answers and give feedback.

2 Students should work individually. Direct them to read the rubric, and to read through the questions. Allow them ten minutes to complete the exercise. Explain to the students why certain answers are incorrect. Explain any unknown words.

Speaking: suggesting solutions, justifying ideas

BACKGROUND: COLOUR IN DIFFERENT CULTURES

Make sure your students are aware of some of the different interpretations of colour in different cultures.

Black	China	colour for young boys
	Western	funerals, death, 'bad guys'
White	Japan	death
	Western	brides, angels, good guys, doctors
Red	China	good luck, celebration, summoning
	South Africa	mourning
	Russia	Bolshevism and Communism
	Eastern	brides
Orange	Western	Halloween (with black), autumn
Yellow	Egypt	mourning
	Japan	courage
	India	merchants
Green	India	Islam
	Western	Spring, new birth, go (at traffic lights)

1 Elicit students' views on black and white. Then give them the information regarding these two colours from the Background feature.

2 Students work individually. Direct them to read the rubric and the information in the box. Make it clear to them that this task is based on Western perceptions of colour, but they can disagree with it. Elicit responses, then give them the Western view, if it differs from their own.

3 Students work in pairs. Allow them time to discuss this. Monitor from a distance.

4 Direct students to read the rubric. Then, tell them to read the 'In other words' feature and answer the questions. They should do this in pairs. Elicit the answers. Refer them back to the exam style task, and the pictures. Allow them three minutes to perform the task. Monitor from a distance, and this time, note down both positive items and mistakes you hear. Give feedback to the class as a whole.

→ Vocabulary Organiser 9.4, page 94

Writing: competition entry

1 Elicit students' opinions about the paintings on the left of the page.

Gauging students' level of interest
Use this exercise to gauge both your students' knowledge of and interest in art. Ask if they know of any other works by the same artists, or have a preference for an artist that is not mentioned here. If students do not seem very interested, have some postcards of a variety of painting styles in the classroom to stimulate further discussion.

2 Direct your students to read the rubric and input material for the sample writing task. Make this active, by eliciting what the competition is about. Students may be confused, and think that the competition winners will be the artists, but it is in fact the person who writes the most convincing nomination who will win a prize.

Justifying choices
3 🎧 9.5 Tell students to read the rubric, and the information in the box. Play the recording twice. Elicit answers and give feedback about their answer choices.

4 Elicit students' own choices for the competition. Note down any useful justifications you hear, or examples of students expressing their idea well, but don't mention these now.

5 Direct students to read the sample answer. Allow them time to underline the justifications.

6 Elicit students' views on the sample. Then, direct them to read the 'Useful Language' box, and add more words and phrases. Allow them time for this, and then elicit answers.

7 Ask your students to read the question. Then discuss ideas about what students are required to write.

8 Ask your students to comment on the paintings on the right of the page, and encourage them to brainstorm ideas. Set the writing task for homework.

Photocopiable activity instructions

1 Activity 9.1 Creative compounds

Before-class preparation:

1 Photocopy sheets to a ratio of one for every three students.

2 Cut out the words, and place them in envelopes. If you wish to keep them for further use, you could stick the sheets to a piece of card before cutting them out, to reinforce them.

In class:

3 Students get into teams of three, and give each team an envelope. They must keep these closed.

4 Explain that the envelopes contain words which can be used in various ways to make compound words.

5 Tell them they will have five or ten minutes (depending on how pressed for time you are, and how demanding you want to make the task) to form as many compound words as possible.

6 Set the clock. Then tell the teams to open their envelopes and start.

7 Monitor from a distance. When the time is up, tell them all to stop.

8 Ask each team how many words they think they have found. Check the words from each team, and write them on the board.

Suggested key: *newsdesk; newspaper; papermill; paperclip; rooftop; windmill; postman; uprising; desktop; upbringing; sunrise; upload; download; overload; overlook; manmade; makeover; manpower; mind-blowing; absent-minded; mastermind; masterpiece; upgrade; downgrade*

Tapescript

Listening 9.1

Joe: Will ya look at this? The amount of work that's gone into it! It's amazing!

Clare: Ummm ... But seriously, Joe, would you really want that hanging on your wall?

Joe: Yeah, why not? So, OK, it's bulky, but it's powerful, and I love the symbolic effect of all <u>those lyrics scrawled across the glass</u> background. <u>Set within the boat like that, it creates the effect of a window on the world as you travel on your voyage through life.</u>

Clare: Wow, Joe! That's a bit deep for you! Personally, I find the colours rather garish for my tastes.

Joe: Well, ya see, Clare, I think they're meant to be. I mean, it's boat paint ... No, I really like it!

Listening 9.2

Interviewer: Good morning, and welcome to this week's Art Corner. On the show today, I'm delighted to have with me a particularly interesting guest. Few of you will have heard of him as yet, but this is not due to a lack of talent on his part. Vasilis Kapodistrias is in fact a man of many talents. An accomplished dentist by profession, he spends most of his spare time creating wonderful works of art. Vasilis, welcome.

Vasilis: Thank you, Judith.

Interviewer: Now, your kind of art is rather unusual, so, can you start by giving us a brief description of what you do?

Vasilis: Yes, well, I do a lot of different things, really, because I love experimenting with materials. I'm not just interested in the look of something, but <u>in how it feels to the touch,</u> if you know what I mean. So, I suppose my work is a combination of three-dimensional painting and sculpture. To give you an idea, I've been influenced by the work of Kostas Tsoklis, a well-known Greek 3-D artist, who I admire a great deal.

Interviewer: Would you say he was the reason you became interested in producing your own work?

Vasilis: He certainly influenced the direction in which my art developed ... <u>But I think really I've always had an interest. My father painted for a hobby also. Landscapes, mainly, and as a boy I remember following him and sometimes drawing, too.</u> Then, at university, it was photography for a while, and I gradually moved on to painting watercolours, and then acrylic. After that, in round about 1985, I started using other materials.

Interviewer: What kind of materials?

Vasilis: At first, I used cardboard, and then plaster ... Err ... Here, my professional work helped. As a dentist, I use plaster, glues and materials for making false plates, wire for braces, and so on. So, it seemed natural to experiment with such materials to develop my hobby. Then, about 15 years ago, I started using polystyrene and fibreglass – what they use to make boats: more durable materials, longer lasting. A major theme in my art is the sea. I live by the sea, and I love boats …

Interviewer: Isn't polystyrene a rather difficult substance to work with?

Vasilis: Yes, and not very healthy, either! I'm attracted to it because of its durability, but I make sure I've got the windows open when I'm working with it! It's so versatile, though, and easy to mix with other materials in order to create different textures. I love that, you see. I haven't followed any art course, so I don't know much about particular techniques. I just follow my heart in a painting. For this reason, I feel I'm a permanent student of art. To describe me as an artist … well, I'm not sure I'm ready for that yet! There is no real beginning or end for me. When I start a new piece, I have no idea how it will turn out. I feel I participate in a painting, but the materials I am using gradually take on a life of their own, and seem to start moulding themselves! It's exciting!

Interviewer: You've produced a lot of work in the last few years. So, why haven't you held an exhibition yet?

Vasilis: My dental practice houses my permanent exhibition! No, really. Many people have asked me that, but it's a difficult question to answer. You see, my art is my hobby, my form of escape. As I get older, the symbolism in my work is increasingly reflective, and very personal. You will have noticed that many of my recent backgrounds contain the lyrics from songs or poems that have a special meaning for me. I don't see myself in a professional light. I've never sold anything. I'm not sure I could put a price on it, since it takes me months to finish one piece. Also, I'm rather shy of publicity, so reluctant to take that step. Perhaps I just don't feel mature enough yet! I don't know …

Interviewer: Well, you should seriously think about it! So, ladies and gentlemen, if you want to see any of Vasilis' work, you'll just have to book an appointment to have your teeth checked! For the time being, anyway. Vasilis, thank you very much for coming to talk to us today, and good luck …

Listening 9.3

Female: I don't know where she finds the time to do all those activities.

Male: Where she finds the time to do all those activities, I don't know.

Female: Although this exercise may seem boring, it is useful.

Male: Boring though this exercise may seem, it is useful.

Male: You need a complete break from the office.

Female: What you need is a complete break from the office.

Male: They are creating unnecessary waste.

Female: What they are doing is creating unnecessary waste.

Male: Don't get upset. You just need to go and talk to your teacher about the problem.

Female: Don't get upset. All you need to do is talk to your teacher about the problem.

Listening 9.4

Vincent Van Gogh cut off his ear after a quarrel with his good friend Gauguin.

Vincent Van Gogh *cut off* his ear after a quarrel with his good friend Gauguin.

Vincent Van Gogh cut off his *ear* after a quarrel with his good friend Gauguin.

Vincent Van Gogh cut off his ear after *a quarrel* with his good friend Gauguin.

Vincent Van Gogh cut off his ear after a quarrel with his good friend *Gauguin*.

Listening 9.5

Michelle: So, who are you going to nominate, Maria?

Maria: Oh, I don't know. I like Paul Klee's work, because it has this childlike quality, but if we're talking about the most popular artists, I'd choose Marc Chagall.

Caitlin: Really? For myself, I prefer Klimt. I mean, the passion in 'The Kiss'. Think about how often you see that painting on people's walls, guys.

Alice: Yawn, yawn. C'mon, Caitlin! Most of us are bored of it! Now, a genuinely provocative artist of the 20th century for me is Takashi Murakami …

Caitlin: Come again?

Alice: Takashi Murakami. His work reflects what's happening in modern Japan, and shows just how far the Manga cartoon images have influenced contemporary art. You see his smiley flowers and Mr Dob figure all over the place.

Tony: You definitely do when you walk into your room, Alice! You've got Murakami posters all over your walls! Who would you choose, Michelle?

Michelle: Well, Tony, my choice would be Wassily Kandinsky, although I don't like all of his work. It's the precision of his shapes. Somehow, you can sense the music in them, as if he composed them in the same way you would compose a piece of music. The colours seem to be in perfect harmony, like a melody.

Maria: I feel like that about Chagall's work, though. His paintings seem to depict aspects of the subconscious mind. Just as Kandinsky speaks to you of music in his paintings, Chagall's paintings remind me of dreams I've had.

Caitlin: They're rather too abstract for me! I think Gustav Klimt's work speaks more directly to us as people – don't laugh, Tony! – certainly in the case of his portraits. It's not just 'The Kiss'. You take a look at some of his portraits of women. He manages to capture their strength and vitality, an inner beauty. It's amazing!

Alice: Well, Tony and I'll stick with the crazily happy images of Murakami …

Tony: Speak for yourself! I like Murakami, but I wouldn't nominate him here … No! My choice would be Miro. I just love those blues, greens and yellows in his landscapes. A particular favourite is 'Ciurana, The Path'.

Maria: And I thought we all had similar tastes in art! … I wonder if any of our choices will be chosen.

Answer key 9

Getting started p85

2 a The blue whale (possibly from a storybook); b drawing of the path and the trees (possibly from a reference book about design); c picture of a mandolin (possibly from an instruction manual).

Reading pp86–7

2 A2; B3; C1
3 1b; 2b; 3b
4 aF; bF; cT; dT; eF
5 1D; 2C; 3B; 4D; 5C; 6D

Language development p88

1 paperclip; rooftop; windmill; desktop; fingerprint; fingernail; footprint
2 a everyday; b computer-controlled; c all-purpose; d time-wasting; e absent-mindedly; f stand-in
3 a footprints; b stand-in; c all-purpose; d paperclip; e absent-minded; f rooftops
4 Answers may vary slightly. Expect something like 'show open admiration for ...' You can also pay homage to a religious shrine, a spiritual leader, etc.
5 1c; 2b; 3b
6 To 'pay you a visit' = come and see you; 'pay for itself' = saves you money (in the long run)
7 1 designs; 2 art; 3 pay; 4 arrested

Listening p89

2 Suggested answers: materials seem difficult to work with; creating the effect of rust could be difficult.
3 The large photograph on the far right [NB it is difficult to see the lyrics on this photograph, but this artwork is the only one set inside a boat].
4 D
5 Joe likes it (is impressed by it); Claire is critical of it.
6 1C; 2D; 3A; 4D; 5D; 6B

Grammar p90

1 a
2 a Poem and painting have already been placed next to each other.
b they haven't been placed together yet, but I plan to do this.
3 1a I thought the poem wasn't written by Auden, and I was right; b I thought it was written by Auden, but I was wrong
2a he's still learning; b he's had his driving licence for two years
3a Sally borrowed the CD, not Paula; b She borrowed a Shakira CD, not a Beyonce one
4a There were several paintings, and Paul bought the one that belonged to an Italian nobleman; b There was one painting, and Paul bought it
5a She used to paint the same things in every lesson; b In one particular lesson, she had painted flowers and trees.
4 1 The second sentence is more emphatic, perhaps to show surprise or frustration.
2 The second sentence is more emphatic, perhaps to show slight impatience.
3 The second sentence is more persuasive.
4 The second sentence is more emphatic, and presses the point home.
5 The second sentence is more persuasive.
5 *Vincent Van Gogh* cut off his ear after a quarrel with his good friend Gauguin (Van Gogh cut off his ear, not Picasso).
Vincent Van Gogh *cut off* his ear after a quarrel with his good friend Gauguin (He didn't chew his ear, but cut it off).
Vincent Van Gogh cut off his *ear* after a quarrel with his good friend Gauguin (He cut off his ear, not his hand).
Vincent Van Gogh cut off his ear after a *quarrel* with his good friend

Gauguin (The quarrel made him do it, not a letter).
Vincent Van Gogh cut off his ear after a quarrel with his good friend *Gauguin* (Van Gogh quarrelled with Gauguin, not Monet).

Use of English p90

1 a ... Mary, it was Peter who ...; b ... though it may be, we are ...
2 1 ... (but) what I don't like ...; 2 ... Claire, it was John, not Paul ...; 3 ... how she manages to stay calm ...; 4 ... not me, but the neighbours ...; 5 ... though it may, the match ...; 6 ... whose paintings were of the sea ...; 7 ... was angry, as ...

Speaking p91

2 Suggested answers (Western view): 1b; 2a; 3d; 4h; 5g; 6i; 7j; 8f; 9c; 10e

Writing pp92–3

2 The competition is to nominate a 20th century artist and persuade the judges to include them in a book on the most popular artists of the century.
3 Maria: Marc Chagall (aspects of subconscious and dream quality)
Caitlin: Gustav Klimt (passion, strength and vitality of his women)
Alice: Takashi Murakami (reflects modern Japan)
Michelle: Wassily Kandinsky (sense of music in his paiting)
Tony: Joan Miro (range of colours).
5 Students should underline most of paragraphs 2 and 3.
6 Answers may vary, but expect students to find it convincing, because she explains why he is popular, and how he reflects the style of modern popular culture, and she also mentions that he is a commercially successful artist, too, which has become increasingly important.

Suggestions for more useful phrases: 1 From the sample answer: 'His work reflects trends ...'; 'Another point worth noting ...'; 2 From listening task, 9.5: His work is 'genuinely provocative'; 'the precision of his' work; 'he manages to capture ...'
7 Expected answer: The students have to nominate one of the five paintings on the right of the page to enter the artwork category of a national arts competition. The nomination chosen will win a prize.

Vocabulary organiser 9 p94

9.1 1 nominate; 2 patent; 3 supersede; 4 gobble up; 5 generate; 6 fiddle; 7 genius; 8 (poker) chips; 9 durability; 10 versatility; 11 flexibility; 12 reliability; 13 indispensable; 14 modish; 15 sustainable; 16 ubiquitous; 17 banal; 18 minimalist; 19 springy; 20 miniature; 21 bureaucratic; 22 absent-minded
9.2 1c; 2b; 3a; 4d; 5b
9.3 1 pay attention; 2 paying her a compliment; 3 paying for itself; 4 pay the penalty for; 5 pay my respects
9.4 1 nostalgia; 2 rebellious; 3 deceit; 4 transition; 5 harmony; 6 stability; 7 joy; 8 unique; 9 balance; 10 sophisticated

Bank of English

2 It means there is something wrong with the design of an object (the accident was the result of a design fault in the machine).
3 a intentionally; b ambitious plans; c wants to acquire/buy it; d art of designing advertisements, books and magazines with a combination of words and pictures; e babies whose parents have chosen the colour of their hair, eyes etc.

Creative compounds

news	desk
paper	up
mill	**rise**
top	bring
make	**sun**
grade	*load*
down	*over*
m a n	**look**
power	*mind*
BLOW	absent
master	**POST**
clip	PIECE
wind	**roof**

10 The good life

Lesson planner

Fast lane: 3 x 1.5 hour lessons = 4.5 hours per unit
(total course = 72–76 hours)

Lesson	Time	Classwork	Exam Booster (EB) homework
28	1.5 hours	Getting started, Reading + Vocab. Organiser (VO)	Getting started + Reading
29	1.5 hours	Check homework, Lang. develop., Listening, Grammar + VO	Lang. develop., Listening + Grammar
30	1.5 hours	Check homework, Speaking, Use of English, Writing + VO	Speaking, Use of English + Writing

Slow lane: 4 x 1.5 hour lessons = 6 hours per unit
(total course = 96–100 hours)

Lesson	Time	Classwork	EB homework
37	1.5 hours	Getting started, photocopiable 1, Reading + VO	Getting started + Reading
38	1.5 hours	Check homework, Lang. develop., Listening + VO	Lang. develop. + Listening
39	1.5 hours	Check homework, Grammar, Speaking, Listening + VO	Grammar, Speaking + Listening
40	1.5 hours	Check homework, Use of English, Writing + photocopiable 2	Use of English; Writing + Coursebook Writing task

Before you begin

Ask your students to describe an ideal world. What would life be like in the perfect utopia?

Topic: family values and ethical living

This unit focuses on ethical lifestyles, choices and dilemmas, and family values. These consist of a variety of issues that tend to concern modern society and can increasingly be found in printed matter and other media, as well as in social conversation or debate.

Unit 10 Wordlist

adversely	custody	penalty
chore	demolish	scruples
commodity	discourse	spouse
commute	infuriate	terminal
conserve	intolerable	undermine
constitute	moderate	unsettling

Getting started

Aim: To focus students on the topic of ethical choices and the decisions that we have to make in order to lead a good lifestyle, and also to introduce some of the topics that will come up in the unit.

1   Hold a class discussion. Elicit from the students that in order to live an ethical lifestyle one needs to think about whether any other people or animals or habitats were maltreated, abused, or destroyed in order to provide us with the things in our lives. Ask students to brainstorm where the clothes they are wearing may have come from, where the food they ate for breakfast may have come from and so on. Ask them to think about what ethical or unethical processes may have been involved in their production, transport, sale and so on.

2   Students look at the pictures and give answers or can work in pairs.

3   Discuss the options with the students. Ask them which ones in the list may present some ethical choices, and what they might be.

Getting started extension

Tell your students to check out the website www.freerice.com to see how good their English vocabulary is. For every correct answer, the charity donates 20 grains of rice through the United Nations to help end world hunger. It's fun too.

→   Vocabulary Organiser 10.1, page 104

89

Reading: gapped texts

In the UK over the past couple of decades, increasing numbers of families are separated for all or part of the year. This is in order for one of the parents to pursue a career in another part of the country, or in another country altogether. This happened less often in the past because the woman didn't usually have a career of her own and so could follow her husband, whereas nowadays, the woman's career is often as – if not more – high-powered than her husband's.

Aim: The purpose of this section is to help students gain a better understanding of the way most texts are structured, and a better understanding of what the text is saying on the whole. This will help them in part 2 of Paper 1 (gapped texts).

Terms to pre-teach:

'Quality of life' refers to material things, wealth etc, that can give you a better quality lifestyle (a big house, two cars, all mod-cons etc).

'Quality time' refers to the time you spend doing something good (time spent with your children doing something fun or constructive together, like flying a kite).

1   Make sure your students understand the terms as defined above and ask them to give further examples of things that would constitute 'quality of life' or 'quality time'. Ask students to justify the reasons for their answers. Students should conclude that a balance is required for a happy life, in other words, if someone doesn't work, he or she won't have any money and therefore will not be able to provide all the material assets required for a higher 'quality of life'. However, if someone works all the time to earn money, they may achieve a higher 'quality of life' but it will be meaningless if they cannot spend any time doing fun things with their loved ones.

Reading extension

Direct your students' attention towards the first paragraph of the text that follows the Exam Spotlight.
1   Ask them what dilemma is being described.

Answer: *that in order for your children to grow up in the country and live in a nice house, most people would have to work in the city.*

2   Ask students what kind of strains can be put on a family that is separated for periods of time due to work obligations.

Possible answers: *One parent has the greater burden of responsibility, the other parent misses his/her family. Distance and time apart can put a burden on the relationship, it is harder to communicate, no time together shared, small every day events/problems are not communicated, resentment builds etc.*

PAPER 1, PART 2 Text structure, paragraph cohesion and coherence

2   Students read the table and do the task individually. Elicit and check answers with the group in order to make sure everyone has located the correct information in the text.

3   Ask the class this question. The point is to emphasise that the last paragraph is different from the others in that it doesn't contain any key information.

4   Tell students to read the text and paragraphs again to find the information. When everyone has finished, check their answers.

Understanding gapped texts

You need to stress to your students the importance of reading the text as a whole, and not just focusing on each gap separately. They need to understand that getting an idea of the structure and understanding the development of the theme of the text are both important prerequisites to doing the task, and the best way to do this is by reading the whole text carefully in the first instance to understand it. Only then should students attempt to find the paragraphs that fit each gap. Students frequently make the wrong choices by selecting an option which fits the text before the gap, and neglecting to check that the text after the gap follows on smoothly.

5   Students should work in pairs. As they have now read the text twice, tell them that they should be able to find the answers to the questions fairly quickly by scanning the appropriate paragraphs.

Paragraph cohesion

Discuss the techniques used by writers and elicit further examples of each kind.

6   Students do the task individually. Check answers with the class and emphasise how useful this technique is for finding the correct order of the missing paragraphs.

7   Students work individually or in pairs. Check answers with the whole class.

Read through the rubric with the class. The point here is to show students some useful techniques for locating the 'odd' paragraph (the one that does not belong in the main text). Point out that students should not simply accept that the last remaining paragraph is always the odd paragraph, but they should apply the same techniques as they did to all the other paragraphs in order to ensure that it doesn't belong somewhere in the text after all. Stress that the information contained in the 'odd' paragraph will of course seem to fit in terms of theme, and may even be from another section of the original text itself, but there should not be any direct links to any of the gaps within the text.

8 + 9 + 10 Students complete the exercises individually or in pairs. Check answers with the whole class.

11 Students should now attempt the final task individually. They should spend no more than ten minutes doing this and they should be able to justify their answers.

→ Vocabulary Organiser 10.2, page 104

Language development:
fixed phrases

1 Students should do the exercise individually or in pairs, or you can go through it with the whole class.

→ Vocabulary Organiser 10.3, page 104

Key word: *pull*

When you *pull* something, you hold it firmly and use force in order to move it towards you or away from its previous position.	*I helped pull him out of the water ...*
When you *pull* an object from a bag, pocket, or cupboard, you put your hand in and bring the object out.	*Jack pulled the slip of paper from his shirt pocket ...*
When an animal *pulls* a cart they move it along behind them.	*In early 20th-century rural Sussex, horses still pulled the plough ...*
When a driver or vehicle *pulls to* a stop or a halt, the vehicle stops.	*He pulled to a stop behind a pickup truck ...*
In a race or contest, if you *pull ahead of* or *pull away from* an opponent, you gradually increase the amount by which you are ahead of them.	*She pulled away, extending her lead to 15 seconds ...*

If you *pull* something *apart*, you break or divide it into small pieces, often in order to put them back together again in a different way.	*If I wanted to improve the car significantly I would have to pull it apart and start again.*
If someone *pulls* a gun or a knife *on* someone else, they take out a gun or knife and threaten the other person with it. (INFORMAL)	*They had a fight. One of them pulled a gun on the other ...*
To *pull* crowds, viewers, or voters means to attract them.	*The organisers have to employ performers to pull a crowd.*
If you *pull* a muscle, you injure it by straining it.	*Dave pulled a back muscle and could barely kick the ball ...*
To *pull* a stunt or a trick *on* someone means to do something dramatic or silly in order to get their attention or trick them.	*Everyone saw the stunt you pulled on me.*
Pull is also a noun.	*The feather must be removed with a straight, firm pull.*
A *pull* is a strong physical force which causes things to move in a particular direction.	*... the pull of gravity.*

2 Elicit answers from the students.

3 Students can use their dictionaries if necessary. They should also make a note of the definition of each phrasal verb in their vocabulary notebooks.

4 Students should use their dictionaries to find the meanings of any they don't know and complete the exercise. They should then add them to their vocabulary notebooks.

5 Do this as a class activity. Answers should include: pulling strings, pulling a face, pulling your weight, pulled along, pulling your leg etc.

→ Vocabulary Organiser 10.4, page 104

Listening (1): identifying speakers

Aim: To help students prepare for the listening task by focusing on key words, and getting them to predict themes and lexical items that they may expect to hear in the recording.

1 Discuss the question with the class. Refer to the photographs and ask the students to tell you in what ways they depict aspects of sustainable living.

Listening extension

Pre-teaching tapescript vocabulary

The following words and phrases all appear in the listening tapescript. Although it is not necessary for students to know the meaning of all words and phrases they hear in order to complete exam tasks, introducing such lexical items before they listen will help them to expand or consolidate their English vocabulary.

phrases: jump on the bandwagon, to do one's bit, impose a fine on someone, on standby, hose pipe bans, turn one's nose up at something

nouns: appliances, detergent, water butt, allotment, compost, fertiliser

verbs: conserve, flush, unravel, recycle, decompose

adjectives: privileged, organic, eccentric

EXAM SPOTLIGHT

PAPER 4, PART 4 Focus on questions
Read the rubric with the students. Make sure they have understood the usefulness of this technique and then direct them to exercise 2.

2   First students need to read and underline the key words. Then brainstorm words that could be associated with them on the board.

3   🎧 10.1 Students attempt tasks one and two individually. They should hear the recording twice. Afterwards, check answers with the group.

4   Discuss the topic with the class. Refer back to the opening discussion at the beginning of this section and ask students to talk about any new things they have learnt, or ask them to suggest any new ways they can think of conserving natural resources.

Grammar: direct and reported speech

1   Elicit that direct speech makes the writing less formal and draws the reader in more. It is generally more lively and engaging than reported speech.

GRAMMAR SPOTLIGHT

Direct speech to reported speech
Ask the students to read through the rubric or read it with them. Ask them why they think it is useful to be able to change direct speech into reported speech. This technique is useful in conversational English, plus when paraphrasing dialogue in written work.

2 Students underline the changes. Check with the class.

3   Students should do this exercise individually before coming together as a group to share answers.

→   Grammar Reference 10.1, page 177

GRAMMAR SPOTLIGHT

Reported speech to direct speech
As before read the rubric with the students. Explain that it may also be necessary to transform reported speech into direct speech, and that the opposite rules will apply.

4 Students underline and point out the change to the sentence.

5   Students do the exercise individually. Check answers with the class.

TEACHING IN PRACTICE

Reporting verbs
Say aloud the following sentence to the class:

> I don't like this soup – it's cold!

Ask the class what you are doing. Elicit that you are complaining. Give a few more examples:

> It wasn't me that broke the window, honest! (denying)

> I know what – I'm going to call my grandmother! (deciding)

6   Students complete the exercise individually. Check answers with the class.

→   Grammar Reference 10.2, pages 177–8

7   Point out that this exercise is similar to part 5 of Paper 3 but has only six questions instead of eight. Students should attempt the exercise individually. Do not allow more than five minutes for the task as students should now be used to doing this kind of task under pressure.

Speaking: organising a larger unit of discourse

EXAM SPOTLIGHT

PAPER 5, PART 2 Organising a larger unit of discourse
Read through the rubric with the class. Ask the students to repeat back to you what they are expected to do in this part of the Speaking Paper.

1 Do this task with the class. Look at the pictures and ask students to decide which two they think are the most interesting. Ask them why. They do not have to agree – each student should be able to justify the reasons for their choice. Ask which pictures seem to have more things to talk about. Point out that the most interesting picture or the one that students like the most, may not always be the one that they can say the most things about, and so they should think carefully before deciding which pictures to discuss.

   a Ask one student to give you a 'descriptive' statement about one of the pictures. Ask another to 'speculate' about something in one of the pictures.

   b Ask a student to 'compare' two things between two of the pictures.

   c Ask a student to 'contrast' two things between two of the pictures.

2 Put students into pairs or open pairs. Ask them to nominate Student 1 and Student 2. Listen to the first pair answering the task in A. Ask the class to comment. Elicit suggestions or offers to attempt the task from other pairs. When you are satisfied that everyone is performing all the functions of the task correctly, tell them to swap roles and attempt task B.

Use of English: gapped sentences

Aim: To familiarise students with preparation tasks which can heighten their awareness of the multiple meanings and/or usage of certain words.

1 Elicit answers from the students after they have read the sentences. Explain that although the same word is used in all three sentences, in each case it has a different nuance of meaning, and that is what they have to learn to be aware of. Ask them to identify a verb, a phrasal verb, and an idiom.

SPOTLIGHT ON VOCABULARY

Lexical contexts
Read through the rubric with the students and make sure they have understood it.

2 + 3 Read the question rubrics with the students and elicit the answers to the questions. Ask them to identify any sentences they would be able to spot and any which are unknown to them.

4 Students should apply the techniques they have just learnt while they do the exercise. Check answers with the class. In each case identify the 'give away' sentence and the 'unknown' sentence. Ask students to point out the different uses (verbs, phrasal verbs, idioms etc) and

to record all new nuances of meaning, with example sentences, in their vocabulary notebooks.

→ Vocabulary Organiser 10.5, page 104

Listening (2): note-taking

BACKGROUND: THE FREECYCLE NETWORK

The Freecycle Network (often abbreviated TFN or just known as Freecycle) is a non-profit organisation that aims to divert reusable goods from landfill. It provides a worldwide online registry, and coordinates the creation of local groups and forums for individuals and non-profit organisations to offer and receive free items for reuse or recycling. The organisation began in Arizona and has since spread to over 85 countries, with thousands of local groups and millions of members.

1 Discuss the topic with the class. If they haven't heard of 'freecycling' before, elicit what other word it reminds them of (recycling) and ask them where or what you may recycle for free!

2   10.2 Tell your students that they are going to listen to three people talking about 'freecycling' and mentioning items they have either acquired, given away, or come across themselves. Explain that their task is to make notes in the box while they listen, although they don't have to catch every item. Point out that this is not an exam task but that it will give them extra practice in listening for specific information.

3 Discuss the advantages quickly with the class. This will lead you into the writing section that follows.

Writing: an information sheet

EXAM SPOTLIGHT

PAPER 2, PART 2 An information sheet
Read the rubric with the students. Make sure they understand what an information sheet is as they may not have had to write one before. Refer them to the model Information Sheet on page 192.

1 Read the rubric with the students and ask them to underline the key words in the exam question. This will give them the headings.

2 Allow students a few minutes to read the freecycling leaflet and write in the headings. Check the answers with the class.

3 Go through the functions in the box with the class. Make sure they understand what each one means and elicit examples of each. Students decide which functions are required in the writing task. Tell them they should get used to doing this every time they do a writing task.

You should get your students used to recognising the different functions required in each task whenever they attempt one. They should also familiarise themselves with the structures and vocabulary relevant to the required functions.

Using register

Read the rubric with your students and make sure they understand what register is. In order to know what register to use, tell your students that they will need to think carefully about who the target reader is for each task. Ask:

> Is the target reader somebody you know or someone unknown to you?

> Is the target reader someone from your school, college or place of work?

> Is the target reader a close friend, family member or someone in a position of authority?

> Do you need to present difficult information politely (as in a complaint) or are you trying to persuade somebody to do something for you?

Point out that students must adopt the appropriate style and tone for the reader, but at all times it is important to have a balance between the function(s) required by the task and the relationship with the target reader.

Note: ESOL advises that students look at past papers and note the vocabulary and structures needed for each Part 2 choice to help them decide which one can best demonstrate their language skills and knowledge.

4 Elicit that information leaflets can be informal, formal, or neutral depending on whom the intended audience is. In this case the audience is likely to be people from the community, in particular people who have things to give away or who don't have much money to spend on new clothes, furniture etc, so the register is more likely to be informal or neutral, rather than formal.

5 Students do exercise 5 in pairs or individually. Go through their choices and ask them to justify their reasons.

6 Ask students to underline vocabulary and structural elements in exercise 5 that indicate the style or register of the sentences. Discuss the questions with the students.

7 Students attempt to rewrite the first three paragraphs individually or in pairs in their notebooks. Offer help where necessary. As well as the words in the box, ask students to consider other choices as mentioned in exercise 6. Suggested answer could be:

1 The Freecycle Network comprises many individual groups worldwide, and consists of an entirely non-profit movement of people who are exchanging articles for free in their own towns. There is no membership fee.

2 The Freecycle Network was started in May 2003 to promote waste reduction and reduce the number of landfill sites that are dominating the landscape. The network provides individuals and non-profit bodies an electronic forum for re-housing unwanted items. One person's recyclable waste can truly be beneficial to another person.

3 When needing to find a new home for items – whether they be a chair, a fax machine, piano, or an old door – you simply communicate by email offering these items to members of your local Freecycle group. Or, maybe you are looking to acquire something yourself. In this case, simply respond to a member's offer, and it is possible that you will be offered it. From that point it is up to the person offering the item to decide who receives the item and to arrange a pickup time for the handover.

8 Students need to spend some time on this and come up with their own answers. They can work alone or in pairs, or it could be done as a class activity.

9 Students write their Information Sheet. As they will have done all the preparation; 15 minutes will probably be enough for most students.

→ Vocabulary Organiser 10.6, page 104

Photocopiable activity instructions

① Activity 10.1 Scruples questionnaire

Aim: To help students discuss their choices and give reasons for what they say.

Instructions:

1 Write the following on the board:

> 1 point = no scruples or ethics whatsoever, no.1 is the only one that matters!
>
> 2 points = got a bit of a conscience, but won't make a big personal sacrifice if it complicates life.
>
> 3 points = morally conscientious and very PC (politically correct)

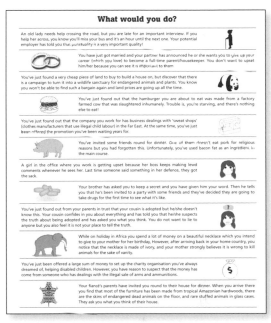

2 Copy the questionnaire once and cut out the dilemmas. Give each student one dilemma. If there are more students than dilemmas then you can repeat some or make up a few more.

3 Each student reads out their question and then names three other people in the group to give answers (offering solutions to the dilemma).

4 Everybody in the group (except the speakers each time) awards a mark of 1–3 to each speaker's answers based on the formula you've written on the board.

5 Go round the room several times, reading the same questions but choosing different people to answer so that everyone has had a chance to answer at least twice.

6 At the end add up the scores: the person with the highest score wins.

② Activity 10.2 Reporting the news

Aim: To help students practise using reported speech when talking about past events.

Instructions:

1 Divide the class into groups of four to six and allocate roles.

2 Photocopy the activity and cut out the newspaper clipping and the character notes.

3 Give one newspaper clipping to each group and tell them to pass it round so everyone reads it. Meanwhile, give each student their own character notes.

4 Students can either stand or swap places for each interview. Alternatively, line up a set of desks with chairs on each side. First, the policeman interviews the two suspects, one at a time, by asking them direct questions. Meanwhile the reporter interviews the two eye-witnesses by asking direct questions.

5 Afterwards, the two suspects, the two eyewitnesses and the policeman and reporter fill each other in on what they were asked and what they said.

6 Finally each person writes up or verbally reports on what they found out.

Tapescript 10

Listening 10.1

Speaker 1: Nowadays, with the climate change crisis, everyone's suddenly jumping on the ecological band-wagon and trying to do their bit. But back in the forties, when the war was on, it was a way of life. <u>We grew up with it. We used to get told off if we accidentally left a light on in another part of the house;</u> it's something that's stuck with me for I always switch the light off when I leave the room – even if it's only for a minute. When my kids were young I even imposed a five pence fine on them if they left the lights on in their room! At night, <u>I switch off all the appliances at the wall sockets</u> because I remember reading somewhere that those little red lights from the TV and DVD left on standby consume enough electricity in a year to power the whole of the UK for a week.

Speaker 2: We've all got used to the hose pipe bans these days but <u>our family always did their bit to conserve water. My father always used the water from his hot water bottle to wash in the mornings as it was still nice and warm. My Mum always had a bowl in the bathroom sink and when it was full from washing our hands and face, we'd tip it into the toilet instead of flushing</u> – did the job just as well. Kitchen water was saved for watering the pot plants, so long as it didn't have detergent in it. We also attached water-butts to the drainpipes around our house and we collected rainwater for watering the garden. The vegetable garden had an old bathtub that used to fill up and during hot summer hose-pipe bans we always had enough water, while everyone else had to watch their gardens dry out.

Speaker 3: Children these days don't know how privileged they are. <u>I remember wearing itchy school uniforms that my mother made,</u> and having to make do with them as long as we could. When our pullovers wore thin on the elbow, <u>Mum simply unstitched the sleeves and reversed them, left sleeve to right armhole, and we wore them until the reversed elbows also began to wear out.</u> Then it was time to unravel the wool and knit it again as part of a stripy jumper. My grandchildren turn their noses up at anything without a label on it – usually on the outside. <u>I still find it hard to buy anything new, and almost impossible to throw anything away if it could be used by someone else.</u>

Speaker 4: <u>Absolutely everything organic that comes out of my kitchen gets composted.</u> Potato peelings, egg shells, banana skins, melon rinds, coffee grounds – you name it. Even newspapers, cardboard egg-boxes, cat hairs. <u>It all gets chucked into my garden compost bin</u> and within a few months nature's done her work and you've got beautiful, crumbly, rich brown compost – the perfect fertiliser for your garden plants, so there's no need for artificial chemical fertilisers and the best thing is knowing that absolutely everything is getting recycled back into nature. <u>I got it from my Mum – she's been composting for as long as I can remember and back in those days she must have been seen as an eccentric in our village.</u> Now everyone wants advice. I hate seeing people throw their organic waste in the bin. I have

been known to slip apple cores and tea bags into my bag while at work in order to bring it home for compost.

Speaker 5: <u>Every time I go to the shops I grab a bundle of plastic bags and take them with me to use again – most of them can be used five or six times.</u> Otherwise they need 50 years to decompose in the ground. I also save the paper bags from market stalls – they can be used to ripen avocados and tomatoes and when I'm done with them, I use them to soak up the fat from fried food. I also use ordinary plastic water bottles as cloches for young garden plants to protect my lettuces from slugs and frost. I just cut the bottoms off and push a thin cane through to stop them from falling over. <u>Another tip that my father passed on was that instead of using expensive hand cream you should just rub sheep's fat into your hand.</u> I know it sounds horrible but if you think about it, most lanolin-based creams are made from mutton fat anyway, only with perfume added to it.

Listening 10.2

Dave: We love *Freecycle*. My girlfriend Helen enforces a policy of household recycling as much as possible and it was her idea to join, because we were about to move in together and had a lot of stuff lying around that was doubled up. We've also used the site to help furnish our new flat. We had absolutely no furniture so it was a big challenge for us. But our *Freecycle* group seemed to offer everything we needed, from <u>three-piece suites to the kitchen sink.</u> After bagging some great stuff in the first few weeks, we were completely hooked. <u>We managed to wangle a bathroom cabinet, a set of bookshelves, a laundry basket and loads of kitchen utensils and crockery.</u> Helen seemed to have more success at claiming things than I did – maybe it was the female touch or maybe it was the sheer speed of her email responses, I don't know. <u>I have shifted, among other things, an old chair, some speakers, and Helen's old curling tongs.</u> It is so much more rewarding to have people pick up the goods from you than just putting things in the bin.

The pinnacle of our *Freecycle* success has got to be <u>claiming a huge shelving unit and a lovely sofa.</u> Helen then requested a <u>sewing machine,</u> which she used to make a cover for the new sofa. We have been able to put other people's unwanted (but perfectly good) <u>furniture</u> to new use. It has also made the cost of decorating an entire flat far easier to stomach. I am now offering a lot more stuff on the site. I'm well and truly converted, and use it more than Helen! I check the site all the time for new offers – come summer, I'd love <u>a garden table and chairs.</u>

Julia: I found out about *Freecycle* when my colleague posted up loads of our <u>ancient office furniture</u> that would have been dumped otherwise. I've been hooked since.

When I drive past the dump, the amount of wonderful stuff I see that's going to waste seems criminal. I'm tempted to give out flyers for *Freecycle* when I go past, to tell people they don't have to throw good things away. There are three main benefits to *Freecycle*. First: people can get things for free. I've got a massive list of things I'm really happy with: <u>shower doors, a sewing machine, a farm gate, a china umbrella stand.</u> I've actually taken more than I've been able to give. Second: people usually post up stuff that they think isn't worth selling, which makes *Freecycle* good for avoiding landfill. Third: people come and collect what you've advertised, so it's very convenient for you. I once offered <u>a broken lawnmower,</u> which somebody snapped up!

Freecycle in Oxford has quite strict guidelines, because everything on the forum should be stuff that could end up on the dump otherwise. People accept the rules, but they also love the community feel of the group, so in order to avoid clogging up the *Freecycle* forum, a subgroup has been set up called the Oxford Freecycle Cafe. The cafe is more chatty and people offer all kinds of things on it, such as <u>wind-fallen apples or spare firewood.</u> It really shows the demand for free community networks.

Anna: My partner and I moved to a smallholding here just over a year ago with the aim of setting up a more sustainable lifestyle. We provide for ourselves by growing produce, raising and eating our own poultry and meat and using our own fuel. We found out about our local *Freecycle* group from an article in our daily newspaper (recycled for composting and firelighting), and its

philosophy seemed to go hand-in-hand with our own, so we thought there would be no better way of offloading some of the <u>excess chicks</u> we had at the time. We instantly got involved with this wonderful system of free exchange, and have since taken many items that have been incredibly useful. Since we started out we have found homes for <u>two cockerels, and we took someone's vacuum cleaner which is now in my son's flat, and we have given away some lovely 'eggs for sale' signs written on slate.</u>

One of the great things about *Freecycle* is that you can choose whom to give things to. You are encouraged to give items to charities if they request it, but otherwise choosing a recipient is entirely up to you and no explanations are necessary. In our *Freecycle* group, there are the 'usual' postings for items like <u>sofas, TVs, computers and cots,</u> all of which are extremely useful to members, but there are also postings which probably would not be found in groups in cities; requests to re-house <u>dogs, geese, a sow and her piglets and sheep.</u> These latter items reflect the fact that here *Freecycle* has become a real aid to those of us who value the idea of sustainability while being part of the farming community.

Answer key 10

Getting started p95

2 Where does the wood for our furniture come from? Have rainforests been cut down to get it?; Where do our clothes come from? Have any animals been killed or harmed to make it? Have people been paid badly or forced to work long hours in bad conditions to make them?; Have any animals been used or abused to test the cosmetics/chemicals/drugs we use in our everyday lives?; Where does the food we eat come from? Has it been organically grown?

Reading pp96-7

2 The Chitnis family: Anthony and Jane, with three children (Asmita, Daisy and Arthur).
The Yardley family: Jonathan and Jean, with four children (names are not given).
The Veninger family: Laurie and Jim, with two daughters (Madeleine and Emma).
3 The last paragraph (conclusion) doesn't belong.

4 Chitnis: they are coping but it is hard; Yardley: they got divorced; Veninger: they are coping but have had enough now.
5 a Tuesday till Thursday
b He has a small flat because he thinks hotels are 'soulless' places.
c They are both committed to what they are doing, they support each other and her parents live next door.
d It would have been difficult to uproot their four children, especially the older ones who were doing their GCSEs, plus their lives were there.
e When Jonathan moved to Tokyo and only came home once every couple of months, he started to miss out on the everyday things.
f The good things about one another.
g It's ironic that they originally decided to spend part of their lives apart in order to give their children a better life, but instead they put an 'intolerable strain' on the family.

6 'the years went by', 'Germany', 'four kids', 'he', … ('he' must refer to Jonathan Yardley – this should help students locate source as gap 4).
8 Paragraph B refers to none of the three families. It mentions reasons why families may live apart.
9 Paragraph C mentions Anne Green. She has not been mentioned anywhere else. Information about long-term commuting and its effect on family life.
10 Both paragraphs seem to have some relevance, but the paragraph about Anne Green seems to stand alone, as she is not mentioned anywhere else in the text, and the focus is on how family separation is more common now than it was 20 years ago.
11 1D; 2F; 3B; 4A; 5G; 6E

Language development p98

1 1b; 2f; 3c; 4e; 5a; 6h; 7g; 8d
2 pull off: make something succeed, be successful at something

3 1 pulled back; 2 pulled down; 3 pull (yourself) together; 4 pull off; 5 pull out of; 6 pull over; 7 pull through; 8 pull up
4 1 pulled a muscle; 2 pull out all the stops; 3 pulled a face; 4 pulling my leg; 5 pull yourself together; 6 pull strings; 7 pulling your weight; 8 pull a fast one on
5 pulling his leg; pulling a face; pulling your weight; pulling you along; pulling yourself up; pulling a muscle, pulling strings.

Listening (1) p99

3 1E; 2F; 3A; 4G; 5B; 6E; 7H; 8C; 9B; 10F

Grammar p100

1 The direct speech in the article makes some points more immediate and engaging. It helps the reader to relate more clearly with the speaker.
2 '… Arthur <u>said to</u> me the other day, 'Why <u>do you have to</u> work in London, Daddy? I like it so much better when <u>you're here with us</u>'; 'The other day, Arthur <u>asked</u> me

why <u>I had to</u> work in London. <u>He said he liked</u> it so much better when <u>I was there with them</u>.'

Rules: tense changes, place changes, subject/object pronoun changes, reporting verb changes.

3 a Anthony said that he missed them all an awful lot but he was lucky he had a small flat in London.

b Jean said it was a good career move for her husband but they knew uprooting their four children would be impossible.

c Laurie said it had been three years since Jim had started working in Holland and the girls had never got entirely used to it. That day her younger daughter had said she was missing her daddy.

4 Reverse the changes normally used to make reported speech: he → I, tense → one step forward (he had been offered → 'I have been offered'; name (Jean) used to clarify who he is speaking to.

5 a I really had a good time in Spain and I can't wait to go back next summer

b I went to the concert last night and I'm feeling rather tired

c I'm not coming because I hate the theatre

6 1 admitted; 2 propose; 3 demanded; 4 swore; 5 begged; 6 suggested

7 1 denied having anything to do with; 2 insisted on inviting me; 3 predicted it was going to snow (that it would snow); 4 apologised for what he had said; 5 objected to me (my getting/having a); 6 recommended (that) we (should) try

Use of English p101

1 a put (vt) = place/position; b put up with (phrasal verb) = tolerate/cope with; c put your back into something (phrasal verb) = work hard to achieve something

2 shut eyes (fairly common use); shut out memories (phrasal verb): less familiar; shops shut (common – though 'close' is more common).

3 a thick skin – idiomatic/metaphorical; b thick slice of bread (common) c; thick accent (idiomatic/metaphorical)

4 1 degree; 2 good; 3 family; 4 notice; 5 fortune

Listening (2) p102

2 Dave acquired: a bathroom cabinet, a set of bookshelves, a laundry basket and loads of kitchen utensils and crockery, huge shelving unit, a sofa, a sewing machine. Dave gave away: old chair, some speakers and Helen's old curling tongs. Dave's other items: three-piece suites to the kitchen sink, garden table and chairs.

Julia acquired: shower doors, a sewing machine, a farm gate, a china umbrella stand. Julia gave away: a broken lawnmower. Julia's other items: ancient office furniture, windfallen apples, spare firewood.

Anna acquired: a vacuum cleaner. Anna gave away: excess chicks, two cockerels, egg for sale signs written on slate. Anna's other items: sofas, TVs, computers, cots, dogs, geese, a sow and her piglets and sheep.

Writing pp102–3

1 How it started; Origins; Background; Aims; How it works; Rules and guidelines; Who can join/take part/participate; How to join, etc.

2 1 Welcome to Freecycle; 2 Background/How it started; 3 How does it work?; 4 Rules and guidelines; 5 Who can use The Freecycle Network?

3 Any of the following: describing, explaining, persuading, outlining, justifying priorities, etc.

4 Informal (words like 'stuff', 'junk' etc)

5 1 ai; bf; cn; 2 af; bn; ci; 3 af; bi; cn

6 Formal sentences tend to be longer and use passive more often. Informal sentences use more slang and colloquial language.

Vocabulary organiser 10 p104

10.1 1 something that can be produced or used without it running out (adj), unsustainable (antonym), sustain (v), sustenance/sustainability (n)
2 something that conforms to a set of principles or moral values (adj), unethical (antonym), ethics (n pl), ethically (adv)

10.2 a consult; b commute; c collate; d uproot; e undermine; f bachelor; g niggle; h impromptu; i frenetic; j intolerable

10.3 1 nitty gritty; 2 rock the boat; 3 take their toll on; 4 tough going; 5 stresses and strains; 6 alarm bells started to sound; 7 up sticks; 8 The bottom line

10.4 1 pulling your leg; 2 pulling his weight; 3 pull off; 4 pulled down; 5 pulling a fast one on us [also pulling the wool over our eyes or pulling our legs]; 6 pull through; 7 pulled strings; 8 Pull over

Bank of English

1 conscience; 2 dilemma; 3 ethics; 4 morals; 5 scruples

Scruples Questionnaire

What would you do?

An old lady needs help crossing the road, but you are late for an important interview. If you help her across, you know you'll miss your bus and it's an hour until the next one. Your potential employer has told you that punctuality is a very important quality!

 You have just got married and your partner has announced he or she wants you to give up your career (which you love) to become a full-time parent/housekeeper. You don't want to upset him/her because you can see it is important to them.

You've just found a very cheap piece of land to buy to build a house on, but discover that there is a campaign to turn it into a wildlife sanctuary for endangered animals and plants. You know you won't be able to find such a bargain again and land prices are going up all the time.

 You've just found out that the hamburger you are about to eat was made from a factory farmed cow that was slaughtered inhumanely. Trouble is, you're starving, and there's nothing else to eat!

You've just found out that the company you work for has business dealings with 'sweat shops' (clothes manufacturers that use illegal child labour) in the Far East. At the same time, you've just been offered the promotion you've been waiting years for.

 You've invited some friends round for dinner. One of them doesn't eat pork for religious reasons but you had forgotten this. Unfortunately, you've used bacon fat as an ingredient in the main course.

A girl in the office where you work is getting upset because her boss keeps making lewd comments whenever he sees her. Last time someone said something in her defence, they got the sack.

 Your brother has asked you to keep a secret and you have given him your word. Then he tells you that he's been invited to a party with some friends and they've decided they are going to take drugs for the first time to see what it's like.

You've just found out from your parents in trust that your cousin is adopted but he/she doesn't know this. Your cousin confides in you about everything and has told you that he/she suspects the truth about being adopted and has asked you what you think. You do not want to lie to anyone but you also feel it is not your place to tell the truth.

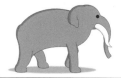 While on holiday in Africa you spend a lot of money on a beautiful necklace which you intend to give to your mother for her birthday. However, after arriving back in your home country, you notice that the necklace is made of ivory, and your mother strongly believes it is wrong to kill animals for the sake of vanity.

You've just been offered a large sum of money to set up the charity organisation you've always dreamed of, helping disabled children. However, you have reason to suspect that the money has come from someone who has dealings with the illegal sale of arms and ammunitions.

 Your fiancé's parents have invited you round to their house for dinner. When you arrive there you find that most of the furniture has been made from tropical Amazonian hardwoods, there are the skins of endangered dead animals on the floor, and rare stuffed animals in glass cases. They ask you what you think of their house.

Reporting the news

Suspect still at large!

Mr Simon Smith, aged 101, was found dead in his home this morning by his housekeeper, Mrs Wiggins. The police are looking into the matter and have not yet ruled out foul play. It appears that the last person to have seen Mr Smith alive, was …

Eyewitness 1: Miss Crimson

- You left your house at 10.30 pm.
- It was dark.
- You saw a man come out of No. 12.
- You didn't see his face.
- You thought he had blond hair.
- He was quite tall.
- You didn't hear anything strange.

Suspect 2: The nephew, Alfred White

- You came to see your uncle at 9 pm and stayed for about an hour and a half.
- The nurse seemed to be in a bad mood with him because he wouldn't take his pills.
- You left the room for 10 minutes to make some tea.
- When you came back the nurse had gone and your uncle was asleep.

Eyewitness 2: Professor Purple

- You were crossing the road at 10.35 pm.
- You heard a loud bang.
- You saw two people running away from No. 12.
- They looked like kids.
- One of them might have been carrying a gun, but you can't be sure.

Suspect 1: The nurse, Sarah Black

- You left Mr Smith at 10.20 pm.
- Mr Smith's nephew was still there.
- Mr Smith was in bed asleep.
- He had always been very kind to you.
- He had taken his medicine at the proper time.
- He seemed in good spirits.

PHOTOCOPIABLE 10.2

11 Making ends meet

Lesson planner

Fast lane: 3 x 1.5 hour lessons = 4.5 hours per unit
(total course = 72–76 hours)

Lesson	Time	Classwork	Exam Booster (EB) homework
31	1.5 hours	Getting started, Reading + Vocab. Organiser (VO)	Getting started + Reading
32	1.5 hours	Check homework, Lang. develop., Listening, Grammar + VO	Lang. develop., Listening + Grammar
33	1.5 hours	Check homework, Use of English, Speaking, Writing + VO	Use of English, Speaking, Writing + Coursebook Writing task

Slow lane: 4 x 1.5 hour lessons = 6 hours per unit
(total course = 96–100 hours)

Lesson	Time	Classwork	EB homework
41	1.5 hours	Getting started, Reading, VO + photocopiable 1	Getting started + Reading
42	1.5 hours	Check homework, Lang. develop., Listening, Grammar + VO	Lang. develop., Listening + Grammar
43	1.5 hours	Check homework, Use of English, photocopiable 2, Speaking + VO	Use of English + Speaking
44	1.5 hours	Check homework + Writing	Writing + Coursebook Writing task

Before you begin

If you have any foreign currency coins at home, bring them to the class to show your students. Alternatively, you could search on the Internet for images of the currencies mentioned below, and print them off to show students.

Write the following on the board:

A 1 yen; 2 dinar; 3 lek; 4 ruble; 5 krone; 6 lev; 7 peso; 8 taka; 9 renminbi; 10 pula

B a Bulgaria; b China; c Belarus; d Botswana; e Japan; f Algeria; g Albania; h Denmark; i Chile; j Bangladesh

Place students in teams and ask them to match the currencies with the country in which they are used. Set a time limit, or state that the first team to find all the correct matches are the winners.

Key: *1e; 2f; 3f; 4c; 5h; 6a; 7i; 8j; 9b; 10d*

Topic: making a living in a foreign country, credit card fraud

This unit aims to look at money and its uses; to discuss the various ways in which people make a living (and whether this makes them happy or not) as well as the topical subject of credit card fraud.

Unit 11 Wordlist

exorcise	middleman	tug
fleetingly	negligible	twiddle
fragment	piecework	unscrupulous
garment	pungent	venture
holdall	rudimentary	weave
lacy	tattered	zip
lint		

Getting started

1   Direct your students to read the quotations, and elicit their responses. Once they have discussed each one in turn, ask them to look at the pictures on the page, then ask them about the meaning of the unit title.

2   Direct your students to read and discuss the statement. Discuss which phrase is a better motto to live by.

3   Elicit from your students ideas about being careful with money before they answer the quiz.

Reading: interpreting literature

1   Students read the question. Gather ideas about why people move to another country to live and work. Then discuss what the potential difficulties are in doing so.

2   Do not give students the background information on the text yet. Tell them to read the extract and decide

whether the statements are true or false. Discuss their reasons for choosing these answers together.

3   Elicit any unknown words before they do the task. Allow them no more than ten minutes to complete the task. Elicit answers and ask students to justify their choices.

Speculating about a reading text

When reading an extract from a novel or short story, it is a good idea to encourage students to speculate about what has happened before in the story, and what will happen next. This gives them useful oral practice in using language for speculating and may also encourage them to seek out the novel and read it.

4   Elicit ideas about what might happen next in the story. Encourage the use of structures such as *may*, *might* and *could* for speculation. Now you may wish to provide your students with the background information on *Brick Lane*.

BACKGROUND: *BRICK LANE* BY MONICA ALI

Brick Lane is the story of Nazneen, a young Bangladeshi woman given into an arranged marriage to Chanu Ahmed, a man almost twice her age. Chanu takes her to London, where he has lived and worked for almost 20 years. Nazneen not only has to learn to live with Chanu, but she has to survive in a whole new culture as well.

In the small Bangladeshi estate community in London, Nazneen meets other Bangladeshi people who cope with their own struggles. Some of them struggle against the traditions they left behind, while others struggle against the new traditions that their English-born children are exposed to. Then Chanu is made redundant, and Nazneen has to find work to support the family. This extract describes the start of her working life in London.

5   Students could work in pairs. Encourage them to use the context to work out the meaning.

→   Vocabulary Organiser 11.1, page 114

SPOTLIGHT ON READING

Literary Devices

6   Direct your students to read the information and rubric in the Spotlight. Elicit answers and check their understanding of the different devices.

7   Ask your students to read through the extract quickly once more to find one more example of each type of literary device.

Language development:
idiomatic phrases with *out* and *money*

1   Direct your students to read the rubric and the two quotations from the text. Elicit the meaning of the underlined phrases.

2   Students work in pairs. Ask them to decide which one is needed to complete each sentence. Discuss their answer choices together.

→   Vocabulary Organiser 11.2, page 114

Key word: *money*

3   Students work in pairs. Tell them to decide which of the verbs in the box can be followed by *money*.

4   Students work in pairs. Direct them to read each sentence carefully, and use the context to work out the meaning of the italicised phrase.

5   Students work in pairs. They won't know all of the definitions, so elicit the ones they do know first. Then, tell them to use a dictionary to find the remaining phrases. Check the answers with the class.

→   Vocabulary Organiser 11.3, page 114

6   Students work individually. Tell students to quickly read through the text. Elicit what it is about. Tell them to look at the words in capital letters, and elicit any unknown words. Allow them ten minutes to complete the exercise. Ask them to compare their answers with a partner.

Language development extension

Ask students if they know of any similar stories. If they show interest, tell them to search the Internet for newspaper articles on further examples of credit card fraud.

Listening: sentence completion

1   Tell your students that you are going to continue with the theme of credit card fraud. Direct them to read the quotations in the speech bubbles. Ask them to compare the use of credit cards with that of cash.

PAPER 4, PART 2 Listening for dates, figures or statistics

Direct your students to read the information in the Spotlight, and the sentences in exercise 2.

2 Tell them to speculate what kind of information they should expect each gap to contain.

3 🎧 11.1 Play the recording twice. Elicit answers and give feedback.

4 Students read the rubric and questions for exercise 5, which is an exam style task. Elicit predictions about what they are looking for.

Maintaining good habits

At this stage in the course, some of the talented students may feel that the introductory prediction tasks are unnecessary. Weaker students, however, often feel intimidated by listening tasks, and will still welcome the support. Training them to predict what they are going to hear every time they are faced with a listening task helps them to feel more confident, and so is valuable even at this later stage in the course.

5 🎧 11.2 Elicit what a credit card fraud agency does. Play the recording twice before asking the students about their answers.

Listening extension

If you have a number of mature students in your class, you may wish to ask them whether their views on using their credit card have changed slightly as a result of listening to what Rodney had to say. Allow them a few minutes to discuss the question of security when using cards, and what precautions they take personally.

Grammar: modal auxiliaries (2)

1 Students work individually or in pairs before you discuss the answers as a class.

2 Students work in pairs or individually. Elicit the use of each sentence. Give feedback.

Plans, predictions, criticism, annoyance, resignation

Read through the information for each modal type and discuss questions/queries.

→ Grammar Reference 11.1, page 178

3 Students work individually. Direct them to read the three mini-dialogues.

4 Allow approximately five minutes for this exercise. Elicit answers and give feedback.

Use of English: multiple-choice cloze

Words of similar meaning, different uses

1 Tell them to read the sentences carefully, before deciding which option is correct. Allow them three minutes to complete the task before asking them to explain their choices.

2 Tell students to form their own sentences with the other words and phrases. Allow them five minutes for this. Elicit answers. If students have difficulty with some items, use the following examples to help them:

> Julia loved walking, and *would often* go for a walk in the park during her lunch break.

> Simon's very busy at the moment, so he *might not* be able to come to the cinema tonight.

3 Elicit views on the board game, *Monopoly*. Most people have played this game at some point in their lives, so ask students to describe how the game is played, whether they still play, and what they like and dislike about it. Tell them to read the text through quickly. Elicit what it is about. Direct them to read the question options. Give them ten minutes to complete the exercise. Hear students' answers and explanations.

p/c 11.2

→ Vocabulary Organiser 11.4, page 114

4 This is a speculative question, as it may only really suggest that someone who is good at the game might make an astute business person, or be good in the property market! It may also suggest that someone is too cautious, and doesn't take risks, may end up working in a small office, or may not be very ambitious. However, there is no golden rule. Welcome students' ideas, and generate discussion.

Speaking: disagreeing with someone else's opinion

1 🎧 11.3 Direct your students to read the rubric, and the Useful Phrases box. Play the recording. Allow students time to tick phrases. Then play the recording again to allow them to check what they've noted.

2 Students work in pairs. Direct them to read the question in the box. They should aim to use some of the useful phrases, where they disagree with their partner's view. Monitor from a distance, and note down items you wish to pinpoint, then give feedback.

Writing: a report – being concise

1 Find out your students' views on the photographs, and how they like to shop. Tell them that this is relevant to the sample writing topic.

2 Elicit what the task is asking them to do. Then ask how long their answer to this question should be. Make sure the students realise that it is a part 1 question, so the answer should be 180–220 words:

3 Students read the sample answer individually. Elicit that it is actually a fairly good answer in itself, but it is far too long, and is repetitive in places.

EXAM SPOTLIGHT

PAPER 2, PART 1 Being concise
4 Students work in pairs. Elicit answers and give feedback. If necessary, provide them with the suggested answer in the Answer key on page 107.

5 Students work in pairs, and discuss what needs to be kept in the sample answer, and what can be deleted, or reduced in length.

6 Students work in pairs, and one does the writing. Remind them to read the 'In other words' feature. Tell them to reduce the sample answer in length, so that it falls within the required word limit. Explain that they will need to change the sentence structure in places, and join points together. See the suggested answer on the right for ideas.

7 Before eliciting answers to exercise 6, direct your students to read exercise 7, and choose suitable headings for each paragraph.

8 Tell students to look at the photographs on the right of the page, and read the rubric for exercise 8. Draw out their answers.

9 Direct your students to read the rubric and input material. Brainstorm ideas as to what is needed in the answer. Then, students write the task.

Suggested answer for 6:

Aims

This report aims to provide an overall view of the current situation in the store, based on comments made by customers, and to make suggestions for improving sales in certain departments.

Successful departments

The Ladies' and Men's Clothing department is experiencing a boom in sales at present. This can be attributed to the fact that customers can try on the wide range of clothing available in spacious changing rooms. Similarly, the practical layout of the Stationery Department provides customers with easy access to all products.

Problem areas

As opposed to this, sales in the Furniture and Children's Clothing Departments have dropped considerably in the last year or so. Complaints have been made that the current range of furniture available is rather limited and old-fashioned in style. In the Clothing Department, concern was expressed over the lack of clothing items in stock for boys, and prices were thought to be too high.

Recommendations

Investment should be made in expanding and modernising the Furniture department to incorporate a wider range of styles, while a wider range of boys' clothing should be made available, at more reasonable prices. If all this can be achieved, then sales will almost certainly improve in these departments, and the store in general will benefit.

[208 words]

Photocopiable activity instructions

1 Activity 11.1 Fiction or fact?

Aim: To provide students with practice in dealing both with different types of reading texts by comparing journalistic and literary styles of writing; and also in producing these two styles of writing.

Instructions:

1 Place your students in pairs for the first part of this activity. Photocopy one page per student.

2 Direct your students to read the two extracts, A and B. Tell them they are based on the same story, but one is an extract from a newspaper article, and one is a narrative account. This should be fairly obvious to them.

3 They should note down: a the differences in style between the two pieces of writing; b the difference in approach to the story.

4 Elicit observations, and encourage class discussion.

5 Direct students to look at the cartoon strip.

6 Tell them to write: a the story as a newspaper article, and then; b as a narrative account.

Question 6 could be set as individual homework. Tell them the pieces of writing do not need to be long, but it is important to use the correct style of writing.

2 Activity 11.2 Monopoly token personality quiz

Aim: To give students further practice in speculating and making predictions, using modal structures.

Instructions:

1 Place your students in pairs. Give each student a photocopy.

2 The students choose the token they would most like to play with, and tell their partner about their choice.

3 Each student then makes predictions about the kind of person their partner is going to be, and speculates what kind of job they might choose in the future.

4 Elicit answers from the class as a whole, and find out your students' opinions of the predictions made.

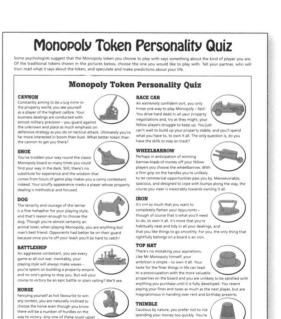

Tapescript 11

Listening 11.1

Analyst: ... Well, the statistics for weekly spending among families in Britain are quite revealing, as they mirror a certain shift in certain social attitudes. Consider tobacco, for example. In 1980, the average household spent £8.60 a week on tobacco, whereas by 2003, this had gone down to only £5.40, reflecting a reduction in the number of smokers. Household goods and services, on the other hand, showed a considerable increase, with families spending approximately <u>£33.80 on household goods in 2003, as opposed to only £22 in 1980.</u> The largest increase by far was in the area of leisure services, which rose from £18.90 in 1980 to £53.60 by 2003. The reasons for this appear to vary. <u>Motoring also saw a steep rise, from £35 in 1980 to £62.70 in 2003, almost twice as much.</u> Here, though, the figures have been greatly influenced by the significant rise in prices. Interestingly enough, <u>families spent less on fuel and power in 2003 than they had 23 years earlier, only £11.70 a week, instead of £15.</u> This clearly represents a growing awareness of the energy crisis. However, other areas such as clothing and footwear and food and drink, showed little change, and I think this can be credited to the ...

Listening 11.2

Interviewer: Now, Rodney, credit card fraud has become a huge problem worldwide in recent years, with global losses reaching almost <u>four billion</u> US dollars, and rising ... Just how bad is the situation for Britain?

Rodney: Well, unfortunately, it's steadily worsening. According to a survey conducted by APACS in 2003 on card fraud, the total value of fraud committed on UK-issued credit cards rose from 406.3 million pounds in 2001 to 411.6 million in <u>2003,</u> and the figures are still rising.

Interviewer: Incredible. Just how is this happening?

Rodney: I think one of the main problems is that consumers fail to realise how easy it is for a determined crook to steal their card details. Many are far <u>too relaxed</u> in their attitude towards keeping their card safe, or not revealing their bank details or personal identification number. There are several ways in which cards can be used fraudulently. The obvious one is actual theft of the card itself. Then there's counterfeiting, or 'skimming', as it's known in the trade. <u>Employees in a shop, restaurant or petrol station</u> may place your card into an electronic reading device, copy your details and then return your card without you noticing. The details can then be used for 'card-not-present' fraud.

Interviewer: What is that exactly?

Rodney: Credit card details are obtained from card theft, or skimming, as I've already mentioned, or going through someone's card receipts – some unscrupulous individuals even go through <u>rubbish bins</u> to obtain these. Then the details can be used fraudulently to buy goods or services online, over the phone, via mail order or by fax, without the card itself needing to be presented. The problem is that customers don't realise that some shop assistants will try to steal their details.

Interviewer: A frightening thought! So what should someone do if they realise their card's been stolen or copied?

Rodney: Call the card issuer right away. This will prevent you from being held liable for any large debts. The most you will have to pay is about <u>£50,</u> and you may not have to pay anything at all. The issuer will cancel your card, so remember not to use it again if you still have it.

Interviewer: But what can be done to prevent fraud from happening in the first place?

Rodney: People have to be more <u>vigilant</u> when using their cards. It always amazes me how relaxed many are about revealing personal card details, and PIN numbers, or lending their card to friends. Also, when paying by card, they shouldn't let the card out of their sight. In the UK, skimming and counterfeiting are the most common types of credit card fraud, whereas in the US, it's actual card theft that's the biggest offender. The implication here is that maybe Americans are more <u>careful</u> when paying by card.

Listening 11.3

Interlocutor: ... Some people say that having any job is better than no job at all. What do you think?

Fernando: Well, <u>I think it depends on</u> the kind of job we're talking about, and the kind of person you are. A university graduate, for instance, would not want to clean the streets for a living! I mean, he'd expect something better than that!

Katrina: <u>Yes, but if</u> there was no other job available, <u>what then? Would you rather</u> be unemployed?

Fernando: I think I would try to create a job for myself. Now, with the Internet, an imaginative person can find a way to earn a living.

Katrina: <u>I'm afraid I don't agree with you.</u> Perhaps you can do that, but it's not always so easy. For me, I would find it frustrating to be unemployed, so I think I would get a job cleaning rather than not work at all. I hate sitting around doing nothing.

Fernando: I think there are certain jobs I would find it embarrassing to do, so <u>I cannot say the same for me.</u> Also, if you are looking for a specific career, you need to be available for interviews etc. So, remaining unemployed until you find what you are looking for is not always bad.

Katrina: <u>Maybe, but that becomes a problem when</u> you are out of work for ... six months! I think a potential employer will be more impressed by someone who shows a general willingness to work.

Fernando: Yes, but ...!

Interlocutor: Thank you. That is the end of the test.

Answer key 11

Getting started p105

3 If you chose mainly A as your answer, you are very cautious about money, and like to be in control of it.

If you chose mainly Bs, you are fairly careful, but want to enjoy yourself as well!

If you chose mainly Cs, you are careless with money, so watch out!

Reading pp106–7

1 Suggested answers: problems with getting your qualifications recognised by the country; employers not wanting to employ foreigners; adapting to ways of working, and customs and way of life of the country; climate; language/local dialect or accent, being accepted.

2 1F; 2F; 3T; 4F; 5T; 6T

3 1D; 2A; 3B; 4B; 5C; 6D; 7A

5 a moisturiser; b beamed; c venture; d fleetingly; e holdall; f rudimentary; g garment; h exorcised; i facilitate; j dispel

6 a3; b1; c2

7 Type 1:'She wanted shampoo now'; 'He noticed Shahara's dress'; 'He seemed uncertain.'

Type 2: 'Yesterday she had refused to wash her hair with Fairy Liquid'; 'For a couple of weeks he puzzled feverishly over calculations ...'

Type 3: 'And don't forget it was we who invented all these weaves of cloths ...'

Language development p108

1 a work out = calculate, solve a problem; b totted up = added together to find the total

2 1 out of the question; 2 out of the blue; 3 out of your mind; 4 out of (respect); 5 out of this world; 6 out of it; 7 out of order; 8 out of luck

3 borrow, charge, earn, inherit, launder, lend, lose, make, owe, pay, raise, refund, save, spend, waste

4 1a; 2a; 3b

5 1d; 2e; 3f; 4b; 5a; 6c

6 1 penniless; 2 financial; 3 fraudulent; 4 insecure; 5 transactions; 6 careless; 7 suspicion(s); 8 conspiracy; 9 criminologists; 10 respectable

Listening p109

2 a sum of money; b date; c comparison of quantity (more/less; higher/lower)

3 a £22; b 1980; c less

4 Answers may vary. Expect to hear: 1 sum of money; 2 date; 3 adjective; 4 noun (type of person); 5 noun; 6 sum of money; 7 adjective; 8 adjective

5 1 four billion; 2 2003; 3 too relaxed; 4 shop assistants; 5 rubbish bins; 6 £50; 7 vigilant; 8 careful

Grammar p110

1 1a; 2d; 3c; 4e; 5b

2 a modal for a plan; b modal for prediction; c modal for prediction

3 1 A 'll/will; B will be/may be; A may/might as well

2 C would; D might as well; won't; C could have

3 E won't; F would; E could; will/may

4 1 you may/might as well; 2 'll become a nanny and; 3 could/

should/might have offered to pay; 4 it would be difficult to persuade; 5 would stop playing basketball

Use of English p111

1 1c; 2d

3 1B; 2A; 3B; 4B; 5D; 6C; 7C; 8D; 9B; 10A; 11B; 12C

Speaking p111

1 'Well, I think it depends on ...'; 'Yes, but if ... what then? Would you rather ...'; 'I'm afraid I don't agree with you. For me ...'; 'I cannot say the same for me'; 'Maybe, but that becomes a problem ...'

Writing pp112–13

2 You must examine the customer's comments on the store's facilities, outline them in a report, and make recommendations for improvements.

3 It's too long and is repetitive in places.

4 Suggested answer: This report aims to provide an overall view of the current situation in the store, based on comments made by customers, and to make suggestions for improving sales in certain departments.

5 Good points: the answer is well organised into paragraphs with headings, and answers the question; Important points to keep: Ladies' and Men's Clothing: plenty of choice and spacious changing rooms; Stationery: successful layout and items easily accessible; Furniture: little choice and old-fashioned; Children's Clothing: not enough

choice for boys and prices too high; Suggestions: need to invest in developing the Furniture department (modernising it); Clothing: more choice needed for boys and reasonable prices.

6 See page 104 for a suggested answer.

7 Paragraph 1: Aims; Paragraph 2: Successful Departments; Paragraph 3: Problem areas; Paragraph 4: Recommendations

Vocabulary organiser 11 p114

11.1 1 ventured; 2 totted up; 3 troublesome; 4 dispel; 5 feverishly

11.2 1T; 2F; 3F; 4T; 5F; 6F

11.3 1 money is no object; 2 gave him a good run for his money; 3 put your money where your mouth is; 4 put my money on; 5 is pumping money into

11.4 Personal noun: counsellor, sponsor

Verb: value, counsel, sponsor

Adjective: valued, valuable, worthy, sponsored, worldly, world-famous

Antonymous adjective: valueless, worthless, unsponsored, world-weary

Bank of English

2 1d; 2c; 3g; 4e; 5b; 6a; 7h; 8f; 9j; 10i

Fiction or fact?

A A 61-year-old woman took the popular game of Monopoly a step further in Denmark last week, when she managed to persuade a bank to exchange 2000 kronor's worth of Swedish Monopoly money for real Danish money. However, she got too greedy, and foolishly returned to the same bank the following day with even more Monopoly money. This time, the bank tellers were ready for her, and she landed on the 'go to jail' square.

B She glanced at the clock. One o'clock. The bank was busy, filled with impatient office workers anxious to get back to work. She hesitated. Could she really pull it off? It was a crazy idea. But she needed the money. It was now or never. She stood in the queue behind a particularly exasperated-looking man. It was a good choice. When his turn came, he managed to intimidate the young cashier to such an extent that she was quite flustered by the time Maggie reached her. Feigning a relaxed manner she didn't feel, she casually pushed the wad of Monopoly notes towards the girl with a sympathetic smile. It worked. Instead of examining the money, the girl looked at her, relieved to see a friendly face.

The glass mousetrap

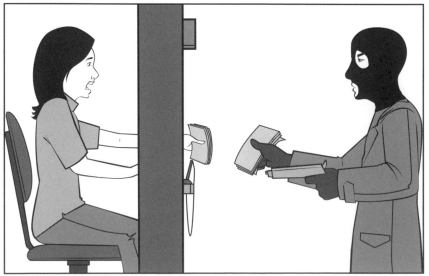
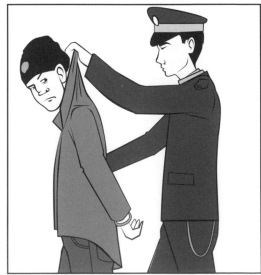

PHOTOCOPIABLE 11.1

Monopoly Token Personality Quiz

Some psychologists suggest that the Monopoly token you choose to play with says something about the kind of player you are. Of the traditional tokens shown in the pictures below, choose the one you would like to play with. Tell your partner, who will then read what it says about the token, and speculate and make predictions about your life.

Monopoly Token Personality Quiz

CANNON

Constantly aiming to be a big noise in the property world, you see yourself as a player of the highest calibre. Your business dealings are conducted with almost military precision – you guard against the unknown and place as much emphasis on defensive strategy as you do on tactical attack. Ultimately you're far more interested in boom than bust. What better token than the cannon to get you there?

SHOE

You've trodden your way round the classic Monopoly board so many times you could find your way in the dark. Still, there's no substitute for experience and the wisdom that comes from hours of game play makes you a canny contestant indeed. Your scruffy appearance masks a player whose property dealing is methodical and focused.

DOG

The tenacity and courage of the terrier is a fine metaphor for your playing style, and that's reason enough to choose the dog. Though you're almost certainly an animal lover, when playing Monopoly, you are anything but man's best friend. Opponents had better be on their guard because once you're off your leash you'll be hard to catch!

BATTLESHIP

An aggressive contestant, you see every game as all-out war. Inevitably, your playing style will always make waves – you're intent on building a property empire and no one's going to stop you. But will your course to victory be an epic battle or plain sailing? We'll see.

HORSE

Fancying yourself as hot favourite to win any contest, you are naturally inclined to choose the horse even though you know there will be a number of hurdles on the way to victory. Any one of these could upset your chances, but your cool head allows you to stay focused on the ultimate goal and, providing you don't let go of the reins, you should end up with your nose in front.

RACE CAR

An extremely confident sort, you only know one way to play Monopoly – fast! You drive hard deals in all your property negotiations and, try as they might, your fellow players struggle to keep up. You just can't wait to build up your property stable, and you'll spend what you have to, to own it all. The only question is, do you have the skills to stay on track?

WHEELBARROW

Perhaps in anticipation of winning barrow-loads of money off your fellow players you choose the wheelbarrow. With a firm grip on the handles you're unlikely to let commercial opportunities pass you by. Manoeuvrable, spacious, and designed to cope with bumps along the way, the course you steer is inexorably towards owning it all.

IRON

It's not so much that you want to completely flatten your opponents – though of course that is what you'll need to do, to own it all. It's more that you're habitually neat and tidy in all your dealings, and that you like things to go smoothly. For you, the only thing that rightfully belongs on a board is an iron.

TOP HAT

There's no mistaking your aspirations. Like Mr Monopoly himself, your ambition is simple – to own it all. Your taste for the finer things in life can lead to a preoccupation with the more valuable properties on the board and you are unlikely to be satisfied with anything you purchase until it is fully developed. You resent paying your fines and taxes as much as the next player, but are magnanimous in handing over rent and birthday presents.

THIMBLE

Cautious by nature, you prefer not to risk spending your money too quickly. You're only too aware that a slip up in your money management could lead to painful ruination. Then again, you're aware of the need to speculate to accumulate. Ultimately, buying well within your means, your prudence is your greatest playing strength.

PHOTOCOPIABLE 11.2

12 Behind the silver screen

Lesson planner

Fast lane: 3 x 1.5 hour lessons = 4.5 hours per unit
(total course = 72–76 hours)

Lesson	Time	Classwork	Exam Booster (EB) homework
34	1.5 hours	Getting started, Reading + Vocab. Organiser (VO)	Getting started + Reading
35	1.5 hours	Check homework, Lang. develop., Listening, Grammar + VO	Lang. develop., Listening + Grammar
36	1.5 hours	Check homework, Speaking, Use of English, Writing + VO	Speaking, Use of English + Writing
Extra	__ hour	Review 3	Can be either set as homework or completed in class

Slow lane: 4 x 1.5 hour lessons = 6 hours per unit
(total course = 96–100 hours)

Lesson	Time	Classwork	EB homework
45	1.5 hours	Getting started, photocopiable 1, Reading + VO	Getting started + Reading
46	1.5 hours	Check homework, Lang. develop., Listening + VO	Lang. develop. + Listening
47	1.5 hours	Check homework, Grammar, Speaking, Listening + VO	Grammar, Speaking + Listening
48	1.5 hours	Check homework, Use of English, Writing + photocopiable 2	Use of English, Writing + Coursebook Writing task
Extra	__ hour	Review 3	Can be either set as homework or completed in class

Before you begin

Tell the class to imagine that they are going to live on a desert island for a year, though miraculously this island has a fully functioning TV/DVD room! They are allowed to choose ten films to take with them to the island. Tell each student to note down their three favourite films. Students take turns naming films, one at a time, and saying why they like the films in question. Write the names of the films on the board. Afterwards take votes from the class for each film that should go. The activity finishes when you have a list of ten films on the board that everyone agrees on. Be careful not to spend too long on this part though!

Topic: film, scripts, Hollywood

Almost everyone loves watching films and many people are interested in the lives of actors and TV celebrities. Talking about films is something that many of us enjoy. In this unit, we focus on Hollywood and reviews of mainstream popular films, while allowing the opportunity to digress into more specialised areas.

Unit 12 Wordlist

adaptation	glamour	offend
adept	hilarious	render
ambivalence	implausible	resemble
anonymous	inspired	restore
blockbuster	intensify	satire
cast	interpretation	slapstick
commercially	intrepid	staggering
convincingly	irresistible	subtle
crew	jest	succinct
cynical	mainstream	suspense
deficiency	mock	tedious
disjointed	offensive	thriller
diverge	paparazzi	trailer
elegant	perseverance	tweak
embellish	plot	uproarious
enamour	portrayal	villain
enigmatic	preposterous	wit
entrance	protagonist	wooden
farce		

Getting started

Aim: This section is meant as a bit of fun, and it's a good way to introduce key words and prepare students for the subject matter of this unit.

BACKGROUND: ACADEMY AWARDS

The Academy Awards, widely known as the Oscars, are awards of merit presented annually by the Academy of Motion Picture Arts and Sciences (AMPAS) to recognise excellence of professionals in the film industry, including directors, actors and writers. The formal ceremony at which the awards are presented is one of the most prominent film award ceremonies in the world. The Oscars, and the Academy of Motion Picture Arts and Sciences itself, were conceived by Metro-Goldwyn-Mayer studio boss, Louis B. Mayer. The 1st Academy Awards ceremony was held on Thursday 16th May 1929.

1   Go through the quiz with the class and elicit responses. Write any new vocabulary on the board so that students can copy it into their vocabulary notebooks.

2   Students can number and discuss the options in pairs at first or just do it as a class activity to save time. Discuss the different elements of a film and ask students to give reasons for their choices.

3   Discuss the points with the class and ask them to give examples of films they know if possible.

→   Vocabulary Organiser 12.1, page 124

Reading: understanding humour, irony and sarcasm

Aim: The purpose of this section is to help students read texts that contain a certain amount of humour, irony or sarcasm, as it is not always obvious to students when a writer is being serious, and this may affect the correct answer of tasks.

1   Tell the class that one of the hardest things to understand in any foreign language is humour. This is because most of the time humour is either based on language or culture and it can be very hard to translate. Analyse the effect on other students of each joke told in English and elicit why it is, or isn't, funny.

2   It is important to establish here that there is not a very great difference between the two, only that sarcasm can often be used rudely or to make a point.

BACKGROUND: 'PENGUIN' FILMS

March of the Penguins is a French nature documentary film which won the 2006 Academy Award for Best Documentary Feature. The film depicts the yearly journey of the emperor penguins of Antarctica.

Happy Feet is an Australian-produced 2006 computer-animated comedy-drama musical film, directed and co-written by George Miller. Though primarily an animated film, it does incorporate live action humans in certain scenes. *Happy Feet* won the Academy Award for Best Animated Feature.

Understanding humour, irony and sarcasm

Read through the rubric with the class. Ask someone to tell you why the words 'understand' and 'appreciate' are in inverted commas. Elicit that neither word is being used in its most literal sense.

3   Students may need guidance with this task, so help them if they are not sure.

Pre-teach the following words: sucrose-enriched (n-adj phrase); upgrade (n); anthropomorphic (adj); deficiency (n); schmaltzy (adj); entrance (v)

Tell students to read the text slowly, and then to paraphrase the gist in their own words. Elicit the answers to questions a and b or help guide students to the answers. Ask:

> Why does the writer mention Elvis Presley?

> What is the 'deficiency' that he mentions?

> What would the writer have expected the humans to have done with this penguin when they found out he could dance? Why?

4   Students now do exercise 4 individually (they should now be able to spot at which points the writer is being sarcastic). Check answers with the group.

5   Point out that this particular reviewer tends to write humorous reviews about the films he dislikes and uses quite a lot of irony and sarcasm in these. He doesn't do this so much with the films he likes.

TEACHING IN PRACTICE

Skimming and scanning

There are two basic ways you could approach this part of the Reading Paper.

1   Read the whole text once all the way through. Then look at each question or sentence in turn, trying to find the text it relates to. This will mean skim reading each text again.

2   Read the whole text once all the way through. Then go back and read each separate part of the text one at a time. Then try to find the question or sentence or sentences that refer to it.

A third technique could be a combination of both methods above, which ensures that if you missed something one way, you are more likely to find the correct answer the second way. A good tip is to underline the parts of the text where you find the answers.

6 Students should work individually as this is an exam-style task. Give them ten minutes, but allow a bit more time if they find this tough. Before they start, go through the techniques for skimming and scanning mentioned above. Tell students they should experiment with both techniques in order to find out which one works best with the text in question, as sometimes the best technique to use depends on the complexity of the text or questions they will be given.

Degree of difficulty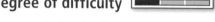

Increase the level: Allow no more than 5–10 minutes for exercise 6. Do not pre-teach any vocabulary or go through the texts until after the students have answered the questions. Elicit justifications and text references for each answer.

Decrease the level: Go through the texts first with the students. Pre-teach key vocabulary, and perhaps go through exercises 7 and 8 before students attempt exercise 6. Ask students to paraphrase each paragraph in their own words. Allow approximately 15–20 minutes for students to complete the task and answer the questions.

Consider pre-teaching the following vocabulary:

cynical	showreel	triumphantly
plead	sans	whingeing
resistance fighter	disjointed	fatigue
gallant	villain	IQ
spine-tingling	boo	outpace
redundant	baddie	gags
enamoured (of)	scamper	mantle
macho	euphoric	absurdity
caulk	implausible	send up
moonstruck	shot	quips
goofy	render up	gadgets
hopscotch	melancholy	preposterous

→ Vocabulary Organiser 12.2 + 12.3, page 124

7 Ask the question to the class. The point is to introduce the film reviewer's particular style of describing certain aspects of a film. This leads on to exercise 8.

8 Students can attempt the exercise alone or in pairs. Check the answers with the class.

Language development:
modifying and intensifying adjectives

1 Students can work in pairs or individually. Elicit the context for each pair of words and get students to say what they describe. Ask them to explain why they think the writer chose these words.

Emphasising adjectives
Go through the rubric with the class. Elicit that when used as modifiers, most adverbs such as 'extremely', 'terribly', 'incredibly' etc, fail to carry their literal meaning and instead are just a stronger form of *very*. (For example, if you say something was 'terribly funny', you don't mean that it was funny in a terrible way, you mean it was very funny.)

2 Students can work individually or in pairs. Elicit responses and go through the answers with the class.

3 Read the sentences with the class and elicit responses. Elicit that 'brilliant' is a non-gradable adjective, so it should be intensified with 'extremely' or other similar adverb, while 'good' is a gradable adjective, and should therefore be graded with 'very' or other similar adverbs.

4 Students can work in pairs or individually. Check answers with the class.

5 Students can work in pairs or individually. Check answers with the class.

6 Students may have come across some of these collocations before, or may have a passive knowledge of some of them. To help them, read the first question with each option and ask the class to raise their hands after the option that they think doesn't sound right.

7 Arrange students in pairs or open pairs, or if you prefer hold an open class discussion. The aim is to let students practise using some of the adverb + adjective combinations they have just learnt in speech when discussing their own views about films etc. If students are not forthcoming with their own ideas, prompt them with questions.

→ Vocabulary Organiser 12.4, page 124

Key word: *quite*

Explain that the word *quite* is different from many of the other quantifiers in that it can have a number of meanings depending on how it is used. Read through the list with the students and ask them to match the examples if they can.

Emphasis on *quite*
Point out that with the word *quite*, the spoken stress in the sentence reveals a lot about the meaning. For example read the following sentence in two different ways and ask students to tell you what you mean in each case:

'I went to the beach at the weekend. It was *quite* relaxing.'
[Strong emphasis on 'quite' meaning it was actually more relaxing than you'd expected it to be.]

'I went to the beach at the weekend. It was *quite relaxing*.'
[Emphasis carries on to the adjective, meaning that it was a bit relaxing, but not very.]

8 🎧 12.1 Play the recording and tell students to think again about their previous answers.

Listening: understanding purpose and function

1 Ask students to look at the pictures and read the comment boxes. For each point ask the students who agrees and who disagrees.

3 🎧 12.2 Play the recording and go through the answers with the class.

4 Discuss the topic with the class.

Grammar: participle clauses

Aim: To give students a little extra help understanding participles and participle clauses.

1 Ask students to read through and match up the examples. Ask students to identify the participle clause in each sentence.

3 Students complete the exercise.

Degree of difficulty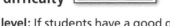

Increase the level: If students have a good grasp of the grammar they should complete exercise 3 individually and should spend no more than five minutes doing so. You could also ask them to add one example sentence of their own using each of the structures.

Decrease the level: Students can work in pairs. You can also provide them with extra help, such as the first word of the first sentence etc.

4 This exercise could be done with the class, individually or in pairs, as you see fit. Tell students to read through the whole text before they make any changes.

8 Students complete the exercise individually.
   → Vocabulary Organiser 12.5, page 124

Speaking: exchanging ideas (parts 3 and 4)

2 Point out that the discussion points in this exercise are similar to the type of questions students will encounter in part 4. Remind students that there are no right or wrong answers to the questions so they should just express whatever ideas they have about each point. Read out the questions one at a time and ask specific students to answer each time rather than waiting for a volunteer. Try to make sure that everyone gets an equal chance to speak.

Use of English: open cloze

Aim: The purpose of this section is to help students identify the missing parts of speech in a cloze text. Sometimes it is not immediately obvious what type of word is missing. Students may need help focusing on the gap and the context around the gap in order to be able to work out what is needed.

PAPER 3, PART 2 Identifying parts of speech

Before your read the rubric ask the class to remind you of the steps required to tackle an open cloze test.

1 Students should be able to do this exercise individually but if you think they need extra help let them work in pairs or tell them to consult their dictionaries. Alternatively spend a bit of time revising different parts of speech and going through some of the examples.

TEACHING IN PRACTICE

Reading the titles

The texts in parts 1, 2 and 3 all have titles. Encourage your students to pay attention to each title as it will indicate the main theme of the text.

2 Students should do the task individually. Allow approximately ten minutes for this. Elicit answers and give feedback.

→ Vocabulary Organiser 12.6, page 124

Writing: a film review

1 🎧 12.3 The films that are described in the Listening task are chosen for being fairly well known Hollywood films, but it is unlikely that all your students will have seen all of them. Some students may not have seen any of these films, and some students may only have seen some of them. Stress that this doesn't matter – the exercise is to help them focus on the section in general. Tell them to make a few notes based on what each speaker says, and then discuss what they imagine the film to be like.

2 Read the rubric with the class. Find out how many students have seen a film recently at the cinema and how many have seen a film recently on TV or on DVD. If any students haven't seen a film recently ask them if they can remember any films they've seen.

SPOTLIGHT ON WRITING

Planning your review

3 Go through the Spotlight with the class, reading the tips in each case and giving students time to follow each of the points. If time is limited here you can speed up this section by eliciting suggestions from students and writing a class answer on the board.

4 Point out that most reviews avoid using personal feelings too often as this makes the review seem too

subjective whereas most reviews tend to aim to be objective.

In other words

5 Read the example sentences with the class and elicit what is wrong with them. Point out that at this stage, students should not be using descriptions like 'very nice'. Raise suggestions for better descriptive vocabulary.

→ Vocabulary Organiser 12.7, page 124

6 Read through the box with the students and ask them which elements they would plan to include in their review. Students then read the review of *The Illusionist* and tick the elements in the box that have been mentioned. Compare with students' own views.

TEACHING IN PRACTICE

Reading reviews

Encourage your students to read as wide a range of reviews as possible, not just for films, but for all kinds of things, including holidays or travel locations, books, television programmes, consumer goods, computer equipment etc. They need to be taught the use of appropriate adjectives, and how to describe and explain. They also need to know how to give an opinion, positive or negative, and make a recommendation.

7 Remind students of the Grammar section and refer back to it if necessary. Students then work individually or in pairs, rewriting the words in italics as required.

PAPER 2, PART 1 + 2 Writing reviews

Read through the rubric with the class. Answer any questions.

8 Students write down their ideas.

Writing extension

Students could prepare plans for any of these as they did in exercise 3.

9 Students could prepare by going through exercise 3 (points 1–4), and just adapting the relevant details.

Photocopiable activity instructions

1 **Activity 12.1 Film images**

Aim: To help students practise articulating their ideas, working in pairs, and summarising narratives.

Instructions:

1   Tell the class: When deciding which films to make, movie studios have to literally choose between thousands of film scripts every year. Because they can't read every single script, producers often make their choice based on the best 'spiel' they receive (or plot summary).

2   Students form pairs or groups of three. Photocopy and hand out the movie picture worksheet.

3   Each pair/group has five to ten minutes to think up an idea for a movie which they have to present to the class. Each of the subjects represented by the images in the picture should appear somewhere in their story, but everything else is up to them. Tell them to be as wacky and imaginative as they can, but the basic story should make some kind of sense and have a clear beginning, middle and an end.

4   When they have finished they have to present their outline to the class. Their 'spiel' should last no more than 60 seconds and should be as visually descriptive as possible.

5   The class votes for the best story idea.

2 **Activity 12.2 'Ellie' Award Ceremony Night**

Aim: To practise using participle clauses.

Instructions:

1   Photocopy the worksheet and hand out to students. (Students can either work individually or in pairs).

2   Tell your students that they have attended the 64th annual Ellie Award Ceremony as reporters for the entertainments section of the local newspaper which they work for. The worksheet contains their own hand written notes based on the events of the evening.

3   Students have to rewrite each award box as only one sentence. Each sentence should begin with a present or past participle. They should use further participles wherever they can.

Tapescript 12

Listening 12.1

a: I think it's time Roger retired.
      Yes, well, *quite*!

b: Gillian is *quite* a little trouble maker isn't she!

c: I think it's *quite* a good idea to take her advice.

d: It's *quite* clear to me that you weren't listening.

e: After the accident, he was never *quite* the same.

f: I thought the script was *quite* ridiculous.

Listening 12.2

Extract 1

Interviewer: So Richard, tell us about what got you started as an independent filmmaker.

Richard: From an early age I was obsessive about film, about directing and cinematography but it never occurred to me that I could do it myself until one day I picked up my Dad's eight millimetre camera and started recording family life. I used to watch films all the time too. My local video shop had a section of 'unclassifiable' films that didn't belong in any section, and these were all my favourite films. They were totally unique, they made up their own rules and they always left me feeling as if something inside me had changed. These films proved that the medium of film had the power to change someone's perception of the world, and that just made me more determined.

Interviewer: And yet you claim that you don't make 'arty' films.

Richard: While I knew I wanted to work in this genre, I also knew how easy it was for experimental films to turn into pretentious rubbish. I wanted to express my message through film, using abstraction and music, but not some over the top art piece. I'm

115

just not interested in art films where I watch ten minutes and know what is going to happen in the next hour.

Extract 2

Woman: Have you seen the latest Narnia film? It's got great special effects and everything, but it couldn't have been more different from my childhood memory of the book.

Man: No, and I don't think I will. I loved the Narnia books and I hate seeing film adaptations of children's books in general, especially if they're books I grew up with. It's almost like they belong to me, if you know what I mean.

Woman: True, but sometimes a bad adaptation can remind you of why you loved the original book in the first place. As soon as I saw the film I went and dug out my old copy and started reading it again.

Man: Yes, but have you noticed how they always make the films with the express intention of not offending any of the 'book fans'? That's why they can never live up to the original.

Woman: Maybe, but in some ways though it's interesting to see another take on the book. To see the characters come to life. And if they choose the right actors to bring out the characters, you might find your understanding of the book to be deepened by the film version.

Man: I just don't think I'll ever be satisfied by any adaptation. You read these children's books so much that you come to inhabit them – every scene in those books has a specific visual reality for me; one that's very difficult to relinquish.

Extract 3

Woman 1: I think it's depressing that women film directors are in such a tiny minority. Did you know that in Britain, only seven per cent of film directors are women? And apart from a couple of obvious commercial successes, like Jane Campion's film *The Piano*, or Gurinder Chadha's *Bend it like Beckham*, how many films can you actually think of that were directed by women? I can't help thinking that if this imbalance were to occur in any other profession, there would be some kind of major outcry. Why is it that film-making continues to be the most unbalanced career in the arts?

Woman 2: Well, obviously there are the difficulties of working in a male-dominated industry. Women need role-models – like the two women you just mentioned. They need self-confidence, and they need tips on how to raise children and commit themselves to their work at the same time. But the truth is that, whether you're

female or male, it is really hard to make films. Creativity is stifled because filmmakers have to spend far too much time fundraising. There is so much courage involved in being a film director because there is so much at stake, and women are not generally raised to gamble with other people's money – a thing that seems to come more easily to men.

Listening 12.3

Speaker 1: Well it's about a pirate, Jack Sparrow, played by Johnnie Depp, who used to be captain of a ship called 'The Black Pearl', but now that ship's been commandeered by a zombie pirate called Captain Barbosa. He has been cursed with living death until he can find the living heir of old 'Bootstrap' Bill Turner, who is actually played by Orlando Bloom and, to that end he has kidnapped the beautiful Elizabeth Swann …

Speaker 2: It's an animated film about an ogre who lives in a swamp. Coming home one day he finds that all these fairy tale characters have moved in, which he is not very happy about, to say the least. Accompanied by a talking donkey that irritates him greatly, he sets off on a fairy tale adventure of his own, and comes face to face with dragons, princesses and even happy endings …

Speaker 3: It's a musical actually, and it's about two brothers, Jake and Elwood, who are on a mission from God to save a convent orphanage from closure. In order to legitimately raise the money they need, they have to put their old blues band back together, no mean feat in itself, despite the fact that the police and all their old enemies are all in hot pursuit. What I love is the wonderful performances by John Lee Hooker, James Brown, Aretha Franklin, Ray Charles, to name but a few …

Speaker 4: The film is based on an actual historical event of course, but the main story is a romance, told in flashback by the old woman, Rose, remembering Jack, whom she met on board the ship for the first time. He is a penniless artist who won his ticket to America in a game of cards; she is an attractive young lady engaged to marry a wealthy aristocrat to pay off her family's debts …

Speaker 5: I love this film – even though it's quite spooky really. I think the actor who plays the scared little boy with psychic abilities is excellent, and Bruce Willis is great as the failed child psychologist who wants to make sure he gets it right second time around. You really need to see it twice because only then do you really appreciate all the details leading to the final twist …

Answer key 12

Getting started p115

1 1 a thriller; 2 a documentary; 3 the cast; 4 the score; 5 a musical; 6 computer graphics

Reading pp116–17

3 a Yes b Key sentences are: 'It's as if executives watched that film and thought: "Mmm, not bad, sick-makingly anthropomorphic,

sure, but only a fraction as anthropomorphic as we'd really like: the penguins still aren't actually singing and dancing and doing Elvis Presley impressions."' (sarcasm)/ '… the humans respond, not by raising ticket prices to $10,000 per head …' (sarcasm) / '… Thank God those penguins can dance just like

humans, eh? It means they deserve to live!' (sarcasm/irony)

4 aF; bT; cF; dF

5 aB, C, D; b B, C, D; c A, E, F; d B, C, D; e students' answers.

6 1E; 2C; 3F; 4B; 5A; 6D; 7A; 8F; 9D; 10C; 11B; 12A; 13F; 14C; 15E

7 dull and lifeless

8 1 cracking; 2 big-hearted; 3 thrilling; 4 spine-tingling;

5 disjointed; 6 pounding; 7 razor-sharp; 8 inspired; 9 preposterous

Language development p118

1 a (hopscotch) dance that the character does (B); b Rocky's attempt to get the world heavyweight boxing title (at his age) (D); c the script /the film (E); d the new James Bond film (F)

2 1 delightfully; 2 tediously; 3 ridiculously; 4 strangely; 5 genuinely; 6 back-achingly

3 a 'brilliant' is a non-gradable adjective, so should be intensified with 'extremely' or similar; b 'good' is a gradable adjective, so should be graded with 'very' or similar adverb

4 annoying, exciting, fascinating, interesting, scary, funny, dull, good

5 absolutely, rather, awfully, incredibly, really, completely, totally, extremely, quite. rather, awfully, really, extremely, quite (can be used with both kinds of adjective).

6 1c; 2a; 3b; 4a; 5d; 6c; 7b; 8d

8 a6; b5; c1; d3; e4; f2

Listening p119

2 a extract three; b extract one; c extract two

3 1C; 2B; 3B; 4C; 5A; 6C

Grammar p120

1 1c; 2a; 3b

3 1 Not knowing what else to do ...; 2 The sea being so warm, they decided ...; 3 (Having been) told off, we stopped talking; 4 Having told Annette ...; 5 Looking for a film to watch, Jackson ...; 6 Having fallen in love with him ...; 7 The manager having retired, Victoria was hoping for a promotion

4 Lara Croft, [who is] one of the world's most celebrated action heroines ... / Facing... / Demonstrating her physical prowess and revealing her courage as never before, Lara proves ... / Knowing that Pandora's box is concealed there, [and that] she must protect the secret ... / the most unspeakable evil [that anyone has] ever known.

5 a

6 b

7 were organically-grown vegetables.

8 a tiring journey; b concerned should come to the meeting; c are French-speaking Swiss people; d faded colours; e barking dogs were getting on my nerves; f retired teacher; g Only balcony

seats were left; h grown-up children

Use of English p121

1 1 preposition; 2 adverb; 3 particle; 4 verb; 5 modal; 6 relative pronoun; 7 quantifier; 8 conjunction; 9 pronoun; 10 article

2 1 do; 2 apart; 3 most; 4 despite; 5 Without; 6 up/of; 7 bring/give; 8 even; 9 on/up; 10 have/want; 11 once/even; 12 until; 13 deal; 14 where; 15 of

Writing pp122–3

1 1 *Pirates of the Caribbean: Curse of the Black Pearl*; 2 *Shrek*; 3 *The Blues Brothers*; 4 *Titanic*; 5 *The Sixth Sense*

2 college magazine, review, outline plot, give opinions: acting, directing, other elements.

4 a The dull script failed to bring life to the story.
b The actors' wooden performances were unconvincing.
c The story was interesting but could have been developed further.

5 a awe-inspiring/stunning; b excellent/talented; c dull/tedious; d atrocious/appalling/terrible

6 genre, acting, plot, reviewer's opinion, script, directing

7 [who is] charismatically played; Discovering he has a talent for magic, he soon ...; being the son of ...; Having changed his name, he is known as ...; Needing an assistant ...; [who is] played ...; a short story [which was] written by ...; making it the setting ...

Vocabulary organiser 12 p124

12.1 1b; 2a; 3c; 4b; 5a

12.2 1 cynical; 2 gallant; 3 redundant; 4 enamoured; 5 disjointed; 6 euphoric; 7 melancholy; 8 implausible; 9 gargantuan; 10 preposterous

12.3 1 call off; 2 set up; 3 turned into; 4 take on; 5 cut back

12.4 1 highly amusing; 2 bitterly disappointed; 3 most kind; 4 deeply offended; 5 seriously injured; 6 perfectly simple

12.5 1 hand made clothes; 2 amusing book; 3 genetically modified fruit; 4 water resistant watch; 5 floating debris on the river

12.6 a unknown/without a name; b produce/create; c difficult/tiring; d add details to make something more interesting; e fiddle with to improve something; f the quality of being able to continue/not give up

12.7 1 acting; 2 characters; 3 story; 4 plot; 5 casting; 6 directing

Bank of English

1 humorist; humorous; humorously; humourless; humourlessly; humourlessness; humoristic

2 dehydrated

Review 3 pp125–6

1 1 tediously dull; 2 ridiculously small; 3 deeply offended; 4 most kind; 5 bitterly disappointed; 6 fully aware; 7 thoroughly annoying; 8 greatly mistaken; 9 deliciously mouthwatering; 10 perfectly reasonable

2 1 notice; 2 money; 3 highly; 4 paid; 5 work

3 1 tough going; 2 out of luck; 3 taken its toll; 4 nitty gritty; 5 out of order; 6 out of the question; 7 rock the boat; 8 bottom line; 9 out of your mind; 10 out of the blue

4 1 awareness; 2 activists; 3 materialistic; 4 unethical; 5 sustainable; 6 unfashionable; 7 penniless; 8 swapping; 9 facilitated; 10 unwanted

5 1 you should do is go out and meet people more
2 wanting to disturb them, I left without saying goodbye
3 he managed to work it out that way, I don't know
4 you need is a break from the computer
5 was the weather, they decided to light a fire
6 dreamed of going to Australia all her life, Grace was extremely excited
7 he gets his bad temper from, I don't know
8 to become an Olympic swimmer, Hannah trained very hard
9 having seen Mike and Helen for several years, we had a lot to talk about
10 though this car is, it is very reliable

6 1 might have got; 2 can't have got; 3 would have phoned; 4 won't/may not have; 5 would be; 6 may/might as well go; 7 'll be; 8 might/could have called; 9 would have done; 10 could order

7 1 apologised for missing/having missed; 2 denied putting/having put; 3 threatened to kill; 4 accused her of lying/having lied; 5 recommended the [Indian restaurant on the corner] to him; 6 admitted to taking/having taken; 7 predicted that; 8 warned us not to go/against going

8 1 might have apologised to her for; 2 insisted on seeing the Manager; 3 having been delayed; 4 pulled strings with the; 5 did not/ didn't cancel as; 6 not knowing where; 7 but what I do enjoy is; 8 someone would tell Nick to

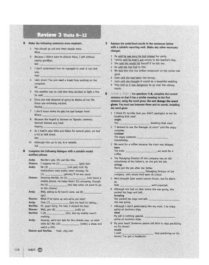

'Ellie' Award Ceremony Night

Best Film

The film had been forecast as the winner by the bookies months ago. It came as no surprise that 'The moment of Truth', walked off with the 'Ellie' for Best film. It clearly deserved the 'Ellie'.

Best Supporting Actor

Everyone was surprised. James Robbins picked up the 'Ellie' for best supporting actor. He had been a clear outsider.

Best Cinematography

'Ice World' was filmed almost entirely on location in Antarctica. It was hardly surprising that it received the award for best cinematography. It earned the award for those amazing rolling vistas of sparkling ice and snow.

Best Director

Caroline Meers didn't believe she would win the 'Ellie' for best director. She hadn't prepared a speech. She nervously stumbled through a long list of thank yous.

Best Supporting Actress

Gloria Goldberg was wearing a red satin dress by Versace. She knew how to pose for the photographers. She won the 'Ellie' for best supporting actress.

Best Documentary

Peter Williams clutched his 'Ellie' tightly. He gave a heart warming speech. He talked about his inspiration to make the film. The film focuses on the plight of the polar bears.

Best Actor

Ronald Smith had been nominated for an 'Ellie' three times previously. He had never won one. It was about time he did. He got the award for best Actor.

Best Original Screenplay

Jannis Patridopoulos had worked for over four years on the script. He was clearly overwhelmed that he had been awarded the 'Ellie' for best original screenplay.

Best Visual Effects

Gillian and Rosemary Craig confessed that ambition had been driving them to make this moment come true. They said they had lived without sleep for almost six months while they worked on the computer graphics for this film.

Best Actress

19 year old Sylvia Watson was the youngest actress ever to be nominated. She burst into tears when she picked up her 'Ellie' for best actress. It made it difficult to hear her speech.

Best Animated Film

The director, producers and animators all crowded onto the stage. They all took turns saying how grateful they were. They received the 'Ellie' for best animated film.

Best Make up / Costume

'The Moment of Truth' producers were grateful to accept their 'Ellies' for Best Costume and Best Make-up. These were the fifth and sixth awards they swept up for the evening.

13 Getting the message across

Lesson planner

Fast lane: 3 x 1.5 hour lessons = 4.5 hours per unit
(total course = 72–76 hours)

Lesson	Time	Classwork	Exam Booster (EB) homework
37	1.5 hours	Getting started, Reading + Vocab. Organiser (VO)	Getting started + Reading
38	1.5 hours	Check homework, Lang. develop., Grammar (1), Use of English, Speaking + VO	Lang. develop., Grammar, Use of English + Speaking
39	1.5 hours	Check homework, Listening, Grammar (2), Writing + VO	Listening, Writing + Coursebook Writing task

Slow lane: 4 x 1.5 hour lessons = 6 hours per unit
(total course = 96–100 hours)

Lesson	Time	Classwork	EB homework
49	1.5 hours	Getting started, Reading, VO + photocopiable 1	Getting started + Reading
50	1.5 hours	Check homework, Lang. develop., Grammar (1), Use of English + VO	Lang. develop., Use of English + Grammar
51	1.5 hours	Check homework, Speaking, Listening + VO	Listening + Speaking
52	1.5 hours	Check homework, Grammar (2) + Writing	Writing + Coursebook Writing task

Before you begin

1   Try to communicate with your students in a different language, or using mime only. If you know anything about Esperanza, you may want to try introducing yourself using this language. Alternatively, use a language that you know but which is unfamiliar to your students. You could use visual prompts and gestures to help you, but do not use English or your students' native language.

2   Students work in pairs. One of them is an alien who is visiting the town. It doesn't speak any human languages. Each pair in turn should try to introduce themselves to each other and the alien should ask for some information. This is intended to be fun, so don't worry about pointing out mistakes.

Topic: sending messages, talking to aliens, communicating ideas

Language is all about communicating. This unit looks at various ways in which we communicate, not only with other people, but with animals as well. We also take a look at the human attempt to communicate with beings beyond this planet, in an attempt to stretch beyond our own boundaries of experience.

Unit 13 Wordlist

ascertain	dignitary	observatory
broadcast	echolocation	ponder
chirp	explain	publicise
clarify	extraterrestrial	publish
cluster	galaxy	random
constellation	impart	squawk
convene	instil	transmit
decipher	kerosene	transparent

Getting started

Aim: To get students thinking about various different ways in which we communicate, to generate the use of 'communicating' language which will be useful for tasks in the unit.

1   Elicit the meaning of the unit title, using the pictures as prompts. Encourage students to talk about the different ways in which we communicate (such as information, ideas, thoughts, needs and desires).

2   Students work in pairs, since they might not be familiar with all of the items. Elicit answers they do know. Then, if necessary, provide them with definitions for the following:

To *convey* information or feelings means to cause them to be known or understood by someone.	In every one of her pictures she conveys a sense of immediacy ... = communicate
If you *impart* information *to* people, you tell it to them. (FORMAL)	I am about to impart knowledge to you that you will never forget. = convey
If you *instil* an idea or feeling *in* someone, especially over a period of time, you make them think it or feel it.	They hope that their work will instil a sense of responsibility in children ...

3 Students work in pairs, or individually. Make sure they are aware that there is more than one possibility in some sentences.

→ Vocabulary Organiser 13.1, page 136

Reading: predicting information

1 Elicit the names of some well-known films about aliens or extraterrestrials. Suggestions: *Close Encounters*, *E.T.*, *Signs*, *Contact*, *Starship Troopers*, *Alien*, *War of the Worlds*. Generate discussion about whether there is life on other planets.

PAPER 1, PART 2 Predicting information
Discuss different types of factual text with the class: a newspaper article reports an event, while a journal or magazine may provide a general article on a particular subject.
2 Elicit answers. Provide further examples if possible.

3 Students predict what they are going to read about. Discuss their ideas.

p/c 13.1

4 Students do this individually. Ask them to read through the text quickly, to see if their predictions were right. Then direct them to do the task. Ask students to give reasons for their choices.

5 Students work in pairs, or individually. Elicit answers, and give feedback.

→ Vocabulary Organiser 13.2, page 136

Reading extension

If your students appear interested in the subject, you could direct them to websites such as the SETI institute website. The article in the unit was published in 2005. You could ask your students to find a more recent one related to this subject. Suggest they search for articles in magazines like *New Scientist* and *Forbes*. Invite discussion on how they think we should try to communicate with extraterrestrial beings.

Language development: nouns followed by particles

Aim: To develop students' awareness of the particles which follow specific nouns, and the fact that some nouns can be followed by more than one particle. The Paper 3, part 5 task will give students active practice using items from this section and the communicating verbs in the Getting started section of this unit.

1 Students may be able to do this without referring back to the text, but tell them to do so to check their answers.

2 Explain that some of the items in this exercise can be followed by more than one particle, depending on the content of the sentence. They must decide which one is suitable in each case. Elicit answers, and discuss which items can be followed by other particles, and give examples of each.

Make sure you look at:

2 In dispute *over* something; you can be 'in dispute *with* someone';

3 Someone *is* 'an authority *on* a subject'; but someone '*has* authority *over* other people';

5 You *have*, or *are in* contact with someone; but we say '*there* has been contact *between* humans and extraterrestrials'.

→ Vocabulary Organiser 13.3, page 136

Key word: *set*

3 Students can work in pairs, or individually. Explain any unknown phrases.

4 The list of phrases here contains items which give the idea of 'preparing' something, rather than starting it. Once students have completed the exercise, you may wish to elicit this slight difference in meaning. For example, 'set the table', 'set a date', 'set a bone', 'set a trap'.

Developing what is done in class
As always, the list of items contained in this section is not exhaustive. Word games such as jigsaw games and word partner games can provide useful practice in using both items from this page, and developing them with other items.

→ Vocabulary Organiser 13.4, page 136

5 Elicit the answers, and emphasise the importance of the use of the correct particles, and structures after verbs etc.

Grammar (1): text references
(*this, that, it, such, these, those*)

GRAMMAR SPOTLIGHT

Reference words
1 Do the first item with the class as a whole as an example. Then, students could work in pairs, or individually. Go through the answers, and explain any points which cause confusion.

2 Elicit the meaning and use of *such* here. If necessary, give a further example to illustrate its use.

→ Grammar Reference 13.1, page 179

3 Direct students to read through the text quickly, then elicit what it is about. If you are in a coastal area, where it is likely that some of your students may have had contact with dolphins, elicit their stories and generate discussion. Allow students to complete the task. Go through the answers.

4 Based on the level of knowledge and interest among your students, develop this question into a discussion.

Use of English: gapped sentences

EXAM SPOTLIGHT

PAPER 3, PART 4 Making educated guesses
1 Elicit which part of speech is required to fill the gap.

2 Students brainstorm possible words here. Encourage words such as *speak*, *discussion* etc, to get students thinking. They may come up with *word* themselves.

3 Hopefully, they will reach a consensus with *word*. If not, tell them, and suggest they write the phrases in their notebooks. They could also try to find other phrases with *word*.

4 Remind students that the word they choose must be in the same form for all three sentences, and that it must fit all three sentences. Elicit answers, and give feedback.

Use of English extension

Building up a list of word groups

Students should be organising their revision for exam preparation now. It is a good idea for them to group together words which are used in a variety of phrases, as a way of preparing for the gapped sentences task. If they haven't done so already, suggest that they go back through the book, and make a list of the vocabulary that has been used in this kind of task, and also a list of key word phrases, where the key word is used in the same part of speech.

Speaking: sustaining interaction

1 🎧 13.1 Remind your students of the importance of interacting with your partner in part 3 of the interview. Emphasise the importance of the two following points in this part:

a You mustn't monopolise the conversation, but encourage your partner to speak as well;

b Do not simply repeat what your partner says.

Tell your students to look at the photographs on page 199. Play the recording. Elicit students' comments on how the two candidates interact.

SPOTLIGHT ON SPEAKING

Sustaining interaction
2 After reading the information in the Spotlight and raising any questions, your students should improve on Fernando's speech in their notebooks.

3 Students work in pairs. Monitor from a distance.

Speaking extension

p/c 13.2

If you are intending to do Photocopiable activity 13.2 on page 129, it's a good idea to decide who are going to be the five speakers, and to instruct them to find out as much as they can about their chosen charity before the next lesson, in order to be able to argue their case in the balloon debate.

Listening: multiple matching

1 This is an extension of exercise 1 in the Getting started section, and aims to provide students with an opportunity to practise and consolidate the communicative verbs introduced in that section. Students may repeat things they said in that earlier section of the unit, but try to elicit more of the target language. Prompt them to say what aspect of communication is depicted in each photograph first, and then encourage them to add more.

TEACHING IN PRACTICE

Consolidating language learned in the unit
You could make this discussion into a kind of game, by telling students they need to use as many different communicative verbs/words as possible. Each time one is used, write it on the board. The next student to speak must try to avoid using the same verb or word again.

PAPER 4, PART 4 Doing multiple tasks at once

2 🎧 13.2 Play the recording once. Elicit answers, but do not give feedback yet.

3 Tell students to listen again and check their answers. Tell them to notice key words which help them. Play the recording again. Discuss any changes that students needed to make.

4 Go through the answers with the class.

5 🎧 13.3 Direct students to read the rubric, and elicit any unknown words. Make sure they know what all the different types of people do. Play the recording twice before getting answers and giving feedback.

6 Students work in three groups. Allocate one discussion point to each group. Allow them to discuss it for a few minutes, and monitor from a distance. Then, elicit a summary of what each group said, and give feedback on the language they used.

Grammar (2): *it / there* as introductory pronouns

1 Find out students' ideas about each pair. Answers may vary.

2 Direct students to the Grammar Spotlight. Answer any queries, and then go through the answers with the class.

3 This could be done orally, to consolidate exercise 2.

Writing: contribution to a longer piece

1 Elicit what students know about the charities mentioned, and any other charity they might know of. Clarify the difference between 'raise money for' and 'donate money to'. If necessary, provide students with the background information in the box above right.

BACKGROUND: CHARITY ORGANISATIONS

Oxfam International is a confederation of 13 organisations working with over 3000 partners in more than 100 countries to find lasting solutions to poverty and injustice.

Amnesty International is an international non-governmental organisation which defines its mission as 'to conduct research and generate action to prevent and end grave abuses of human rights and to demand justice for those whose rights have been violated'.

The World Wide Fund for Nature (WWF) is an international non-governmental organisation for the conservation, research and restoration of the environment.

The United Nations Children's Fund (UNICEF) was created by the United Nations General Assembly on 11th December 1946, to provide emergency food and healthcare to children in countries that had been devastated by World War II. UNICEF provides long-term humanitarian and developmental assistance to children and mothers in developing countries.

Greenpeace is an international non-governmental organisation for the protection and conservation of the environment. Greenpeace utilises direct action, lobbying and research to achieve its goals.

2 Check that students understand what the question is asking them to do.

3 Students work in pairs, or small groups. Brainstorm ideas about the points which should be included in the answer. Elicit ideas, and allow some discussion, if disagreement arises.

4 Tell students to underline the relevant points covered in the sample answer. Check answers, and discuss any discrepancies with students' own views.

5 Elicit students' views on the tone of the sample answer, and then ask them to compare the alternative paragraph with the original. Ask them to give reasons for their views. If necessary, explain why the alternative is more suitable, at the same time, making it clear that neither is actually wrong.

→ Vocabulary Organiser 13.5, page 136

6 Students work in pairs, or individually. They should rewrite the phrases in italics, but may also need to make slight changes to the sentence structure in places.

p/c 13.2

Suggested answers:

'Without doubt, it is very important to achieve …' could become 'Try to achieve the right balance …'

'One shouldn't be too formal, for instance' becomes 'You shouldn't be too formal …'

'A friendly, semi-formal approach is invariably the most desirable' becomes 'The best approach is to be friendly, yet polite.'

'The value of research before preparing one's presentation cannot be ignored' becomes 'Do some research into …'

'It is important to know as much as possible …' becomes 'Make sure that you know something about …'

'Another point to consider is appealing to …' becomes 'Appeal to their sense of justice, but be careful not to make them feel guilty.'

'Emphasis of the fact that …' could become 'A useful trick is to emphasise the fact that …'

7   Students work in pairs, or as a class for the brainstorming task. Elicit ideas, and give feedback.

8   Students do this individually.

Photocopiable activity instructions

1 **Activity 13.1 Reading skills worksheet**

Aim: The reading text is quite demanding, so this worksheet should be used as an aid for preparing the students to tackle the reading task in the unit.

Instructions:

1   Prepare a copy of worksheet 1 for each student, and worksheet 2 for every two students.

2   Hand out copies of worksheet 1 only. Students should initially work individually on questions 1, 2 and 3.

3   Students work in pairs. Each pair compare their answers to questions 1, 2 and 3, and then work together on question 4. Tell them they need to give reasons for their choices.

Key: *2 1iii; 2iii; 3ii; 3 1C, 2A, 3B*

2 **Activity 13.2 Charity Balloon debate**

Instructions:

1   Hand out copies of the activity, and elicit what students know about each charity. Students nominate or volunteer to be representatives of each charity.

2   Each speaker researches their charity at home, and makes a list of five points why their charity is important.

3   In class the following lesson, each speaker makes one point in favour of their charity in turn, then the class votes to decide which speaker should be thrown out of the balloon.

4   Then, the remaining speakers make another point, and the class votes again, until there is only one speaker left in the balloon. This person is the winner.

Tapescript 13

Listening 13.1

Interlocutor: Now, I'd like you to talk about something together for about three minutes. Here are some pictures showing different ways of advertising a product. First, talk to each other about the merits and limitations of using these forms of advertising. Then, decide which one would be the most effective to promote a new language school in your area. All right?

Carlos: Yes ... Well, I think the billboard is a very effective way of advertising, as it can be seen by everyone in the area. Also, people are not so angry at seeing billboards, whereas they get annoyed when people push leaflets under their door ... Do you agree, Magda?

Magda: Yes, you're right. They don't like leaflets ... Erm ... not at all ...

Carlos: Er ... I know I usually throw leaflets away without looking at them! But I think it depends on what product you want to advertise. Leaflets might be a good idea for a new language school, because you can include information on courses, and photos of the classrooms and facilities in the school ... and a bold advert in the local newspaper is a good idea, as most people read the newspaper, and so they will see it. But I still think the billboard is the best idea, don't you?

Magda: Yes, I agree with you. It will be seen by the largest number of people, and so will be most effective ... Erm ... That's all.

Listening 13.2

While observing gorillas at Zurich Zoo – one of my favourite places for study – I was witness to something very special. The Gorilla House was celebrating the recent birth of a baby gorilla, and so was chock-a-block with visitors. Next to where I was sitting quietly making notes, there was a couple with a nine-month-old baby in a pushchair. The woman sat down in front of the compound and took her baby out of the pushchair, presumably to show him the gorillas. Within seconds, the gorilla mother appeared in front of her, proudly sporting her own offspring, sat down and proceeded to play with it. It was as if she was saying, 'Look, I've got a baby, too! And isn't he adorable, just like yours?'

Listening 13.3

Speaker 1: Communication is one of the most complex skills we can learn, but it's frequently taken for granted by parents, childcare workers and policy makers. In consequence, the barriers, problems and exclusion experienced by children with poor communication skills are ignored along with the importance of speech and language development for all children.
'I CAN' is a non-profit-making organisation that encourages the development of communication skills for all children through UK-wide programmes with a special focus on those kids who find this hard: children with a communication disability.

Speaker 2: Getting it right with ad copy is a sensitive business. The worst kind of advertising exaggerates to grab your attention, while the best gets your interest without appearing to try. I believe the skill is in finding exactly the right words, and making every word count in getting your message across to the public. If you use long-winded, wordy copy – you've lost your audience, simple as that. Make your point quickly and effectively, to create an impression that lasts.

Speaker 3: English is peppered through and through with idiomatic phrases. You could ask someone 'What's cooking?', 'What's up?' or 'What's going on?' and expect the same response. Someone who asks 'What's the damage?' may want to know how much he's got to pay for something. The meaning of such phrases is apparent to native-born Americans, but can cause bewilderment in a multicultural setting, such as the area of health care. Nowadays, more and more health care providers are from multicultural backgrounds, making effective communication problematical. As managers, we're concerned that immigrant staff cannot understand guidelines or instructions, and nurse-patient communication is often adversely affected.

Speaker 4: We head on into the school with our mobile cell block, and give students an authentic taste of what it's like to be locked up. The kids follow the inmate's routine for the day, supervised by myself and two other professional officers. We usually discover that a few minutes spent stuck inside the cell is more than enough to dispel the myth created by TV of prison being like a hotel. The reality is extremely different, I can tell you! The message we're trying to put across is that you have choices in life, but what you need to think about is the consequences of those choices. Our workshops are very effective in showing the cost of making the wrong choices.

Speaker 5: The guy next door asked me how I would deal with an annoying colleague. I told him that, for example, if I was having trouble with a neighbour's children kicking their ball into my garden all the time, I would never go over and tell the neighbour to get control of their kids. I would go over casually, talk about the weather, gossip a bit, then say something like, 'I see you've got material over there to build that fence you were talking about. I've got some time today to help'.
'That seems so indirect', he said.
'Well, here's the thing', I replied. 'My way the children aren't a problem any more, and I'm still talking to my neighbour. Your way, you're at war with your neighbour, and his kids'.

Answer key 13

Getting started p127

1 Message in a bottle (idea of a call for help); TV news reporting; communicating with/training dolphins; advertising a mobile phone/telecommunications; sign language for deaf people; air traffic control.

2 Ideas: convey, clarify, instil, exchange, broadcast, publish.
Information: broadcast, send, exchange, publish, publicise, share, reveal.
Messages: transmit, send, convey, exchange.
Knowledge: impart, publish, exchange, share, convey, reveal.

3 Answers may vary: a clarify/ explain; b send/transmit; c convey/ reveal; d impart/convey; e instil

Reading pp128–9

2 1b; 2a

3 Possible answers: communicating with aliens/the question of life on other planets/films about making contact with aliens

4 1C; 2E; 3A; 4G; 5D; 6F

5 a extraterrestrial; b dignitaries; c irrelevant; d decipher; e slime; f drowned out; g ponder; h trench; i convene; j with intent

Language development p130

1 a for; b at; c to; d of

2 1b; 2d; 3a; 4b; 5c; 6d; 7c; 8c

3 Only two NOT possible: a desire; money

4 1h; 2c; 3f; 4b; 5j; 6g; 7i; 8e; 9a; 10d

5 1 in dispute over; 2 impart knowledge and ideas to; 3 convey an impression of; 4 is set on going; 5 the general public access to; 6 I was witness to a terrible; 7 clarified the idea he was; 8 were (all) set to go on

Grammar (1) p131

1 a the proposals for communicating with aliens;
b the numbers that made up the Arecibo message of 1974;
c the attempts made by Drake and Sagan to send messages to aliens;
d create an optical message, using lasers;
e something visual;

2 *Such* refers to ideas like that of studying communication in animals in order to understand our own ability to speak.

3 1 Such; 2 this; 3 These; 4 they; 5 This; 6 them; 7 this; 8 that/this; 9 that; 10 that

4 Possible answers: we could learn the extent of their own intelligence, but also we may learn more about how closely we are related to them, and how we have evolved; why it is that we developed sophisticated language patterns, while they did not.

Use of English p132

1 noun

3 word

4 1 talk; 2 set; 3 connection; 4 communicate; 5 image

Speaking p132

1 Katrina is not responsive. Fernando controls the conversation too much.

Listening p133

2 1a; 2a; 3b

4 The following point to the answers in each case:
1 observing gorillas at Zurich Zoo (one of my favourite places for study)
2 I was witness to something very special
3 It was as if she was saying, 'Look, I've got a baby, too! And isn't he adorable, just like yours?'

5 1D; 2G; 3E; 4H; 5A; 6E; 7H; 8F; 9G; 10C

Grammar (2) p134

1 1a 'It' can be used as an impersonal subject when describing the time, weather or temperature b 'There' is followed by a general noun, to describe the overall situation
2a A general comment about the distance between two places
b More specific, with a noun followed by an infinitive
3a Impersonal subject to describe time; b There + noun + infinitive.

2 a3; b2; c7; d4; e8; f1; g5; h6

3 1 it; 2 There; 3 There, It; 4 there, It; 5 It, there; 6 There, it

Writing pp134–5

2 semi-formal

3 Points to include: Learn something about the target company before you visit them; Emphasise the positive marketing effects support of the charity will have on the company; Make sure you know a great deal about the charity, so that you will be able to answer any questions that may be asked; Try to assess the level of your audience when talking to them, in order to achieve the right tone.

5 Although the model answer covers all the necessary points and answers the question, it is too formal in places. For that reason, the alternative paragraph 2 is more suitable in tone for the specific task outlined in exercise 2.

7 This task requires a slightly more formal approach, as it is for a guide book.

Vocabulary organiser 13 p136

13.1 1 broadcast; 2 reveal; 3 published; 4 publicise;
5 exchange/share; 6 instil; 7 impart; 8 explained

13.2 1 pondered; 2 decipher; 3 convene; 4 dignitaries; 5 irrelevant

13.3 Nouns followed by *of*: effect, matter, product, question, result, threat
for: admiration, argument, respect, search
to: access, alternative, approach, connection, solution, threat, witness
on: authority, effect
over: authority, dispute
with: argument, connection, communication, contact

13.4 1 set a date: arrange a day when something will happen
2 set a precedent: do something for the first time, and provide a valuable example for others to follow
3 set a task: tell someone to do a specific task, or job
4 set your heart on: want to have or do something very much
5 set your eyes on: see something for the first time
6 be set against: oppose something strongly or examine one argument in relation to another
7 set about (doing): start doing something
8 a set menu: a fixed menu
9 set the stage for: prepare the way for a course of action to take place
10 set the scene: create the atmosphere (at the beginning of a story)

13.5 1c; 2e; 3g; 4f; 5d; 6b; 7h; 8a

Bank of English

1 collaborated; 2 communicated/ conversed; 3 cooperate; 4 communicate; 5 contacted

Reading Skills worksheet 1

1 Read paragraphs 1–3 below, and decide which type of article they come from. This will help you understand what kind of information is likely to follow.

2 Decide which of the following types of information you would expect to follow each paragraph. Underline the key words and phrases which help you reach your decision.

i background information

ii an opposing point of view

iii a supporting point for clarification

1 'The advantage exists because of the nature of electromagnetic waves. Although electromagnetic radiation can travel very fast (about 6.7 million miles per hour), it disperses and weakens across space. That's why a flashlight beam only shines brightly enough to see over short distances, and why a parent has to shout more loudly at her child, the further away the child is.'

2 'Rose and co-author Gregory Wright, a physicist at Antiope Associates in Fair Haven, N.J., published that surprising conclusion in the journal Nature in 2004. But they did not set out to make the headlines on the best way to contact 'E.T.''

3 'The idea of sending physical objects into space is nothing new. When NASA's Pioneer 10 spacecrafts went plunging into space in 1977, they carried twin 12-inch disks bearing words, music and images selected by a team of scientists to represent life on Earth. Now at the edge of the solar system, the Pioneer 10 craft may represent the best approach, says Rose.'

3 Match each paragraph (1–3 above) with one of the subsequent paragraphs A, B, or C below.

A 'Rose's research began with a grant from the National Science Foundation to study how to make wireless communications on Earth more efficient. The project's goal, he explains, was to figure out how to 'get the most amount of information across for the least amount of energy'. While investigating that subject, it occurred to him that this work might have implications for interstellar communications as well.'

B 'Like much good news, however, this discovery comes with a catch: A physical package could not travel as fast as radio or light waves. At a reasonable speed, Rose estimates a package could take 20 million years to reach distant stars. That's but a blip in time, given the galaxy's 10 billion-year history, but it doesn't inspire hope for the kind of 'contact' made famous by Jodie Foster in the movie of the same name.

C 'In other words, the farther a light beam travels, the more it spreads out. Any message encoded by it will have likewise faded in the voyage. The same is true for radio waves: for a message to retain its meaning over a long distance, it must be beamed out with high energy. A message inscribed on an object, on the other hand, remains as legible when it reaches its destination as on the day it was sent, no matter how far it has gone.'

4 Now look at the whole text. The three paragraph pairs have been removed. Decide which pair goes into each gap.

Reading Skills worksheet 2

Getting a message across the universe: would E.T. send a letter?

10ᵗʰ March 2006

The prospect of communicating with intelligent life beyond Earth has long captured human imagination. For decades, scientists have been sending hopeful messages in the form of radio signals into space and patiently scanning the skies for signs that someone, somewhere, is doing the same.

So far, that search has been fruitless. But we might be wise to look as well as listen, says Christopher Rose, a physicist and professor of electrical engineering at New Jersey's Rutgers University. By his calculations, it's vastly more efficient to send large messages across space not in the form of radio waves or beams of light, but in physical packages. That's right: If we want to send a note to outer space, Rose says, we should consider sending a message in a bottle.

Likewise, we should anticipate messages that might arrive here as physical artefacts – embedded in a meteorite, perhaps, or falling to Earth after hurtling across the cosmos on a comet's tail.

[…]

[…]

In wireless communications, transmitting information with radio waves makes sense because speed is a critical consideration. But in some instances – such as when two people are just around the corner from each other – it's more efficient, from an energy conservation perspective, to simply deliver a letter than to use radio waves or some other form of electromagnetic energy.

"That was the jumping off point," says Rose. "I thought, 'Huh, there's a fundamental issue here. When is it better for me to hand over the information than to radiate it?' And that was the kernel of the idea."

Rose calculated how much energy would be required to ship a message 1,000 light years into space. A package travelling a million kilometres an hour (about 670 000 miles per hour) would need a million years to reach its destination. A radio transmission would get there in only a fraction of that time – an obvious advantage when the sender can't tolerate a delay, as in the case of cell phone conversations on Earth.

But when timing is irrelevant, Rose found that sending a physical message makes more sense.

[…]

[…]

What's more, once a physical message arrives at a given destination, it stays there. A radio signal must be intercepted at the moment it passes by in order to be "received."

While it would take a serious amount of protection – thousands of pounds of lead, in Rose's estimation – to prevent damage by cosmic waves in transit, the energy required to package information and hurtle it across space would be far less than that required to beam out high-powered electromagnetic signals on a regular basis. The further a message must go, and the longer the message is, the greater the advantage of sending that message in a physical form.

The advantage is strong enough, Rose says, to compensate for the fact that thousands, or even hundreds of thousands, of messages might need to be sent to cover the range of potential star systems that could potentially pick up a single radio signal.

If, for instance, we wanted to send a very large message – say, all of the information inside the Library of Congress – to a star 10 000 light years away, it would be a hundred billion times more efficient to encode it in silicon chips than it would be to radiate the same amount of information from the world's largest radio telescope.

[…]

[…]

For simple messages meant to convey only "I am here," Rose says radio waves are still more efficient. And because radio waves travel so quickly, they offer the possibility of two-way communication. So the efforts of researchers looking for signals with giant radio telescopes – like those at the California-based SETI Institute – are worthwhile, he says.

Still, says Rose, there's something to be said for sending a message out for "posterity," and for devising ways to look for physical messages that other life forms may have shipped across space, hoping to find us.

Rose's Nature paper was the first quantitative comparison of the costs of the different ways of delivering information across space. Since then, Rose has been working on the next logical question: If sending a physical message is the most efficient way to communicate, in what form might these message arrive, and how should we look for them?

He stops short of guesswork, though, preferring not to speculate about what an extraterrestrial life form might say or why it might want to communicate with people in the first place. For Rose, it's not about psychology or science fiction: "It's just the physics, ma'am."

CHARITY BALLOON DEBATE

UNICEF (international children's charity)
WWF (world wildlife fund)
Cancer Research Fund
Doctors Without Borders
CND (campaign for nuclear disarmament)

PHOTOCOPIABLE 13.2

14 Gaia's legacy

Lesson planner

Fast lane: 3 x 1.5 hour lessons = 4.5 hours per unit
(total course = 72–76 hours)

Lesson	Time	Classwork	Exam Booster (EB) homework
40	1.5 hours	Getting started, Reading + Vocab. Organiser (VO)	Getting started + Reading
41	1.5 hours	Check homework, Lang. develop., Grammar, Listening + VO	Lang. develop., Grammar + Listening
42	1.5 hours	Check homework, Speaking, Use of English, Writing + VO	Speaking, Use of English + Writing

Slow lane: 4 x 1.5 hour lessons = 6 hours per unit
(total course = 96–100 hours)

Lesson	Time	Classwork	EB homework
53	1.5 hours	Getting started, photocopiable 1, Reading + VO	Getting started + Reading
54	1.5 hours	Check homework, Lang. develop., Grammar + VO	Lang. develop. + Grammar
55	1.5 hours	Check homework, Listening, Speaking + VO	Listening (1), Speaking + Listening (2)
56	1.5 hours	Check homework, Use of English, Writing + photocopiable 2	Use of English, Writing + Coursebook Writing task

Before you begin

Warm up the class by asking them to brainstorm a list of questions about the Earth. Don't worry if you don't know the answers yourself; treat it as an exercise in discovery for the whole class – including the teacher. Ask:

> Where is the Earth in our solar system?

> How old is the Earth?

> How was the Earth formed?

> How fast does the Earth spin around the sun?

Afterwards get students to read out their questions. If anyone knows the answers they raise their hands and attempt to answer them.

Topic: history of the Earth, life on Earth, Gaia theory

The planet Earth is our home. In this unit we aim to look at the history of the Earth and bring our own existence into perspective; to discuss 'Gaia theory' and its implications for life on Earth; to examine the biodiversity of life on Earth and to consider the consequences of an expanding human population.

Unit 14 Wordlist

abundance	diminish	inconstant
accelerate	drastic	inherit
adapt	ecosystem	legacy
biodegradable	equilibrium	optimum
biodiversity	evolve	pristine
brink	exacerbate	refuge
colonise	flourish	regulate
conquer	ignorant	resource
conservation	imbalance	vague
deplete	incompatible	

Getting started

1   Start the unit with the discussion question. Ask students for their ideas. Some may know, while some may be surprised to discover the age of the Earth. This is a chance to get students focused on the theme of the unit and the Reading text to follow. Make a note on the board of any topic vocabulary that may come up.

2   Ask students to mark their guesses on the timeline, elicit responses from the class and then write the correct

answers on the board. Check to see how many people were correct – or close! Point out that in fact most of the life on Earth today was formed during only the last billion years, and our primitive ancestors appeared less than one million years ago (which is approximately represented by the thickness of the last white line next to the zero. Modern humans have been around for one tenth of that white line).

BACKGROUND: THE AGE OF THE EARTH

Planet Earth is 4 600 million years old. If we condense this inconceivable time-span into an understandable concept, we can liken the Earth to a person of 46 years of age. Nothing is known about the first seven years of this person's life, and whilst only scattered information exists about the middle span, we know that only at the age of 42 did the Earth begin to flower. Dinosaurs and the great reptiles did not appear until one year ago, when the planet was 45. Mammals arrived only eight months ago and in the middle of last week, human-like apes evolved into ape-like humans, and at the weekend, the last Ice Age enveloped the Earth. Modern Humans have been around for four hours. During the last hour, Humans discovered agriculture. The industrial revolution began a minute ago and during those 60 seconds of biological time, Modern Humans have made a rubbish tip of paradise. They have multiplied their numbers to plague proportions, caused the extinction of 500 species of animals, ransacked the planet for fuels and now stand like a brutish infant, gloating over their meteoric rise to ascendancy, on the brink of war to end all wars. A human life in this time span lasts a mere 18 seconds ...

3 🎧 14.1 This exercise offers an opportunity for students to practise listening to fairly long texts that contain a lot of detailed or specialised information. In this case they are listening out for dates and should just write down the number that represents the million of years since something happened. Tell students that they will hear the numbers in the correct order, so if they miss one they should just leave it blank and try to fill it in on the second listening. Play the recording twice. Check answers with the group.

Reading extension

p/c 4.1

After the listening, brainstorm the students' memories of what they heard and elicit what they learnt about the age of the Earth. Ask them to recall the name of different species that were mentioned, and if necessary, write them on the board.

Reading: multiple choice questions

Aim: To show students that different words and structures can be used to convey the same meaning or different

meanings can be conveyed by using similar words and structures, thereby creating confusing false options.

1 Some students may well answer 'no', in which case ask them to look at the picture of the Earth and hazard a guess. If no guesses are forthcoming, move straight on to exercise 2.

BACKGROUND: GAIA HYPOTHESIS

The Gaia hypothesis is an ecological hypothesis proposing that the biosphere and the physical components of the Earth (atmosphere, cryosphere, hydrosphere and lithosphere) are closely integrated to form a complex interacting system that maintains the climatic and biogeochemical conditions on Earth in a preferred homeostasis. The theory is named after the Greek supreme goddess of Earth. The hypothesis is frequently described as viewing the Earth as a single organism.

2 Ask students to skim read the text to find out who or what 'Gaia' is and to write a sentence in their own words. This will help them practise their skimming technique when searching for specific information. Don't let them spend more than three minutes on the task.

SPOTLIGHT ON READING

Matching gist to detail

3 The purpose of this exercise is to show students how many of the words found in a piece of writing are reused in the stem questions and how other words are changed, while the meaning is kept the same.

4 There are various answers to this question, but it will help students focus on how question distractors are written and how they can cause confusion by using information that is in the text. If time is pressing you could do this as a spoken activity instead and ask students to volunteer possible incorrect options. You could write these on the board so that you have three incorrect options as in the multiple choice questions.

5 Students should attempt the task and then explain the reasons for their answers. This can be done individually, as pairwork or altogether in class.

6 This task is an extension of exercise 5 but can be done with the whole class. It is really meant to serve as a reminder of an important tip. Ask students how many of them don't bother to mark the answers in the text because they are confident they know the answer just from reading it.

7 Students should attempt the task individually. They can now read the text carefully and should follow the techniques outlined so far. They should spend no longer than ten minutes on it.

→ Vocabulary Organiser 14.1 + 14.2, page 146

Language development: idioms from nature

Pictures and idioms
A good way to help students remember idioms is by association with images. Ask students to think of an appropriate visual image to describe each idiom. If they are good at drawing they could try to draw a picture, or alternatively, have them assemble a photo-montage or collage by taking images from magazines.

1   Direct students' attention to the picture and ask them what they think the picture is trying to tell us about the relationship between these two people. Then ask them to try and think up an idiom using the word 'world' that would make a good caption to the picture.

Afterwards, students complete the exercise individually or in pairs. Allow a few minutes for this, and let them use dictionaries if you like.

Language development extension

Hold an art competition. The students should choose one of the idioms and draw a picture that shows what it means.

SPOTLIGHT ON VOCABULARY

Adjectives followed by particles
Read through the rubric with students and remind them that correctly used particles can sometimes make the difference between a good English speaker and an average one!

2   Students should refer back to the reading text on page 139 to check their answers.

3   Most students will know the correct particle to follow each adjective, but focusing on the gap in context will help to reinforce good habits. Remind them that it is a good idea to note down any new pairs in their notebook if they are not familiar with them. You could extend the task by asking students to suggest other adjective pairs for each particle.

→   Vocabulary Organiser 14.3, page 146.

4   Students can work individually or in pairs. Allow them to use dictionaries if necessary. Check answers with the group and elicit example sentences for each phrase.

→   Bank of English, page 146

Grammar: unreal past

Aim: The purpose of this section is to consolidate the different structures which form the unreal past in English and to familiarise students with their many uses.

1   This exercise will allow you to lead into the section and help students focus on the structure with 'as if'. Elicit answers from the students and ask why they chose their answers.

SPOTLIGHT ON GRAMMAR

Unreal past
Elicit examples of past tense structures that are used to talk about the present or the future.

2 Students work individually or in pairs. Check that they understand they have to compare the tense used with the meaning of the sentence.

→   Grammar Reference 14.1, pages 179–80

3   Students should now be able to do this exercise, either individually or in pairs. Allow them to refer to the Grammar Reference section again if necessary.

4   Students should do the exercise individually. This will confirm whether any students are still having any problems with certain structures. Check the answers with the group, and in each case elicit which other words in the sentences define the structures required. Students should highlight or underline these or make further notes in their grammar notebooks.

TEACHING IN PRACTICE

Eliciting answers from the class
When checking the answers to a class exercise it is obviously better if you can elicit the correct answers from students, rather than just 'telling' them what the correct answer is. In most cases at least one student in the class will know the correct answer (you hope!) but there may be times when you are greeted by a sea of blank expressions.

5+6 Students should complete both exercises individually and under exam conditions. Allow no more than ten minutes for each task and check answers with the group afterwards.

Listening: sentence completion

1   Discuss the question with the class and elicit various ideas. The aim here is to introduce the subject of the listening tapescript which explains how different amounts of oxygen in Earth's history have both helped and hindered the survival of various species. If students don't seem to

know what to say prompt them with some questions. Ask:

> Why can't I live on the moon?

> There's no oxygen.

> Why can't I live on Mercury (the planet closest to the sun), or Neptune (the planet furthest from the sun)?

> It's too hot/too cold.

> What covers over two thirds of the Earth's surface and makes it possible for all life to exist?

> Water!

PAPER 4, PART 2 Focused listening

2 To emphasise once more the importance of reading the questions first, read through the rubric with the class and the example sentences, and then ask students to raise their hands with suggestions of a word that could fill the gap. (You will probably find that several will rush to say: 'disappearance' because this is what is most often talked about in relation to the dinosaurs.) Continue reading the rubric with your students and ask if anyone has changed their mind. Then ask students to answer the questions in exercise 2. They should all therefore now realise that the missing word is in fact 'appearance'.

3 Explain that students will be given enough time in the exam to study the question and examine the key words in the sentence. Let them spend about one minute doing this before you move on to the next exercise.

4 Do this as a class activity, thereby reinforcing the usefulness of this technique.

5 🎧 14.2 Make sure you play the recording twice, giving time between listenings and afterwards for students to complete or correct their answers.

Speaking: evaluating

1 Discuss the question with the class. This will get your students' thoughts focused on the content of the listening section and photos that they will have to look at. It's more than likely that most students will select fairly obvious animals as their favourites and express qualities such as cute, cuddly, intelligent, friendly, loyal etc (qualities we admire in our own species) and will select other animals as their least favourites because they are dangerous, scary, revolting,

scaly, slimy, creepy etc. However, there will probably be a few students with totally different ideas, which could make for an interesting class discussion. Make a note of all descriptive vocabulary and new animal species on the board.

PAPER 5, PART 3 Making choices

2 🎧 14.3 Play the recording, twice if necessary, and check students' answers. The point here is to highlight that not only is it perfectly alright to change your mind during this part of the Speaking Paper, it can actually help to expand your discussion time and give you more things to say.

3 Each pair or group of three should work simultaneously while you monitor from a distance. Afterwards select pairs or groups to demonstrate to the class what they have practised. Time them and make sure they speak for three minutes. If they end too soon, give them the signal to keep going. If they are still speaking when the three minutes are up, cut them off. This is what the interlocutor will do, so they need to get used to it!

Use of English: word formation

Suffixes

Read through the rubric with the students. Brainstorm examples of suffixes that they can think of and write them on the board.

1 Go through exercise 1 with the students and make sure they pay attention to the standard patterns.

2 Students work individually. Check the answers with the class.

3 Ask students to read the text all the way through first. Allow three to five minutes for this according to the level of the group. Then ask questions to see if they have understood the gist of it, such as:

- How many species are on Earth?
- Why should we hurry up if we want to study biodiversity?
- What could happen by the year 2020?
- What implications could this have for humankind?
- What should we do in order be better able to protect the biodiversity of life on Earth?

Only when you are satisfied that students have a good understanding of the text allow them to attempt to complete the gaps.

→ Vocabulary Organiser 14.4, page 146

Writing: an essay (discussing issues that surround a topic)

Aim: This section intends to show them how to organise their ideas and plan their work efficiently, as well as developing their vocabulary skills at the same time.

→ Writing Guide, page 187

1 Before you start, analyse the title of this section with your class and elicit what is meant by 'issues that surround a topic'. Students then read and discuss the sample question. Encourage a brainstorming of different answers and write key words and points on the board.

2 Students work individually at first. Check answers with the class and for each issue ask students to provide at least one reason why they think it is serious.

3 Students work individually, reading the essay and underlining reasons, or do it as a class activity. Elicit the points which would not be relevant in this essay and ask students to justify their reasons.

4 Elicit answers from the class. Write ideas on the board.

In other words

5 Students work individually or in pairs. Allow a few minutes for this. Check answers with the class.

→ Vocabulary Organiser 14.5, page 146.

Discussing issues that surround a topic

6 The main purpose of this exercise is to help students brainstorm all the different issues surrounding a central issue. Allow them to work in pairs or individually, and check answers with the class.

7 Depending on the time available, ask students to do just a brief paragraph plan, or they could write key sentences, or whole paragraphs. As an extension they could write the whole essay.

8 The topics are deliberately similar but different enough for students to think up new ideas. For example, the first topic asks students to discuss serious issues in society. This will allow them to focus on issues such as crime, unemployment and drug abuse, which were not tackled in the sample. The second essay topic allows for a bit more free thinking but it is hoped that students will be able to draw on information provided in the unit.

Degree of difficulty

Decrease the level: With some classes you may feel it would help your students to briefly discuss these issues before they work on the spidergrams and possibly to note key points on the board.

Increase the level: Allow your students total freedom to choose which topic they wish to answer and let them plan it in the class.

9 Students should spend no more than 30 minutes writing up their essays.

Photocopiable activity instructions

① Activity 14.1 Odd animal out!

Aim: To help students learn the names of animals and some animal groups.

Instructions:

1 Give student pairs a copy of the animal grid which you have cut into strips. Tell them to place the strips face down on the desk between them.

2 Write the following animal groups on the board:

1 invertebrates; 2 fish; 3 amphibians; 4 insects; 5 reptiles;
6 birds; 7 mammals (excluding apes); 8 apes

3 Students take turns picking up one strip at a time. If they can name the animal group that three of the animals belong to and identify the odd one out, they can keep the strip. They should write the name of the animal group on the strip and put a cross through the odd one out. If not they have to put it back on the table.

Key:

1 *Group: Reptiles. Odd-one-out: worm (a worm is an invertebrate. It doesn't have a backbone)*

2　Group: Insects. Odd-one-out: spider (a spider is an arachnid along with scorpions, and has 2 body segments and 8 legs, insects have 3 body segments and 6 legs).

3　Group: Fish. Odd-one-out: snake (reptile).

4　Group: Mammals. Odd-one-out: goose (bird).

5　Group: Apes (mammals). Odd one out: spider monkey.

6　Group: Invertebrates. Odd-one-out: tuna (a tuna is a fish and therefore a vertebrate, it has a backbone).

7　Group: Birds. Odd-one-out: pterosaur (a pterosaur, now extinct, was in fact a dinosaur that could fly).

8　Group: Amphibians. Odd-one-out: platypus.

 Activity 14.2 Ideal world

Aim: To give students extra practice at using the unreal past.

Instructions:

1　Students form pairs or groups of three. Photocopy, cut out and give one eight box table to each group.

2　Students have to discuss the idea of an 'ideal world' and come up with some suggestions about what they believe would make an ideal world.

3　Each idea that they agree on should be written into the boxes using the cues provided.

4　When everyone has completed their box, they have to 'present' their ideal world to the rest of the class.

5　When everyone has presented their ideas, the class votes as a whole to decide which pair/group has the best ideas.

Ideal World

Write down your hopes for an ideal world ...

If only ...	I'd rather ...	Were it possible ...	Suppose ...
I wish ...	I'd prefer it ...	It's time ...	Imagine ...

Write down your hopes for an ideal world ...

If only ...	I'd rather ...	Were it possible ...	Suppose ...
I wish ...	I'd prefer it ...	It's time ...	Imagine ...

Write down your hopes for an ideal world ...

If only ...	I'd rather ...	Were it possible ...	Suppose ...
I wish ...	I'd prefer it ...	It's time ...	Imagine ...

Tapescript 14

Listening 14.1

Palaeontologist: The earliest multi-celled animals might have been sponges, which although they look like plants are actually animals. They most likely appeared around 700 million years ago. Invertebrates, which are the first animals that could get around, such as flatworms and jellyfish, are believed to have evolved around 570 million years ago. And then, about 500 million years ago, vertebrates, the group which includes fish and other animals with a backbone, suddenly appeared.

About 470 million years ago, the first plants began to grow out of the water, and this is when life on land established itself. Insects originally appeared on land about 380 million years ago and were followed, relatively soon after that, by the first amphibians, which surfaced from the water to become land animals approximately 350 million years ago. Essentially, they were fish that evolved lungs to breathe air. They employed their fins to crawl from one pond to another and these gradually became legs. The next group to emerge, about 300 million years ago, were the reptiles.

For the next 50 million years, life on Earth prospered – but about 250 million years ago, the Earth experienced a period of mass extinction, which meant that many species disappeared. Around this time, one group of reptiles, called 'dinosaurs', started to dominate all others. Their name means 'terrible lizard'. They were the commonest vertebrates and they controlled the Earth for the next 150 million years.

Throughout this time, a new type of animal began to evolve. These animals were the mammals. They gave birth to live young, which they nourished with milk from their bodies, and they first appeared about 200 million years ago.

The closest living family to the dinosaurs is believed to be birds. The first known bird, 'Archaeopteryx', appeared about 150 million years ago. It existed for around 70 million years, before becoming extinct, and was replaced by the group which includes modern birds, believed to have appeared around 60 million years ago, at the same time that the dinosaurs became extinct.

The group of mammals to which humans belong – the primates – emerged from an ancestral group of animals that ate mainly insects, around 50 million years ago. But it wasn't until about three million years ago – about the time the last ice-age started – that intelligent apes, with the ability to walk on their back legs, appeared in southern Africa. Simultaneously, their brains evolved and they learnt to make and use tools. Although called *Homo habilis,* meaning 'handy man', these creatures were more like apes than men. About two million years ago, *Homo habilis* evolved into the first people called *Homo erectus.* Their bodies were like ours, but their faces were still apelike. They evolved in Africa and spread as far as South East Asia. Modern people (*Homo sapiens*) appear to have evolved in Africa about 100 thousand years ago (although the date is far from certain).

Listening 14.2

Jeremy Sargon: One of the things we all take for granted is the air we breathe, and the oxygen essential for our survival. But you might be startled to hear that the Earth's atmosphere didn't always contain oxygen! In fact, for most of its history there wasn't really any oxygen in the air at all! It's only been during the last 600 million years that there's been enough to support life, which, as it happens, is how long there has been life on land. From that time then, the amount of oxygen in the atmosphere has swung wildly between tiny amounts – as little as 12 per cent compared to today's 21 per cent – to huge proportions – up to 30 per cent oxygen during one particular period. This variation has of course had a massive impact on the animals living on Earth at any particular time. Animals have either taken advantage of the sudden increases in oxygen in order to evolve and colonise the land, or they have faced being made extinct during the periods when oxygen was scarce.

Palaeontologists have always had an interest in the occurrences that may have caused species to become extinct. The leading causes have been attributed to meteors, ice-ages, climate change, and so on, but fascinatingly enough, proof now exists which demonstrates that each mass extinction on Earth coincides with times of reduced oxygen. These periods have usually been followed by bursts of much higher oxygen levels, which again have coincided with a time of incredibly fast evolution in animal species. In most cases it appears that the most successful animals to inhabit the land during these times were those that developed more advanced respiratory systems. For example, invertebrates appeared on land for the first time around 420 million years ago – at a time when oxygen levels were higher than today's. Yet soon after that, approximately 400 million years ago, oxygen levels suddenly fell dramatically and most of these animals disappeared: either becoming extinct or returning to the ocean. Oxygen levels did not increase again for another 50 million years or so, during which time only a small number of animals could survive on land.

Then 350 million years ago, oxygen levels suddenly started to rise, reaching their highest ever levels around 280 to 300 million years ago. This is when reptiles appeared, for they thrived in this rich atmosphere, but as oxygen levels started to fall once more over the next 50 million years, they had to make some swift adjustments, or they were destined to suffocate for lack of air.

The animals that did this most efficiently were the dinosaurs … and what they did was to add another pair of air sacs next to the lungs. This enabled them to extract even greater amounts of oxygen from the thinning air. Because of this evolutionary adaptation, it appears that they were the only animals that managed to do well during the late Triassic mass extinction of 200 million years ago. This was the time with the lowest recorded oxygen levels. We can still see these air-sac adaptations in their descendants left on our planet today – the birds – and it's actually this which then allows some birds to fly at altitudes with little oxygen.

Listening 14.3

Interlocutor: Now, I'd like you to talk about something together for about three minutes. I'd like you to imagine that you want to give your support to an important ecological campaign. Here are some of the ecological issues that need our immediate attention. First, talk to each other about how serious each of these issues is. Then decide which campaign you would most like to support. All right?

Elisabeth: OK … well, at first glance I would say that 'deforestation' is probably the most important ecological issue. What do you think?

Giovanni: Yes, I agree. It is terrible that they are cutting down the rainforests so fast. These forests are important because they are the home to so many species of animals and plants. If they are all cut down there will be many problems.

Elisabeth: Yes, and the forests also control the weather and the Earth's temperature, I think, don't they? However, we shouldn't ignore the issue of 'pollution'. That is another very serious issue.

Giovanni: Yes, you're quite right. Pollution is dangerous for our health and it's also is dangerous to wildlife. Some species may disappear for ever because their habitats have been destroyed by pollution. On the other hand, 'the extinction of species' is a very serious issue. It says here that if we don't do something now, over half the Earth's species could be extinct in the next 100 years.

Elisabeth: Yes, and that is a frightening idea! But I believe that there's not much point in saving all these endangered species if there's nowhere for them to live. Personally I think 'habitat destruction' is the biggest issue facing wild animals at the moment and so I would probably choose to support the campaign for 'conservation of natural habitats'.

Giovanni: I agree it is a serious problem, but I would not choose that one because I think we have to tackle the issue of climate change before it's too late. All life on Earth is being threatened by this at the moment, and if the planet keeps getting hotter and all the ice melts, most of the land will be under water, and then what difference does it make if you have put all your money into 'habitat conservation'? So the issue of 'climate change' would be my first choice.

Interlocutor: Thank you.

Answer key 14

Getting started p137

2 a 4 billion years ago; b 100 thousand years ago.

3 a The first multi-celled animals appear 700 million years ago; b Animals without back-bones (invertebrates) appear 580 million years ago; c The first animals with backbones (vertebrates) appear 500 million years ago; d Plants appear on land 470 million years ago; e Insects appear on land 380 million years ago; f Fish develop lungs and leave the sea 350 million years ago; g Reptiles appear 300 million years ago; h Dinosaurs appear 250 million years ago; i Mammals appear 200 million years ago; j Birds appear 150 million years ago; k Primates appear 50 million years ago; l Apes that use their hands to make tools appear 3 million years ago; m Apes that walk on two legs appear 2 million years ago; n Modern humans appear 0.1 million years ago.

Reading pp138–9

2 Gaia is the name that James Lovelock gave the planet Earth as a self-evolving and self-regulating system that adjusts itself to support life.

3 It is almost impossible to know how many species there used to be or calculate how fast they <u>disappeared</u>, but in studying the vertebrates and molluscs in <u>the fossil records</u> over the past 65 million years, one notices that the <u>average</u> life of a species is approximately 2 to 3 million years, and <u>one species per every million</u> seems **to have become extinct per annum** during that time.

4 B Possible sentences that would be wrong: one species has become extinct per year for the past 65 million years; scientists have calculated how many vertebrates have become extinct; few species can survive for longer than 3 million years; scientists are close to calculating the number of species that have become extinct.

5 D

6 In other words, he knew that <u>when looking at the Earth</u> in this way, what he was seeing was not so much a planet that just happened to be suitable for sustaining life, <u>but a self-evolving and self-regulating living system, that could adjust itself to support life.</u> This seemed to qualify the Earth as a living entity in her own right.

7 1B; 2C; 3A; 4A; 5D; 6C; 7B

Language development p140

1 1b; 2a; 3a; 4b; 5a; 6a; 7b; 8a

2 a to; b on

3 1 of; 2 about; 3 with; 4 at; 5 to; 6 by; 7 for; 8 in; 9 from; 10 on

4 1d; 2g; 3b; 4e; 5f; 6h; 7i; 8c; 9j; 10a

Grammar p141

1 b: 'as if' indicates a comparison. The verb: be is being used in the subjunctive.

2 1 were (present time); 2 had (present/future time); 3 didn't smoke (present/future); 4 wouldn't have been fined/hadn't dropped (3rd conditional – past hypothetical situation); 5 was going to be (past/future); 6 Were (present); 7 did (present); 8 hadn't had (past)

3 1c; 2g; 3f; 4b; 5a; 6h; 7e; 8d

4 1 were; 2 were; 3 had not made; 4 took; 5 took; 6 Were; 7 would not buy/had not bought; 8 had not told; 9 was/were; 10 had seen

5 1 only; 2 was/were; 3 as; 4 were; 5 had; 6 have; 7 rather/sooner; 8 than; 9 wish; 10 time; 11 lived; 12 if/though

6 1 high time you switched off
2 would rather try to save/we tried to save
3 wish I had not/hadn't been
4 if you (should) see/saw
5 had not/hadn't been so polluted
6 sooner go to
7 I changed career I would join
8 as if she knows everything but

Listening p142

2 1 a circumstances, leading up to, dinosaurs; b are not often questioned = few people wonder; c extinction

3 Underline: 1 years
2 per cent/gases
3 animals/leave the water/the land
4 animals underwent/stage of
5 species/became/oxygen levels fell
6 higher oxygen/enabled/to flourish
7 animals/died/not adapt quickly/ periods low oxygen
8 Birds/fly at high

4 1 a number (of years)
2 a number (percentage)
3 verb meaning 'live in a place'
4 noun meaning 'change'
5 adjective showing the effect on a species of not enough oxygen
6 noun (species)
7 verb (connected to dying)
8 noun that can be described by 'high'.

5 1 600 million; 2 21; 3 colonise;
4 evolution; 5 extinct; 6 reptiles;
7 suffocated; 8 altitudes

Speaking p142

2 Elisabeth mentions: deforestation, pollution, habitat destruction. Giovanni mentions: extinction of species, climate change.
Yes, they do change their minds.

Use of English p143

1 They all use al: a + *isation*, b + <u>ise</u>, c + *ly*

2 a affectionate; b evolution;
c activate; d historical; e diversity;
f development; g modernise;
h childhood

3 1 confidence; 2 scientific;
3 broaden; 4 destruction;
5 extinction; 6 biological;
7 madness; 8 indefinitely;
9 intellectually; 10 superiority;
11 identify; 12 knowledge

Writing p144

2 international/national issues: poverty/famine, illness/disease
social issues: drug abuse/addiction
environmental issues: pollution, species extinction/loss of

biodiversity, depletion of Earth's resources

3 Increase in human population is the most serious issue because it causes depletion of the Earth's resources, pollution, climate change, species extinction. Crime and drug addiction would not be appropriate here because they are not global issues.

4 It's too short, has no paragraph structure, and doesn't deal sufficiently with the issues surrounding the question to provide a conclusive answer. Also the student does not provide reasons for his/her opinions. It's also repetitive in style and reuses the same words.

5 1 make worse; 2 very fast; 3 using up; 4 different species

6 1 depletion/overuse of natural resources; 2 climate change/global warming; 3 loss of biodiversity/ extinctions; 4 poverty/famine/ starvation; 5 disease; 6 warfare

Vocabulary organiser 14 p144

14.1 a salinity; b metabolism;
c phenomenon; d entity; e biosphere;
f diversity; g void; h myriad;
i equilibrium

14.2 a profound; b attain;
c postulated; d imprecise;
e provoked; f optimum; g sustain;
h allotted

14.3 a of; b about; c with; d at; e to;
f by; g for; h in; i from; j on

14.4 a ridiculousness; b postage;
c courageous; d affectionate;
e insecticide; f refugees;
g diversification; h ecological

14.5 1 exponentially; 2 Depletion;
3 exacerbate

Bank of English

1 a biosphere; b geography;
c biology; d geology; e biographer;
f geometry; g biodiversity;
h biodegradable; i geophysicist;
j geopolitical

Odd-animal-out

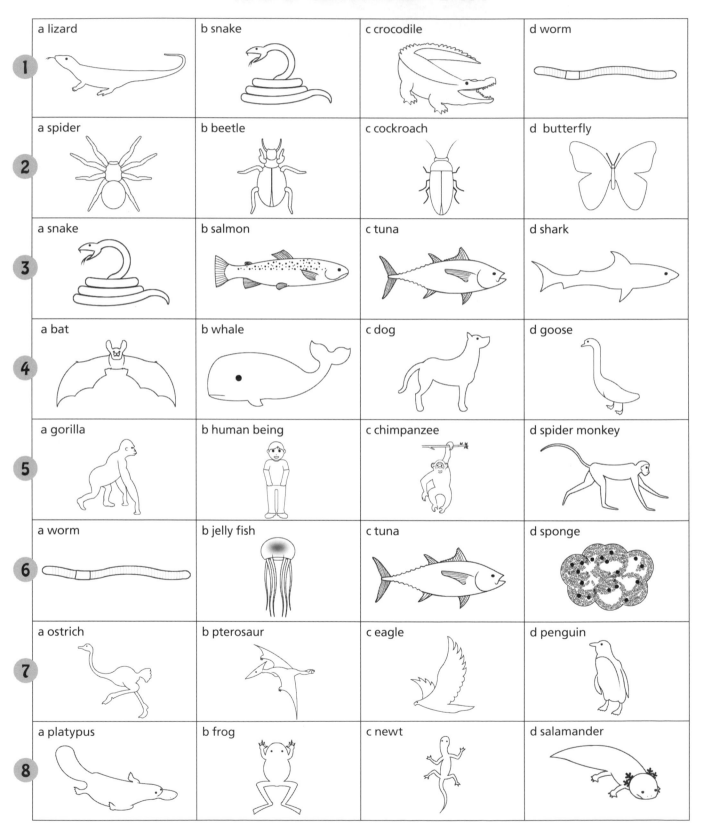

1	a lizard	b snake	c crocodile	d worm
2	a spider	b beetle	c cockroach	d butterfly
3	a snake	b salmon	c tuna	d shark
4	a bat	b whale	c dog	d goose
5	a gorilla	b human being	c chimpanzee	d spider monkey
6	a worm	b jelly fish	c tuna	d sponge
7	a ostrich	b pterosaur	c eagle	d penguin
8	a platypus	b frog	c newt	d salamander

PHOTOCOPIABLE 14.1

Ideal World

Write down your hopes for an ideal world …

If only …	I'd rather …	Were it possible …	Suppose …
I wish …	I'd prefer it …	It's time …	Imagine …

Write down your hopes for an ideal world …

If only …	I'd rather …	Were it possible …	Suppose …
I wish …	I'd prefer it …	It's time …	Imagine …

Write down your hopes for an ideal world …

If only …	I'd rather …	Were it possible …	Suppose …
I wish …	I'd prefer it …	It's time …	Imagine …

PHOTOCOPIABLE 14.2

15 Our global village

Lesson planner

Fast lane: 3 x 1.5 hour lessons = 4.5 hours per unit
(total course = 72–76 hours)

Lesson	Time	Classwork	Exam Booster (EB) homework
43	1.5 hours	Getting started, Reading + Vocab. Organiser (VO)	Getting started + Reading
44	1.5 hours	Check homework, Lang. develop., Listening (1), Speaking, Grammar + VO	Lang. develop., Listening, Speaking + Grammar
45	1.5 hours	Check homework, Use of English, Listening (2), Writing + VO	Use of English + Writing

Slow lane: 4 x 1.5 hour lessons = 6 hours per unit
(total course = 96–100 hours)

Lesson	Time	Classwork	(EB) homework
57	1.5 hours	Getting started, photocopiable 1, Reading + VO	Getting started + Reading
58	1.5 hours	Check homework, Lang. develop., Listening (1), Speaking + VO	Lang. develop., Listening + Speaking
59	1.5 hours	Check homework, Grammar, Use of English + VO	Grammar + Use of English
60	1.5 hours	Check homework, Listening (2), Writing + photocopiable 2	Writing + Coursebook Writing task

Before you begin

Ask students to prepare for the lesson by doing research into one unique culture or custom of their choice from another country. This can be anything they like, from how people in

Denmark celebrate Christmas, to how the Yanomami Indians of the Amazon rainforest remember their dead. They can prepare by searching Internet sites (in English) and make a short presentation at the beginning of the lesson. This can be done in pairs or small groups, to save time. There is the possibility of extending this task into a larger project to be submitted as a longer essay at the end of the unit.

TEACHING IN PRACTICE

Teaching in multicultural groups versus monocultural groups

When teaching multicultural groups, it's important to watch out for anything that may cause offence. However, there is the possibility for you and your students to share information and find out so much more about different cultures. Another advantage with multicultural groups is that students are forced to communicate with each other in English, and it makes a good opportunity for pairwork, as students from different countries also have different problems speaking English and they can help each other.

Topic: cultures, customs, civilisations

Nowadays we come face to face with other cultures, belief systems, traditions, languages and environments far more frequently than ever before. It is therefore necessary to learn more about other people, the places they come from, and the way that they do things there.

Unit 15 Wordlist

abolish	ethnic	prohibit
adolescence	etiquette	prospective
anecdote	gesture	restrict
attend	heritage	rite of passage
bond	idiosyncrasy	ritualistic
cement	impending	rural
clash	improper	stipulate
compatibility	instinctive	taboo
conflicting	irreverence	transgress
convention	liberty	transition
deport	ludicrous	violate
despise	misinterpret	vulgar
endearing	obscene	
esteem	ostracise	

Getting started

BACKGROUND: THE GLOBAL VILLAGE

The term 'Global Village' was first popularised in the 1960s, but today it's mostly used as a metaphor to describe the Internet and World Wide Web. On the Internet, where physical distance does not exist, social spheres are greatly expanded by the ease with which people can interact with others in online communities. This has fostered the idea of a unified global community.

1   Discuss the title of the unit with the class and elicit ideas about what they think it means. Then invite students to look at the pictures and identify the countries or traditions shown. Talk about any other issues that may come up connected to the subject and note down key vocabulary.

2   Students either work individually, in pairs or you could do this as a class activity.

    →   Information File 15.1, page 203

3   A possible game here would be along the lines of 'Ten Questions', where a student does a short mime of a traditional custom and the other students take turns asking questions in order to guess what is. Questions should take the form of yes/no answers only. For each 'yes' answer a student receives, he/she gets to ask another question. For each 'no' answer, play moves on to the next student.

    →   Vocabulary Organiser 15.1 + 15.2, page 156

Reading: purpose and main idea

Aim: To help students look at a selection of texts with a common theme and to quickly understand the purpose and main idea of each text.

1   Ask students to look at the pictures to get them started. (The pictures show a Hula dance from Hawaii; a Native American Indian dance from North America; a traditional dance from Thailand; and Flamenco from Spain.) Try to encourage a few volunteers to describe some national dances, costumes etc. Give help with vocabulary wherever necessary.

2   The purpose of this exercise is to help students identify and understand basic information about a text by quick reference to it. Allow no more than a few minutes for this. Check answers with the group.

BACKGROUND: MORRIS DANCING

A Morris dance is a form of English folkdance usually accompanied by music. It is based on rhythmic stepping and the execution of choreographed figures by a group of dancers. Implements such as sticks, swords, and handkerchiefs may also be wielded by the dancers. In a small number of dances for one or two men, steps are performed near and across a pair of clay tobacco pipes laid across each other on the floor.

3   Tell your students not to worry about vocabulary at this stage. Let them refer back to the text again and underline the answers. Again, they should only spend a few minutes doing this. Check answers with the group.

SPOTLIGHT ON READING

Texts from different sources

Read through the rubric with students and check that they have understood it.

4 Tell students you are only going to give them one minute to skim read all three texts and decide which one comes from which source. Check answers with the group and ask for justifications.

As an extra activity, consider asking your students to summarise the main idea behind each of the texts.

5   Allow a full ten minutes for students to read the texts properly and answer the multiple choice questions. Afterwards, check answers with the group, elicit justifications.

6   Generate a discussion on any of the topics that interests the group.

Reading extension

Homework assignment could be a continuation of the warm-up activity if it hasn't already been done, including finding texts on cultures, customs or taboos and either writing a review or giving a report to the class.

→   Vocabulary Organiser 15.3 + 15.4, page 156

Language development: phrasal verbs and phrases with *pass*

You could start the section by brainstorming any phrasal verbs or phrases with *pass* that students remember. Write them on the board, or elicit example sentences of each one.

1 + 2   Students continue with the exercises individually or in pairs. Check answers with the class.

3   Students may be familiar with some of the idioms, but not all of them. Either allow them to use their dictionaries or let them try to guess the answers. Afterwards, check answers with the group by eliciting further examples, or encouraging students to describe possible cartoons for each idiom.

Key word: *pass*

4   Go through the exercise with your students. Point out that this is a common mistake, even with native speakers.

5 + 6 Students work individually or in pairs. Go through the exercises with the class and make sure they have correctly understood the different meanings.

7 Allow enough time for students to write their own sentence. Tell them that the sentences need to be simple but clear enough to denote the meaning. Afterwards students swap their sentences with their partners who try to match them. You can either go round the class checking answers or ask each student to read their sentences and definitions after the activity.

→ Vocabulary Organiser 15.5, page 156

Listening (1): multiple speakers

1 Discuss the questions with the class. With multicultural groups there may be a variety of answers here that would be interesting to compare. With monocultural groups, elicit the general answers for that country and discuss how it may be different to other cultures. Tell students to look at the four pictures and describe how each one shows a different kind of kiss and a different relationship in each case.

SPOTLIGHT ON LISTENING

Attitude and opinion

2 🎧 15.1 Point out that this is not an exam task but that this activity will help students focus on a useful skill: identifying who said what. Students read through the questions first. Tell them that for this task you will only play the recording once.

3 As students have heard the recording once already they may not need two listenings for this task, but decide that according to the level of the group. Allow enough time for students to read the questions. Afterwards check answers with the group and refer to the tapescript if necessary.

You may want to pre-teach some of the words from the multiple choice questions: prospective mates = possible future partners; groom (v) = to clean fur; offspring (n) = young, child/children; primates (n pl) = order of mammals which includes apes and monkeys; bestow (v) = to give (formal); constitute (v) = to be something; denote (v) = to mean something.

Speaking: talking about your country, culture and background

TEACHING IN PRACTICE

Preparing for part 1 of the Speaking Paper
In the Speaking Paper, it's possible to prepare your students for part 1 to a certain extent. They will most likely be asked

questions about themselves, their families, their occupations or studies, hobbies and interests. They may also be asked some questions about their country, culture customs or taboos. Get your students to practise talking about these things, either in class or with a partner. However, don't let students memorise set speeches for the interview, as this will not win them any marks!

1 In multicultural teaching groups the advantage here would be to mix students so that they are with partners from different countries. In mono-cultural groups one student in each pair can pretend to be from another country, asking questions to find out more about their partner.

2 Students continue to work in pairs or open pairs. Monitor them in the class.

Degree of difficulty

Decrease the level: To make it easier for younger or weaker students to answer these questions, have a brainstorming session before they begin the pairwork, and write general ideas and suggestions on the board. Most students, however, should be able to say some things about the customs and traditions in their countries.

Increase the level: More advanced students shouldn't need any further guidance with these topics, and should also have a few things to say about question 3. Get them to close their books and not use the Useful Language feature.

Grammar: adverbial clauses

1 Students should read the extract from the tapescript and try to think of other words to explain the same thing or to explain what the purpose of the words in bold are. Prompt them if necessary or guide them to the Grammar Spotlight first, or the Grammar Reference section. You could also direct students to review the tapescript for further examples of adverbial clauses when they have finished the section.

GRAMMAR SPOTLIGHT

Clauses of time, purpose, reason, concession and result

2 Elicit answers from the group, and then further examples of similar sentences.

3 This exercise can be done as a class activity if you think some students need extra help, or it can be done in pairs or individually. You may have to pre-teach 'concession' although this already has an example.

→ Grammar Reference 15.1, page 180

4   Students work individually to choose the best option. Afterwards, check the answers with the class. You could also elicit example sentences for the two options which are not used.

5   Students should attempt the task individually in the class. Allow approximately ten minutes for this. Elicit answers and iron out any problems.

Grammar extension

Extra practice with adverbials …

Write on the board, or dictate the following sentences. Students should complete them in their own words.

1 I haven't seen Bertie *since* _____.

2 I had *so* little money _____.

3 Be home by midnight or *else* _____.

4 *In spite of* the weather we _____.

5 Smart *though* Sara is _____.

6 He decided to take a taxi *for fear of* _____.

Key: The following answers are examples only.
1 1975 (point in time); 2 that I couldn't afford a bus ticket; 3 you'll be in big trouble; 4 decided to go for a walk; 5 she'll fail her exams if she doesn't do some work; 6 being late again

---

Use of English: open cloze text

Aim: The aim of this section is to give further practice of open cloze texts and to use this as an opportunity to consolidate much of what students have learnt in the Grammar section. It should therefore be taught after the Grammar section as many of the gaps are based on adverbial clauses.

1   Students work individually. Allow approximately ten minutes for the exercise. Check answers with the group.

2   Students work individually or in pairs. Check answers with the group.

3   This is another opportunity for students to have a go at part 4 of the Use of English Paper. Don't give them any assistance at first. Let them have a go at it by themselves, then check answers with the group and go over any problems. Students note down any new meanings or expressions in their vocabulary notebooks.

→   Vocabulary Organiser 15.6, page 156

Listening (2): short extracts

1   🎧 15.2 Students should read through the questions and identify key words. Elicit from students as much information as they can give you about what they expect to hear, from the questions they have read. Play the recording twice. If time allows there is more material for discussion here.

Writing: an article (2)

Aim: To show students how they can write an article about a personal experience or something that involves a degree of description, narrative or anecdote.

1   Discuss the points with students and elicit a few personal descriptions of some of them. If necessary explain or give definitions for any unknown events. Refer to the pictures at the bottom of page 154 for examples of some.

BACKGROUND: SOME TRADITIONAL CEREMONIES

A baby shower is a party in which parents or expectant parents receive gifts for their newborn or expected child. By convention, a baby shower is intended to help parents get items that they need for their baby, such as baby clothes. In some countries this party is not celebrated until the baby is born.

A name day is a tradition in many countries in Europe and Latin America of celebrating on a particular day of the year associated with one's given name. The custom originated with the Catholic and Orthodox Calendar of Saints, where believers, named after a particular saint, would celebrate that saint's feast day.

A wake is a ceremony associated with death. Traditionally, a wake takes place in the house of the deceased, with the body present; however, modern wakes are often performed at a funeral home. While the modern usage of the verb 'wake' is to 'become or stay alert', a 'wake' for the dead harks back to the antiquated 'watch or guard' sense.

---

2   Read through the question and the advertisement with the students or get them to read it individually and underline key words. Elicit what is required in the task.

3   Students should read the extract individually. Elicit suggestions about what is wrong with it, and then go straight on to the Spotlight on Writing which students can read for themselves.

SPOTLIGHT ON WRITING

Using description and anecdote
Discuss why the example given here is an 'anecdote' and how it may improve an article or piece of writing.

4 Students should read the article and answer the questions individually. Allow a few minutes for this. Tell students not to worry about unknown vocabulary or Japanese words at this point. Note: If you have any Japanese students in the class, this would be a good chance to encourage them to speak up about their own experiences of *Seijin Shiki*.

In other words

Read through the rubric with the class and make sure students understand the main point here. You could also elicit some examples of words in the students' own languages that probably cannot be translated directly into English and may need to be treated in this way.

5 + 6 Students work individually or in pairs. Check answers.

→   Vocabulary Organiser 15.6, page 156

7   Students can work individually – in which case encourage students to try and think up two or three ideas and choose the best one – or you can do a class brainstorming session and write a few ideas on the board. Allow some time for them to carefully plan their headings and arrange their ideas.

8   Encourage students to spend a few minutes thinking about this before they start writing. Get them to write a few notes explaining it, but remind them that they shouldn't spend too much time planning in detail, and they have to remember to check their word count.

TEACHING IN PRACTICE

Writing in pairs
Sometimes getting students to write in pairs can be very useful for them, as it enables them to see how other students express themselves in writing. It also forces students to explain what they want to say out loud and to justify their ideas. A combined writing effort means students have to decide together what sounds good and what doesn't, what should stay and what should go, and there are two people suggesting vocabulary and checking grammar instead of one.

9   Students either write individually, or in pairs.

Photocopiable activity instructions

 Activity 15.1 Home exchange holidays

Aim: To justify choices, explain reasons, debate pros and cons. This is also an opportunity for students to use adverbial clauses and can be used in conjunction with the grammar section.

Instructions (for groups with 6–12 students):

1   Divide the class into two equal groups: 'home-seekers' and 'property owners'.

2   Photocopy and cut out the 'home-seekers' and 'properties' on offer. Give each student either a home-seeker card or a property card.

3   Each home-seeker should write a short description of the kind of property they think would suit them. Each property owner should write a short description of the kind of family/individuals they think their property would best be suited to.

4   When everyone has finished writing the teacher calls on students at random to talk about who they are and what they are looking for (home-seekers) or to describe their properties and the families or individuals they think their home would be suitable for (property owners).

5   As soon as someone from either group thinks they have identified a close enough match, they should raise their hands and explain why they think the home exchange would work.

6   The aim is to match up all the pairs if possible. If someone doesn't think a particular property or home-seeker is suitable, they should identify the one they do think is most suitable and explain their reasons.

Home exchange holidays

Tapescript 15

Listening 15.1

Interviewer: Today we're here to discuss the subject of 'kissing' and its origins. With me in the studio are two anthropologists: Professor Rosemary O'Bryan and Dr Andrew Peters. Professor O'Bryan, is kissing learned or instinctive behaviour?

Rosemary: Affectionate kissing is a learned behaviour that most probably originated from a mother gently touching or nibbling her child's body with her lips, to cement the bond between them, or it may have arisen from <u>premasticating food to make it easier for her child to swallow.</u> From there it developed into a way of showing affection towards family members, close friends or other members of society and as a sign of respect to older, senior group members.

Interviewer: And yet, according to some anthropologists, kissing is an echo of an ancient form of communication that was necessary for the healthy and successful continuation of the species. Dr Peters …

Andrew: Yes, kissing in humans is an instinctive behaviour which most likely evolved from grooming behaviour common in mammals. However, recent research has indicated that this kind of behaviour had a much more serious biological function than just social bonding. Kissing, or rubbing noses, actually allows prospective mates to smell or taste each other's pheromones …

Interviewer: … You mean the chemicals which give off information about our biological make-up?

Andrew: … Correct, and thus we get more information about our biological compatibility. Women are more attracted to men who are more genetically compatible to them, and a woman picks this up by breathing in his pheromones. <u>Any resulting offspring will have better resistance to a greater number of diseases, and will consequently have a better chance of survival.</u> That's why we still like to kiss – to maximise our chances of sampling each other's aroma.

Interviewer: So that's why couples are more likely to bond if they have the right 'chemistry'.

Andrew: Yes, and it's not just a mating tool. <u>Chimpanzees, for instance, use it for reconciliation, by kissing and embracing after fights, providing good evidence that kissing in the higher primates has the function of repairing of social relationships.</u>

Interviewer: So when did the romantic act of kissing one's sweetheart on the mouth as a form of affection actually develop?

Rosemary: Well … not until comparatively late in the evolution of love in fact. In antiquity, kissing – especially on the eyes or cheek – was mainly a form of greeting, but <u>there's no evidence of it being romantic.</u> One of the earliest descriptions of kissing as a form of love and affection comes from the 6th century, in France. Around that time it seems to have become fashionable for a young man to give his betrothed a kiss on the lips as a seal of his affection.

Interviewer: But the rest of the world did not practice kissing as a sign of affection?

Rosemary: In the years before cinema the lovers' kiss was largely a Western habit – unknown in other parts of the world. <u>By the end of the Second World War Western motion pictures had carried the image of romantic couples engaged in a kiss to many other parts of the world.</u> Until quite recently, it was only in North America and Europe that kissing was an important aspect of courtship, which puts paid to the notion that kissing must be instinctive in all people. For instance, the Chinese and the Japanese never kissed on the lips.

Andrew: Yes, but in other cultures affection was expressed in a number of ways – for instance, in Samoa, lovers would express affection by sniffing the air beside each other's cheek; in Polynesia affection was shown by rubbing noses together. The same goes for Eskimos and Laplanders, as with many animals who smell each other or rub noses to smell each other's pheromones. <u>This indicates that it's still instinctive …</u>

Rosemary: <u>It's hardly the same thing …</u>

Andrew: … What about monkeys? Bonobos? They'll kiss each other on the lips for just about any excuse at all. They do it to make up after fights, to comfort each other, to develop social bonds, and <u>sometimes for no clear reason at all – just like us …</u>

Listening 15.2

Speaker 1: My identity is most certainly Nigerian. It's vital to establish that differentiation because in the United Kingdom, we are all described as either African or perhaps West Indian. What isn't taken into account is that black people are really quite territorial – and in Nigeria we even go slightly further because we have three tribes and take immense pride in our tribe. Since I'm an Ibo, I wouldn't like to be called a Yoruba or a Hausa. <u>I was born in Nigeria and came to England when I was 13.</u> I have a huge family here, but still the allure of Nigeria is very strong. The responsibilities of family need to be taken very seriously. There is no getting away from our background, no matter how much we want to belong in our new home and integrate well. <u>We look and are different, but London is so ethnically mixed, especially where we live in West London which helps.</u> I'm bringing up my daughters to value and recognise their roots … but still to appreciate the culture they are growing up in.

Speaker 2: Being a Greek Cypriot isn't about religion, but a way of life. It's 100 per cent about the family – and that means the extended one, too. If you are some kind of blood relation, no matter how tenuous, you're considered part of the family. This can be a blessing and a curse, believe me! <u>Being Greek means making decisions collectively, forever in a crowd: essentially, it's a community experience. Now, perhaps that might sound a little claustrophobic, but it has many advantages. There is always support and love.</u> Even though the film My Big Fat Greek Wedding was a caricature of this lifestyle, it was also very true. When the girl tells her American boyfriend about her 27 first cousins, I had to laugh. I have 74! Our parents were first generation immigrants, and so were determined to preserve their culture because it was all they had. We are much more confident of who we are, but can also dip in and out of the British way of life and not be excluded. Our children likewise appreciate their background, but don't have a particularly close attachment to Cyprus, unlike their grandparents.

Speaker 3: You cannot escape from who you are culturally but, given the opportunity, you can create your own traditions and become a more improved person. We are Persian-Iranian. Our culture is very rich in so many areas, like in our history, our language, our literature and food and our music. These are all what we want to save and pass down to our next generation and then the generation after that. In our own country, our modern principles came under attack, so we left and have learned not to keep looking back. I am a person who likes to welcome the future and I am not afraid of change. As parents, we believe in giving our children the knowledge of their heritage. But we don't want to force our values on them; we have faith in their reasoning. I feel we are truly fortunate to be able to understand two cultures and it is beneficial not only to us as immigrants, but to our host country, too. This process – it is two-way.

Speaker 4: I'm a British Muslim and am very proud to call myself both. My parents came from Gujarat and settled in Batley where I was born. But although I've never been to India, as a young boy I always had a sense of who I was, where I was from. I was happy with this, even though growing up I endured a lot of racial jeering – many of the kids at school told me to go back to my country. There's a huge Gujarat community in Batley – we've more relatives here than in India! So, together with my parents,

this community gave me my ethnic identity. Now that I too am a father I will do the same for my children. My wife is from the same background and we feel strongly that we must keep our customs and traditions because this is what gives us a sense of ourselves. Being Indian is not what our identity is about; I have a British passport, and if I go to India I need to have a visa. My ethnic identity is a religious one, not a geographic one. It's inevitable that our religion, language and customs will vanish if we don't pass them on to our children.

Speaker 5: My ethnic identity is of great importance to me, but I didn't realise the extent of this until my daughter was born. I came to England as a student and I always believed I would be returning home to Osaka. But then I ended up getting married to an English guy that I met here, and realised I'd be staying in this country – and raising my daughter here. I knew that I would always remember my roots and cultural heritage, but I also wanted Lily to know as well. I wanted to bring her up to be both English and Japanese. I realised how hard this task would be that I had set myself for, without effort on my part, she was bound to become more British than Japanese. Of grave importance to me was that she learnt the language so that she could converse with her grandparents and truly understand the culture, so I spoke to her only in Japanese, and left it to her father to speak English with her. The Japanese language is very poetic, there are several different words to describe the moon; just being able to use those words in the correct sense makes a huge difference and shows a true understanding of the language. The other day Lily looked out of the window. She told me that she could see a 'natsu no tsuki', which means a summer moon. I was so pleased.

Answer key 15

Getting started p147

1 Chinese dragon (Chinese New Year), Jack o'lantern (Hallowe'en/UK/Ireland/USA), Japanese Geisha (Japan/Sado/tea ceremony), red eggs (Easter/Southern Europe), African ceremonial dance.

2 1a; 2c; 3b; 4a; 5c; 6a; 7b

Reading pp148–9

2 a from a leaflet, website or information book about traditional dances

b to give information about 'Morris Dancing', its origins, costume and variations

c that there are several different types of Morris Dance.

3 1T; 2F; 3F; 4T; 5T; 6F; 7F; 8F

4 a text b; b text a; c text c

5 1C; 2A; 3 D; 4B; 5D; 6A

Language development p150

1 a to teach to the next generation; b hand down

2 1 over; 2 on; 3 up; 4 off; 5 away; 6 as; 7 out; 8 by

3 1b; 2c; 3a; 4c; 5a; 6c; 7b; 8a

4 b is incorrect: The correct answer would be 'walked past me' because pass is a verb and past is a preposition.

5 b

6 d

Listening (1) p151

2 1A; 2B; 3B; 4A; 5A; 6A; 7B; 8B

3 1C; 2D; 3A; 4A; 5B; 6C

Grammar p152

1 *thus*: so/therefore/in this way
by: the manner in which they do it
consequently: as a consequence/result/after a fact
That's why: explains the reason, *to*: explains the purpose

2 it tells us 'when' (time).

3 Time (I'll meet you *when* I've finished); Place (She wanted to know *where* I'd been); Manner (He asked me *how* I'd done it); Comparison (It was as bad *as* I feared); Cause/reason (I walked fast *because* I was late); Purpose (She smiled *so that* I'd feel welcome); Result (It got *so* hot *that* I couldn't concentrate); Condition (If I'd known you'd be late I'd have started without you); Concession (She won the game *although* she'd never played before).

4 1 Due to; 2 in order to; 3 the minute; 4 Nevertheless; 5 No matter how; 6 Seeing as

5 1 had the plane stopped when; 2 and consequently I got; 3 in order to make; 4 seeing as it is/it's such; 5 being the only person; 6 otherwise I will/I'll tell; 7 in spite of the fact that; 8 reason why I took up

Use of English p153

1 1 so; 2 take; 3 example/instance; 4 to; 5 as/because/since; 6 reason; 7 should/must; 8 other; 9 with; 10 unless; 11 mean/signify/indicate; 12 such; 13 it; 14 is; 15 which

2 … your host's customs *so that* (purpose); in Thailand, as (reason) the foot is the lowest part of the body; and *to point* (purpose) a foot at someone; Likewise, *as/since/because* (reason) the head is; For *this reason*, (reason) a pat on the head; do not mix at all *unless* (concession/conditional) they are family.

3 1 sight; 2 leave; 3 party; 4 return; 5 howling

Listening (2) p153

1 Task one: 1F; 2E; 3H; 4A; 5C
Task two: 6C; 7A; 8E; 9D; 10G

Writing pp154–5

2 Students should identify: 'write an article', 'describe one of these events', 'unique and unusual customs', 'first hand narrative description' 'event you have witnessed or taken part in'.

3 It is just an informative explanation of what 'coming of age' means and how it is generally celebrated in different cultures. It contains no first hand narrative descriptive accounts of a specific celebration and does not emphasise any unusual or unique customs.

4 a most of the account is a description; b the final paragraph is anecdotal.

5 *seijun shiki*: coming of age ceremony in Japan
furisode: a kind of traditional dress (usually worn by young, unmarried women)

kimono: traditional formal dress in Japan (usually worn by women)
hakama: traditional formal dress (usually worn by men)
zori slippers: traditional Japanese footwear.

6 limping, wobbly, staggering: the writer uses them because they emphasise the way the people are walking (limping – because the shoes are painful or difficult to wear, wobbly and staggering because people have probably had too much to drink.

Vocabulary organiser 15 p156

15.1 a dyed eggs; b sado; c lobola; d piñata; e Jack o'lantern; f henna

15.3 1 passed down; 2 rural; 3 wield; 4 blunt; 5 distinctive; 6 aloft

15.4 Text A: 1 violate, 2 transgress, 3 ostracise
Text B: 4 abducted, 5 take stock, 6 grumble
Text C: 7 spouse, 8 patrilineal, 9 exclusively

15.5 1 pass away; 2 pass (something) on; 3 pass out; 4 pass up; 5 pass off (as); 6 pass with flying colours; 7 let something pass; 8 pass the buck

15.6 1 ignorant; 2 obscene, offensive, vulgar, insulting; 3 inferior; 4 pat (on the head), bow, clasp hands, crook a finger

Home exchange holidays

Ms Camelia Rhodes from New York, USA

Single professional businesswoman, 40s, seeks to travel in Europe, for shopping and entertainment.

The Dirkin family from Canada

We are a family of two adults and two young children, one boy aged six and one girl aged eight. We would like to explore and see new things. A child-friendly house would be nice.

Pete and Sue, Jim and Emily from Australia

We are two married couples in our 30s, no children, looking for an exciting break somewhere warm. We all love sports, relaxation, history and culture.

The Wilkinson family from Chicago, USA

We are a family of five: two adults, two boys aged 15 and 17 and one 13-year-old girl. We would consider an exchange anywhere either Europe or further afield. Something comfortable and pleasant.

Mr and Mrs Roberts from Ireland

Retired couple in their 70s who want to travel – nothing too adventurous though. We like arts and culture and going somewhere new.

The Joneses from Devon, UK

Adventurous family of four (children 14 and 11), we love outdoor sports, summer or winter activities, exploration and leisure activities. Open to all offers.

PHOTOCOPIABLE 15.1

Phuket, Thailand

Treat yourself and your family to a unique getaway at Phuket's loveliest beach. This unique, private home is built in traditional Thai style and features a central pool, silent air conditioning, ceiling fans, a state of the art entertainment centre. There are over 1000 square metres of tropical landscape and adjacent 5000 square metre park; maid service and pool cleaning three times per week. Hear the surf from the pool deck! NOTE: With its deep pool and high waterfall, this villa is not suitable for children under 12 or for those who cannot swim.

Alberta, Canada

Our home is surrounded by huge fir trees and there is hiking and cross-country skiing. There is also a very good golf course nearby. Our home has approximately 3500 square feet of living space, two fireplaces, large recreation rooms and a hot tub. Half an hour drive to the beautiful National Parks and the Rocky Mountain Range. Excellent ski hills in the area in winter as well as fabulous camping facilities and hiking trails in summer. Also, the Dinosaur National Park and the Royal Tyrell Museum (a world heritage site) are a 90 minute drive from our home.

Nairobi, Kenya

Small three-bedroomed bungalow set in a lovely well-kept half acre garden with lots of shade. Located to the west of central Nairobi with easy access to shops and the city. The exchange potentially comes with a four-wheel-drive car that enables self-drive safari travels for up to four people to nearby national parks (day trips and weekend trips). Child seats available. The house is well equipped for small children, has satellite TV and Internet connection, and a home help to do cleaning, washing and cooking.

Red Sea, Egypt

One minute from the beach we have newly furnished apartments fully equipped for comfortable self-catering holidays. The area is a fascinating holiday destination with plenty of bohemian charm, world-class scuba diving and windsurfing. It is also popular for yoga breaks, relaxation and safaris. The apartments have two bedrooms with sea views, and a spacious open plan living area with a fitted kitchen. The comfortable lounge area opens onto the balcony with views over the rooftops and minarets of the Bedouin village to the Sinai mountains beyond.

London, England

Stylish contemporary modern apartment in one of the best squares in London. The flat is one bedroom and overlooks a picturesque quiet residential square. Large studio room with full height windows, separate double bedroom and modern contemporary bathroom and fully equipped kitchen with all mod-cons. The beautifully maintained apartment is situated in an 1820s Georgian House within easy walking access to the museums, Harrods, Knightsbridge shops, the West End and the royal parks. The flat also has a high speed Internet connection.

Sydney, Australia

Our two-bedroomed house is three minutes walk to the bus stop and there are many shops and restaurants nearby. Our street is a quiet cul-de-sac but is still within walking distance to the Aquatic Centre, Rowing Club and the Bay Walk. Sydney Opera House, Harbour Bridge, The Rocks Precinct and the Olympic site are all within easy reach. The Blue Mountains and the wine growing Hunter Valley are both within two hours drive. Our house is low maintenance and there are no lawns to mow as the garden is small. A home help will clean twice a week.

16 Endings – and new beginnings

Lesson planner

Fast lane: 3 x 1.5 hour lessons = 4.5 hours per unit
(total course = 72–76 hours)

Lesson	Time	Classwork	Exam Booster (EB) homework
46	1.5 hours	Getting started, Reading + Vocab. Organiser (VO)	Getting started + Reading
47	1.5 hours	Check homework, Lang. develop., Listening, Grammar + VO	Lang. develop., Grammar + Listening
48	1.5 hours	Check homework, Use of English, Speaking, Writing + VO	Use of English, Speaking, Writing + Coursebook Writing task

Slow lane: 4 x 1.5 hour lessons = 6 hours per unit
(total course = 96–100 hours)

Lesson	Time	Classwork	EB homework
61	1.5 hours	Getting started, Reading, VO + photocopiable 1	Getting started + Reading
62	1.5 hours	Check homework, Lang. develop., Listening, Grammar + VO	Lang. develop., Listening + Grammar
63	1.5 hours	Check homework, Use of English, photocopiable 2, Speaking + VO	Use of English + Speaking
64	1.5 hours	Check homework + Writing	Writing + Coursebook Writing task

Before you begin

Consider handing out 'Just a Minute!'
(Photocopiable Activity 16.1, page 158) to your class.
Instructions can be found on page 154.

Topic: saying goodbye

To show that the book has come full circle, and that every ending opens the door to new beginnings,

this unit touches upon a variety of subjects that do just that.

Unit 16 Wordlist

abort	extinguish	relegate
cease	finalise	ruthless
complete	finish	scavenge
conclude	forsake	settle
cursory	forsaken	slaughterhouse
comprehensive	grindstone	slog
compulsive	heed	terminate
confounding	professed	treadmill
cumbersome	reform	threshold
demote	regenerate	transient
discontinue	rejuvenate	unwieldy
dormant	relapse	wrench
downgrade	relativity	wrinkled

Getting started

1   Ask students to compare the 'pairs' in the bottom left-hand corner of the page, in order to elicit the idea that for everything that comes to an end, something new takes its place. Then ask them to compare the title strip with that of Unit 1, as well as the pictures in the bottom right-hand corner. Elicit suggestions about what is coming to an end/beginning in each one.

2   Students work in pairs. Go through the answers together, but do not expect them to know all of the combinations. Elicit and, if necessary, explain the difference between 'cease fire' and 'extinguish a fire'; 'finalise a business deal/ contract' and 'terminate a deal/contract'; 'complete a rescue operation' and abort a rescue operation'.

Degree of difficulty ▰▰▱▱▱

3   **Decrease the level:** If your students struggled with exercise 2, you could allow them to continue working in pairs.

Increase the level: If they found exercise 2 fairly straightforward, they could do this exercise individually. Check the answers with the whole class and clarify any points which cause confusion.

4   Students work in pairs, or individually. Make it clear to them that not all of the items in exercise 3 can be replaced by a phrasal verb. Elicit suggestions, and give feedback.

Reading: multiple matching texts

1 Encourage students to talk about how they would feel if they had to leave their home permanently.

2 Students work in pairs. Explain to them that they should create a picture to match their ending to the story. Each pair should tell their story to the rest of the class.

6 Students do this individually. It is a good idea to time them. Check answers and give feedback, if needed.

7 Students work in pairs, or individually. Discuss the answers as a group.

8 This could be done with the whole class. Elicit ideas, and discuss any differences in opinion.

→   Vocabulary Organiser 16.1, page 166

Reading extension

At this late stage in the course, there probably won't be time for a follow-on discussion of the topic, but students may wish to comment on one or more of the moral questions raised in these extracts. The question of banning the TV, for instance, is potentially controversial! Also, vegetarianism and home-schooling could raise some interest. If so, then transform it into practice of a Paper 5, part 4, by placing students in pairs, and asking each pair a specific exam-style question, allowing them only two or three minutes to answer it.

Language development: word partners

1 Tell your students that one of the options in each item forms a phrase which appears in the Reading extracts on page 159. You could direct them to find out which one in each case, before they complete the task.

a – shocked me out of my ignorance (D)

b – drastic action (A)

c – expound a theory (B)

d – confirmed meat eater (D)

e – staple diet (B)

f – cloud my conscience (D)

g – dispel the myth (D)

h – be cut off from the rest of the world (A)

Check answers, and clarify any points which may cause disagreement.

→   Vocabulary Organiser 16.2, page 166

Key word: *end*

2 Students work in pairs, or individually. Do not expect them to know all of these items. Elicit answers.

→   Vocabulary Organiser 16.3, page 166

3 + 4 You may like to do these as timed exam practice tasks. Students work individually. Explain to them that some items revise words and phrases from earlier units. Check answers with the whole class.

→   Vocabulary Organiser 16.4, page 166

Grammar: making and intensifying comparisons

1 Students work individually. Check answers, and clarify any problem areas.

2   Tell students to use the Grammar Reference to help them complete this exercise. Elicit suggestions and give feedback.

3   Students should be able to do this without referring back to the text. You could ask them to refer to the text to check their answers once they have finished.

4   Elicit as many different comparisons as possible.

5   Do this as a class exercise. Elicit comparisons. If they haven't discussed the question of living without a TV, you could ask students what they think of the idea now.

6   🎧 16.1 Direct students to read the rubric and the gapped text. Play the recording. Elicit answers. If necessary, play the recording again.

7   Gather some ideas from the students, and allow some discussion.

Use of English: multiple choice cloze

1   Elicit titles from students, and gauge the level of interest in the subject. If students are interested, provide them with further suggestions for reading or viewing: *The Time Machine* by H. G. Wells; *Thief of Time* by Terry Pratchett; *Time Wars* by Simon Hawke; *TimeLine* by Michael Crichton; *The Time Traveller's Wife* by Audrey Niffenegger; *If I Never Get Back* by Darryl Brock; *Time and Again* by Jack Finney; *Woman on the Edge of Time* by Marge Piercy; *Doctor Who*; *Back to the Future* and so on.

2   Direct students to read through the gapped text. Then, elicit their views on the subject.

3   Explain some of the unknown vocabulary in the text before allowing your students to tackle the task. Do not set a strict time limit. If, however, you are confident that your class can cope by now, ask your students to complete the task within a set time limit. Check answers and clarify any problem areas.

→   Vocabulary Organiser 16.5, page 166

5   Allow for some free discussion here, so that students can relax a little.

Listening: three short extracts

2   🎧 16.2 Direct students to read the rubric. Play the recording twice. Check answers, and, if necessary, clarify any problem areas.

Listening extension

Checklist for the Listening Paper

To round off this section, you may like to give your students a quick general reminder of the task format for each part of the Listening Paper, by outlining the content and task type:

PART 1

Task type: multiple choice

Focus: feeling, attitude, opinion, purpose, function, agreement, course of action, gist, detail etc.

Format: three short extracts from exchanges between interacting speakers with two multiple choice questions on each extract.

Number of questions: six

PART 2

Task type: sentence completion

Focus: specific information, stated opinion

Format: a monologue (which may be introduced by a presenter) lasting approximately three minutes. Candidates are required to complete the sentences with information heard on the recording.

Number of questions: eight

PART 3

Task type: multiple choice

Focus: attitude and opinion

Format: a conversation between two or more speakers of approximately four minutes; six multiple choice questions, each with four options.

Number of questions: six

PART 4

Task type: multiple matching

Focus: gist, attitude, main points, interpreting context

Format: five short themed monologues, approximately 30 seconds each; each multiple-matching task requires selection of the correct options from a list of eight.

Number of questions: ten

Speaking: individual long turn

Aim: To get students thinking about different ways of making comparisons, and to encourage them to vary their language as they speak.

1   Elicit ideas from the class. Students in pairs for the rest of this section.

In other words

2   Direct students to the 'In other words' feature. Suggest they refer to the Grammar Reference section on page 182 for help. Elicit answers from each pair.

3   Do this as exam practice, and time it as such. Remind students that in this part, they must talk for about a minute. Allocate parts A and B to each pair. Direct them to read the rubric as you read it aloud. Time the speakers, and monitor the pairs from a distance.

4   Read the question out to students B. They should direct their response to their partner.

5   Direct students to turn to the pictures on page 201. Direct students B to read the rubric on page 163 as you read it aloud. Students turn back to the pictures and answer the questions.

6   Read the question to students A. They should direct their response to their partner.

At the end of the Speaking section, give general feedback to the class. Highlight positive aspects of their performance where possible.

Writing: a letter of reference

Aim: This final writing section aims to look at writing letters of reference, and also focuses on encouraging students to check their work thoroughly.

1   Elicit what students know about letters of reference. Brainstorm ideas about what information you should include in such a letter.

2   Direct students to read the question. Discuss the key points, and make sure students cover all of them.

A letter of reference
Direct students to read the information, and elicit any queries students may have.

3   Students work in pairs. Elicit who the writer is, the writer's relation to the person they are recommending, and who the target reader is. Students complete the plan. Check answers.

Eliciting students' ideas
By now, your students will have a good idea of what is required in this paper, so many of these exercises are designed to consolidate what they know. For this reason, throughout the section, elicit instructions from your students, instead of giving them yourself.

PAPER 2 Final reminder – check your work!
Direct students to read the Checklist, and then look at exercise 4.

4   Students work in pairs, or individually. Tell them to use the checklist and go through the sample answer carefully. Students should tick the following in the checklist:

Relevance (yes, the letter does answer the question satisfactorily)

Register (on the whole, it is fairly formal, but unfortunately, it ends informally)

Use of language (there are some careless mistakes in tenses at the beginning)

Range of vocabulary (fairly good, although some words are inappropriately used)

Spelling and punctuation (these are both very good, with only a few mistakes)

Organisation (yes, the answer is well organised)

Length (221 words, just within the lower limit)

Students should underline the following mistakes:
was asked; refrence; I know since; teach Maria for;
had; relates us; skilful; took up; entertained; serene;
efficiently, recommending you her; Yours. Suitable mark:
Answers will vary, but aim for band 3 or 4.

5   Direct students to read the question rubric. Brainstorm
    ideas about the key points to include in the answer.
    Students do this task individually.

TEACHING IN PRACTICE

Ways of revising vocabulary
You may wish to discuss vocabulary revision with your
students. Recap the different ways in which they can organise
this by eliciting ideas from the students themselves. Invite
questions on how they may capitalise on their revision time,
and draw their attention to items you have found effective
during the course, such as grouping words of similar meaning
together; words centred upon a theme; synonyms/antonyms;
word webs and spidergrams etc.

Photocopiable activity instructions

1 **Activity 16.1 Just a minute!**

Aim: Students practise sustaining a monologue describing their feelings about
a subject for one minute. This is relevant to the Paper 5, part 2 practice that
they will be doing in the Speaking section of this unit.

Instructions:

1   Photocopy the Just a minute! sheet and cut out the questions in
    the boxes.

2   Make sure you have a watch or clock with a hand that counts the seconds.

3   Hand out a question to each student. Tell them they must answer their
    question, describing their feelings and why they would feel that way, and
    keep talking for one minute.

4   Time each student, and interrupt them as soon as the minute is up.

2 **Activity 16.2 Advanced Particles Dominoes**

Aim: To revise phrases and collocations learned throughout the course book.
[Note: for ease of reference, all the word combinations used in
the game have been taken from the Language Development sections].

Instructions:

1   Photocopy the Advanced Particles Dominoes page, and cut out
    the square cards.

2   Students play in two teams. Deal each team 25 cards.

3   Toss a coin to see which team places a card on the table first.

4   The other team must match one of their cards to it to make
    a phrasal verb, noun, verb or adjectival phrase.

5   The winners are the first team to use up all their cards.

Just a minute!

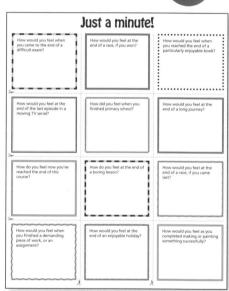

Advanced particles dominoes

pass	of	blame	to	ashamed
with	inform	bring	communication	over
accuse	about	turn	serious	eligible
away	authority	search	out	good
up	pull	convict	back	confide
derived	in	witness	by	contact
admit	through	take	access	for
look	off	alternative	on	arrest
from	deficient	from	keen	out of
obsessed	make	distressed	into	convinced

Tapescript 16

Listening 16.1

James: Here you are, Sally. I've finished it.

Sally: Hmm? Oh, *The Last Will*! Thanks, James. What did you think of it? Great, wasn't it?

James: Actually, I found it rather disappointing in comparison with his other books. Not so believable, if you know what I mean.

Sally: Really? I find that hard to believe. I thought it was by far his best ever! Far superior to *Waiting to Die* and *A Just Cause*, for instance.

James: I feel just the opposite. Compared to his first novel, the plot in this one is far fetched and unrealistic, to say the least …

Sally: You're joking! For a start, we see a lot more courtroom drama in this book, which is lacking from his others. They tend to focus purely on lawyers playing detective, which is not always very convincing.

James: It keeps things interesting, though, wouldn't you say?

Sally: Perhaps. But you have to admit that the courtroom drama in this novel lends weight to it, makes it even more believable.

James: Well, admittedly, the courtroom scenes are the most exciting in the book, quite gripping in places in fact, but the rest of the book is often slow and boring. I mean, all that description during the search in South Africa – I practically fell asleep!

Sally: But the protagonist is significantly more rounded and better developed here, wouldn't you say? The way we are led through his drug-induced self-pity to his struggle to redeem himself is cleverly created.

James: It was exactly this that I found just too good to be true! Our hero goes from being a total waster to becoming a knight in shining armour, against a background of support characters who are singularly wooden in their weakness and selfishness. They're nowhere near as realistic as the cast in A Just Cause, where good and bad qualities are more evenly shared out.

Sally: Funny! I didn't feel that way at all when I read it, and I thought you'd like it more than that. A pity …

Listening 16.2

Extract 1

Man: … For a while, it felt like we were on a second honeymoon. But then the quiet started getting to us.

Woman: Yes, well, I won't say I don't miss Mike, but quite frankly I was glad when he left to go to university. It was as if the house was no longer big enough for the both of us. We both like our independence, and I think the pressure of feeling responsible towards someone else was getting us both down.

Man: But don't you feel lonely in the house?

Woman: Well, that's just it. I like having the house to myself, but I can see Mike when we both feel like it. I also think it's good for him to know that I'm not waiting by the phone for his every call. That puts a hell of a lot of pressure on any child.

Man: Too right! Jan gets frantic if more than three days go by without a phone call from one of the boys, and I know that bugs Davy, in particular! I try to tell her to relax about it, that 'no news is good news', and all that.

Woman: Mmm, at their age, it can be restrictive to have to account for their movements all the time. They don't want to be thinking about us right now, but about enjoying themselves as much as possible …

Extract 2

Interviewer: So, how did you feel when you first retired?

Man: Guilty, basically.

Interviewer: Guilty? About what?

Man: The fact that I wasn't going to work. As the weeks went by, I became bored and irritable. The change was hard on my wife as well, because I started making demands on her time. I'd expected to do more things together, while she thought that she would go on as before, meeting up with her friends for coffee, going on shopping sprees, all without me. That was difficult for both of us. I had to find my own interests, and she had to make some room for me.

Interviewer: So how do you feel now?

Man: Well, I wonder how I ever had the time to go to work! I find I'm busy nearly all the time now. I think the secret to enjoying your retirement is firstly, health, and then having enough money to do the things you really want to do. Those two elements prevent you from being a burden on your children. Having a good circle of friends has helped. We see the kids when we can, of course, but we're not under their feet, and they're not under ours, either! So, life is fairly good now …

Extract 3

Woman: My decision to go out on my own was all about money. I was stuck in a poorly paid job, with virtually no prospects. I saw an opportunity and grabbed it. Being a Mum, however, I knew I'd need some kind of routine to my working day, and there'd be too many distractions at home! Difficult to ignore the pile of washing up in the sink, and the ironing waiting by the ironing board! So, I opened an office, and I think that was the key to making it work – keeping work and home separate.

Man: Yes, I can see that. Working at home just didn't work for me. I also found it stressful having to rely on myself for all the decision-making. Sometimes, I wanted to share ideas with someone, to get some feedback before putting things into operation, and there was no one. That began to get to me. Now, I'm back in an office, with other people around me, and I feel part of the team again.

Woman: That's it, I've never really been a team player. I like the independence of making my own decisions. I won't say it always works, but on the whole, we've got a better quality of life …

Answer key 16

Getting started p157

1 The end of a race; the destruction of a house, and a new building going up (in its place, perhaps?); the 'death' of a plant, and a new one growing; a couple kissing – perhaps the start of a new relationship? – at midnight on New Year's Eve – the end of one year, and the beginning of another; the rainbow signifying the end of the rain, and the beginning of a sunny day.

2 complete: a course, a form, a questionnaire, a plan, a race, a rescue operation, operations, production, school
cease: fire, production, trading
abort: a plan, a pregnancy, a rescue operation
discontinue: manufacturing a product, production
extinguish: a fire, hope
finish: a course, a race, school
finalise: a business deal, a contract, a plan
terminate: a business deal, a contract, a pregnancy
settle: a dispute, a lawsuit, an argument, differences

3 1 discontinued/ceased; 2 settle; 3 extinguish; 4 concluded/finished/completed; 5 terminate; 6 completed/finished; 7 finalising/finishing/completing; 8 finished; 9 abort; 10 cease

4 1 broke off; 2 – ; 3 put out; 4 rounded off; 5 break off; 6 wound up; 7 rounding off; 8 – ; 9 call off; 10 –

Reading pp158–9

3 1C; 2D; 3A; 4A+C

4 1 'Saying goodbye to the place that had been our home for 35 years was a huge wrench'; 'Heartbreaking though it was'; 'It was a very emotional time, and we didn't always see eye to eye'
2 'not allowing the glaring ethical dilemma to cloud my conscience';

'a documentary about the horrors of battery farming and the slaughterhouse shocked me out of my ignorance'
3 'Friends accused us of going too far, the kids blamed us for cutting them off from the rest of the world, but this was countered by the fact that my son lost ten pounds within a month'
4 'The last straw, however, came when my son was diagnosed as obese', 'Then my wife fell and broke her hip, and that clinched it.'

5 B

6 1B; 2D; 3E; 4C; 5A; 6A/D; 7A/D; 8C; 9E; 10B; 11A/E; 12A/E; 13D; 14A/B; 15A/B

7 a obese; b relegated; c dormant; d the box; e treadmill; f wrench; g that clinched (it); h professed; i forsaken; j slaughterhouse; k agonised; l heeded

8 the box; treadmill; wrench

Language development p160

1 Odd one out: a knowledge; b talk; c enthusiasm; d man; e mind; f temper; g the freedom; h the road

2 1b; 2a; 3a; 4a; 5a; 6b

3 1 disposed; 2 death; 3 draw; 4 close; 5 end

4 1 shocked me out of my; 2 wrong end of; 3 a confirmed bachelor; 4 the law down; 5 cloud my conscience; 6 to dispel rumours of

Grammar p161

1 a far more enjoyable than (ever before); b Nothing compares to; c significantly more expensive than; d wasn't so spectacular as; e The more … the healthier; f isn't nearly as tasty as

2 1 … is not nearly as happy …; 2 This is by far the best holiday …; 3 … is nowhere near as calm as …; 4 …was far more interesting than …; 5 … works a lot harder than …;

6 … considerably more time for …; 7 … a lot earlier, so he's got significantly more energy …; 8 … considerably longer to … than …

3 a much, a lot; b By far; c both … than; d never; e far

5 Answers will vary. Possible answers: The family have a lot more time to talk to each other than they did before. They are far more active than they were before. The children were not nearly as interested in talking about themselves when they had the TV. The son is considerably healthier than he was before. The children are significantly more interested in their daily lives than before.

6 1 not so/not as; 2 by far; 3 best; 4 compared to; 5 a lot more; 6 the most exciting; 7 significantly more; 8 nowhere near as

Use of English p162

3 1C; 2C; 3B; 4B; 5A; 6B; 7A; 8D; 9C; 10B; 11C; 12A

4 Answers may vary, but obvious ones are: 1=3; 2=8; 3=7; 4=11

Listening p163

1 1F; 2T

2 1B; 2C; 3C; 4A; 5A; 6B

Writing pp164–5

1 Say how you know the person/ your relationship to them; describe their character, qualities; talk about the skills/experience they possess which are relevant for the job/ position they are applying for; give reasons why you think they are suitable for the job/position.

2 'student of yours'; 'good at dealing with small children'; 'knowledge of first aid'; 'your student's character and personal qualities and skills'; 'previous relevant experience'; 'reasons why they should be considered'

3 Paragraph 2: Talk about their qualities and relevant skills, previous experience with children, and whether they know first aid. Paragraph 3: Emphasise the reasons why you think they are suitable for this job.

Vocabulary organiser 16 p166

16.1 a skinny; b promote; c useless; d doorknob; e trial; f confuse; g take up; h annoying; i teach; j provide; k be in pain; l involve

16.2 a drastic changes; b expounding theories; c dispel rumours; d confirmed bachelor; e shocked me out of my complacency; f staple ingredient; g cut off from the rest of the world; h cloud my conscience

16.3 1d; 2c; 3e; 4a; 5b

16.4 1 change; 2 good; 3 time; 4 confirmed; 5 drew

16.5 a single; b winked; c compulsive; d resulted; e transient; f emerged; g Although; h pull out; i consistent; j ran; k pleasure

Bank of English

rebuild (V); reconsider (V); reform (V/N); reformist (N/A); regain (V); regenerated (V/A); reintroduction (N); rejuvenate (V); relapse (V/N); remake (V/N); remix (V/N); renewal (N); reorganise (V); repeatable (A); replay (V/N)

Review 4 pp167–8

1 1 ludicrous; 2 ruthless;
3 contagious; 4 biodegradable;
5 compulsive; 6 incompatible;
7 baffled; 8 vague; 9 cursory;
10 obscene

2 1 pass out; 2 die out; 3 laid off;
4 drown out; 5 stands/stood out;
6 pass on/down; 7 wind up; 8 wore
me down

3 1 set fire to; 2 bogged down in;
3 got wind of; 4 deep water; 5 end of
my tether; 6 fell flat; 7 are at a loose
end; 8 let it pass

4 1 shock – d; 2 drastic – g;
3 expound – a; 4 confirmed – b;
5 staple – h; 6 cloud – c; 7 dispel – e;
8 (be) cut off – f

5 1 obsessed with; 2 immune to;
3 deficient in; 4 derived from;
5 eligible for; 6 ashamed of

6 1B; 2C; 3B; 4D; 5C; 6A

7 1 when; 2 theirs; 3 it; 4 that/
when; 5 with; 6 at; 7 instead; 8 This;
9 why; 10 if; 11 would; 12 their;
13 its; 14 but; 15 until

8 1 would rather cook something
fresh than; 2 would not/wouldn't
have learned so much; 3 would be
better if I/we found; 4 in spite of
the fact that; 5 had the lightning
struck when; 6 is significantly
more expensive than it; 7 is not/
isn't nearly as tasty as; 8 and
consequently he had

Review 4 Units 13–16

1 Complete the sentences below with a suitable adjective from the box below. There are two extra words you do not need to use.

baffled	biodegradable	compulsive	compatible
contagious	cursory	incompatible	ludicrous
obscene	pristine	ruthless	vague

1 I've heard some lame excuses in my time, but your story is utterly _____.
2 If you want to cut this down to fewer than two hundred words you're going to have to be _____.
3 Sally had to stay in her room for an extra day in case her measles were still _____.
4 You can throw the banana skin in the compost – it's completely _____.
5 I wouldn't believe a word Mike says – he's a _____ liar you know!
6 I'm not surprised Tim and Sue didn't get on – they're such _____ types!
7 I was a bit _____ by the puzzle until John showed me there was a simple solution.
8 I asked Peter what he thought of the film, but his answer was a bit _____.
9 Roger asked his teacher to check his work, but she only gave it a _____ glance.
10 I'm not going to repeat the _____ word that boy said to me!

2 Complete the sentences below with a verb from the box below in its correct form, and one or more particles to form a phrasal verb that means the same as the word in brackets.

| die | drown | lay | pass |
| pass | stand | wind | wear |

1 Miriam has been known to _____ _____ at the sight of a drop of blood. (faint)
2 If we don't do something soon, millions more species will soon _____ _____. (become extinct)
3 Over fifty workers were _____ _____ when the company started losing money. (made redundant)
4 I turned the music up but still couldn't _____ _____ the sound of the neighbours' arguing. (cover with sound)
5 Wilson, with his red hair and pale skin, always _____ _____ in a crowd. (is noticeable)
6 Lucy said she wanted to _____ _____ her diamonds to her great granddaughter. (leave in a will)
7 If you're not careful, you'll _____ _____ unemployed. (become as a result)
8 I told Jack I wasn't going to come, but he _____ me _____. (destroyed my resistance)

3 Replace the underlined part of the sentences that follow with an expression which uses the word in capitals.

1 When he was five, Bob nearly burnt the house. SET
2 He explained that he had become completely absorbed in the accounts. BOGGED
3 The party was supposed to be a surprise, but somehow Geoffrey heard about it. WIND
4 If you're not careful, both you and Martin are going to be in a lot of trouble! WATER
5 I couldn't cope any more – I had reached the limit of my patience! TETHER
6 It was supposed to be a joke but it failed to work as intended! FLAT
7 If you have nothing to do, I can give you a few chores. LOOSE
8 Will could have been really annoyed by what happened, but he decided to ignore it. PASS

4 Write down the word or phrase that completes the collocation in each of the sentences in the column on the left. Choose a further example of nouns that collocate with each group from the column on the right.

| cloud | confirmed | (be) cut off | dispel |
| drastic | expound | shock | staple |

1 _____ someone out of their ignorance   a a view / an idea
2 _____ action   b bachelor / atheist
3 _____ a theory   c mood / mind
4 _____ meat eater   d complacency / daydream
5 _____ diet   e the rumours / the fears
6 _____ my conscience   f civilisation / society
7 _____ the myth   g measures / changes
8 _____ from the rest of the world   h excuses / ingredient

5 Complete the gaps in the sentences with a suitable word from the box below and one suitable particle.

| ashamed | deficient | derived |
| eligible | immune | obsessed |

1 Lucinda has been _____ _____ this particular rock band for the past three years!
2 Rupert's _____ _____ to criticism; you can say what you like, but he won't care at all.
3 If you're _____ _____ vitamin C, you'll suffer from all kinds of problems.
4 This shampoo is _____ _____ various plant oils.
5 My next door neighbours are _____ _____ a building grant from the council.
6 Laura was so _____ _____ her brother's behaviour that she told him to walk home alone.

Review 4 Units 13–16

6 Choose the best word from the options A, B, C or D to complete each of the sentences below.

1 The human ear is unable to hear the dolphins' signals, but we have developed machinery which can pick _____ up.
   A these   C it
   B them   D those
2 One area of study that scientists are particularly interested in is _____ of communication between mother dolphins and their offspring.
   A such   C that
   B what   D one
3 I'd rather you _____ the bus every day instead of driving.
   A take   C were taking
   B took   D will take
4 _____ you had the chance to do one selfless act. What would it be?
   A As if   C Had
   B Were   D Suppose
5 _____ the fire, many birds lost their nests.
   A Because   C Due to
   B Consequently   D As a result
6 _____ it hadn't rained all week, I watered the garden.
   A Seeing as   C In case
   B Therefore   D Notwithstanding

7 PAPER 3, PART 1 For questions 1–15, read the text below and think of the word which best fits each gap. Use only one word in each gap.

Saturn runs rings round all the other planets

Why are Saturn's rings so astonishingly stunning? It could be that the planet managed to cling on to a moon (1) _____ all the other gas giants in our solar system had already lost (2) _____. Today's rings formed when the moon was shattered.

Astronomists at the university of Diderot, Paris, suggest (3) _____ was during the 'late heavy bombardment', 700 million years after Saturn formed. (4) _____ a fragment of debris collided (5) _____ one of the planet's moons. Because the moon was orbiting (6) _____ just the right distance from Saturn when it exploded – within what's known as the Roche limit – the tiny pieces created the rings (7) _____ of dispersing.

(8) _____ could explain (9) _____ other planets don't have rings like Saturn's. Even (10) _____ other planets had moons within their Roche limits at the birth of the solar system, the French astronomists' calculations show that the moons (11) _____ soon have been yanked down into the planet or unchained from (12) _____ orbits. Yet Saturn's rapid rotation meant it could hold a satellite within (13) _____ Roche limit until the bombardment.

Other astronomers around the world say the French way of showing Saturn's uniqueness among gas giants is, interesting, (14) _____ that their hypothesis cannot be proved (15) _____ we have better ways of replicating in model-form the evolution of the solar system.

8 PAPER 3, PART 5 For questions 1–8, complete the second sentence so that it has a similar meaning to the first sentence, using the word given. Do not change the word given. You must use between three and six words, including the word given.

1 Instead of finishing the leftovers, I'd prefer to cook something fresh.
   rather
   I _____ finish the leftovers.
2 Anthropologists have learned a lot about human behaviour by studying dolphins.
   so
   If anthropologists hadn't studied dolphins they _____ about human behaviour.
3 I'd sooner find out some things about their culture first.
   better
   It _____ out some things about their culture first.
4 Even though he hated cartoons, he agreed to watch it with the kids.
   fact
   He agreed to watch it with the kids _____ he hated cartoons.
5 No sooner had the lightning struck than all the lights went off.
   when
   Hardly _____ all the lights went off.
6 Two months ago this dress was quite a lot cheaper.
   significantly
   This dress _____ was six months ago.
7 My dad's pie is far tastier than this one.
   nearly
   This pie _____ the one my dad makes.
8 He had to get off the bus because he didn't have a valid ticket.
   consequently
   He didn't have a valid ticket _____ to get off the bus.

Just a minute!

How would you feel when you came to the end of a difficult exam?

How would you feel at the end of a race, if you won?

How would you feel when you reached the end of a particularly enjoyable book?

How would you feel at the end of the last episode in a moving TV serial?

How did you feel when you finished primary school?

How would you feel at the end of a long journey?

How do you feel now you've reached the end of this course?

How do you feel at the end of a boring lesson?

How would you feel at the end of a race, if you came last?

How would you feel when you finished a demanding piece of work, or an assignment?

How would you feel at the end of an enjoyable holiday?

How would you feel as you completed making or painting something successfully?

Advanced particles dominoes

pass	of	blame	to	ashamed
with	inform	bring	communication	over
accuse	about	turn	serious	eligible
away	authority	search	out	good
up	pull	convict	back	confide
derived	in	witness	by	contact
admit	through	take	access	for
look	off	alternative	on	arrest
from	deficient	from	keen	out of
obsessed	make	distressed	into	convinced

CAE set book

Writing about a set book
(Paper 2, part 2: question 5)

Teaching notes

Aim: The activity worksheets on page 161 and 162 are to be used if your students show an interest in studying for the optional question 5 in Paper 2, which asks them to write about one of the set books. This worksheet offers you some suggestions for generating interest and ideas among your students as they read. Since the set titles change regularly, we have kept the suggestions very general, so that you may adapt them to suit the particular book you choose to do.

1   Before embarking on the worksheet with your students, consider carefully how you want to tackle the reading of the set book. You may wish to ask students to read up to a point in the novel, and then elicit their views on it, before giving them the worksheet to complete. Alternatively, you could ask them to complete at least the character analysis activity as they read. Decide on a method that is suitable for both the book in question, and your students' capabilities.

2   Introduce your students to the question types that are used for question 5. These include an essay, a review, an article or a report. Remind students that if they choose to write about a set text, they should make sure they get practice in answering all the task types which are likely to appear. The question is likely to ask about the characters, relationships and themes in the book, and whether they would recommend it to others. They need to know the story fairly well, so that they can back up their views with examples from the book. When answering the question, they must think carefully about the target reader, and plan their answer accordingly. Remind them that question 5 is a part 2 question, so they will be expected to write between 220–260 words.

3   It is a good idea to pre-teach some key vocabulary connected with talking about literature, so that students can use this in their writing. Suggested words: *protagonist*; *plot*; *villain*; *sub-plot*; *central theme*; *climax*; *narrative*; *narrator*. Add any others that you consider relevant to the book in question.

4   Hand out a copy of the worksheet to each student.

Notes on activities

Activity one: Direct students to read the adjectives to describe character in Activity one. Tell them to decide which adjectives apply to the protagonist, and write down at least one example in the book where he or she displays this quality. Brainstorm further suitable adjectives that might be used for this character. This will help them build up a character study, and at the same time provide them with useful words to talk about the character. You could develop this to include other characters in the book. Set some time aside in the classroom for discussion, to allow students to brainstorm ideas.

Activity two: Once students are further along in their reading, they should be able to form ideas about the relationships between characters. Activity two shows only a diagram of the protagonist's relationship with other characters in the book. If there is more than one protagonist, you may wish to develop this. Ask students to examine the main characters' relationship with others in the book, and how they are affected by them. They should note down examples from the book to support their views.

Activity three and four: This asks them to examine the themes, and the relation between them. Where suitable, adapt this and look at how the central characters develop/ are affected by the central theme. The diagram could also be reproduced to examine the main plot in relation to sub-plots. There are various ways you could adapt this. It is a good idea to ask students to prepare some notes at home, and then brainstorm/discuss ideas in class, before they complete the diagram. For each activity, encourage them to make a list of useful vocabulary for writing about the book.

There is also a list of suggested writing tasks on the worksheet. You could ask students to do one as they complete each activity. In each case, elicit the required format for the task type, to make sure they know what is expected of them.

Set book activity worksheet

The set book question in Paper 2, part 2 will focus on your knowledge of the following: central characters (the protagonist/s), relationships, plot and themes within the book. Based on your reading, complete the three activities below. Then use the information you have gathered to practise answering the various writing tasks.

1 Character analysis

Add to the list of adjectives below:

afraid	cruel	immature	narrow-minded
brave	determined	insensitive	proud
confident	gentle	intelligent	self-centred
considerate	greedy	loving	weak

Name of protagonist (1)	Adjective	Evidence in the book
Name of protagonist (2)		

2 Relationships

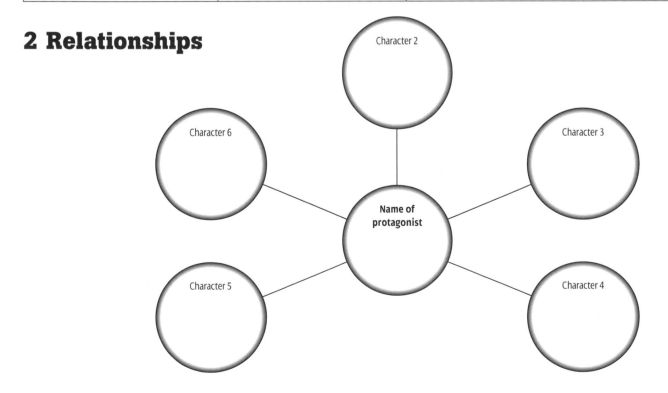

3 Themes

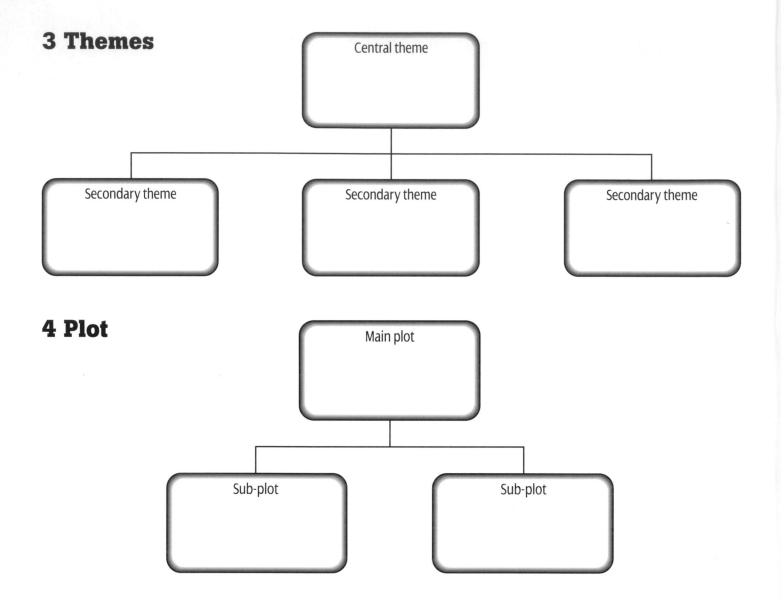

4 Plot

Sample questions

1 Your teacher has asked you to write an essay on the following topic, based on your reading of the book: 'The strength of the novel lies in the way the protagonist overcomes his initial weakness.' Discuss this statement in relation to the protagonist in the book you have been reading. Use examples from the book to illustrate your points.

   Write your essay.

2 Your teacher has asked your class to write a review of a book you have read examining how the relationship between two of the main characters affects developments in the story. You must include examples from the book to illustrate your views.

   Write your review.

3 The manager of the book store where you work has asked you to write a report on the popularity of certain themes in fiction. You have decided to write a report on the book you have been reading, outlining its main theme and why this interests readers of today.

   Write your report.

4 The literary supplement of your local newspaper has invited readers to send in articles in response to the following statement one of their regular critics made in a review recently: 'Why is the fictional hero nearly always so classically good? Can't we have a protagonist with weaknesses, for once?' You have decided to write an article in response to the statement, citing aspects of the protagonist's character in the novel you have been reading to illustrate your views.

   Write your article.

Exam Booster key

Unit 1

Getting started p1

1 **Across** 1 inaugurate
5 prompts
6 trigger
8 kick off
10 produce
11 launch
12 stimulate

Down 1 initiate
2 embark
3 provoke
4 establish
7 generate
9 found

Reading pp 2–3

1 a Text 3   b Text 2   c Text 1
2 1 C   2 B   3 D   4 C   5 C   6 D
3 1 The 'zeroists' were adamant that the new century started when 1899 gave way to 1900 ...
2 Others made their way to church or chapel, keeping the tradition of the night-watch service and listening in solemn silence for the first stroke of the midnight hour.
3 But a mouse cannot transmute into a cat. A fox cannot transmute into a penguin. A monkey cannot transmute into a human.
4 To ascertain by experimentation how fast each species learns from danger – then, perhaps, to take specimens on board, and see if their offspring really can receive their parents' newly acquired knowledge at birth.
5 ... undertaking environmental sampling, monitoring and assessment. Accountable for the data generated from your survey sampling and analysis
6 ... experience in the operation and maintenance of mechanical or electronic instrumentation being an advantage.
4 make up [one's] mind; make [one's] way; make a special study of

Language development p4

1 1 start from scratch, go back to the drawing board, start from square one
2 make a fresh start, turn over a new leaf, wipe the slate clean
2 1 f   2 g   3 i   4 a   5 e   6 b
7 h   8 j   9 c   10 d
3 1 made off
2 make it up to you
3 make out
4 made up
5 made off with
6 make up for

Grammar p5

1 1 had ever seen
2 had been walking
3 was listening
4 have never been
5 didn't call
6 takes
7 is going/is going to go
8 have been sitting
2 1 have eaten
2 was walking
3 has been working
4 broke
5 chopped
6 haven't read
7 is having
8 have you been doing

4 1 haven't forgotten
2 had expected
3 had been training
4 woke
5 was shining
6 put
7 waited
8 arrived
9 were already doing
10 have been training
11 marched
12 tossed
13 blew
14 passed
15 cheered
16 were putting
17 was beginning
18 saw
19 kicked
20 was

Listening p6

1 1 B   2 C   3 B   4 A   5 B   6 A

Use of English p7

1 1 I had had enough pie
2 have known each other for
3 (been) ages since we
4 has been under construction for
5 to make the most of
6 was three years before I heard
7 not as easy to get
8 make ends meet

Unit 2

Getting started p9

1 1 march
2 bound
3 heave
4 wade
5 clamber
6 wrestle
7 wander
8 tiptoe
The word 'movement' is spelt out.

Reading pp10–11

1 a Three people are mentioned.
b Two people speak.
c Joseph Hooper and his son, Edmund.
2 a **After gap 2:** 'But I came through ... He felt exonerated.'
After gap 5: 'Though he remembered ... the high windows.'
Paragraph A: 'Looking up now ... his own son was pale.'
Paragraph B: 'Mr Hooper coughed ... his own father.'
b the son
c A book he is reading, and a boy called Kingshaw, who bothers him.
3 1 D   2 B   3 G   4 F   5 E   6 A

Language development p12

1 1 down in the mouth
2 did not/didn't bat an eyelid
3 (just) gave me the cold shoulder
4 was all fingers and thumbs
5 is a pain in the neck
6 have never seen eye to eye
7 had a (brilliant) brainwave
8 too wet behind the ears.
2 1 take your pick
2 pick your brains
3 picked it up
4 picked her way
5 pick you up
6 pick up the pieces
7 picked holes in
8 picked up on

163

3 1 office 4 counter
  2 risk 5 engine
  3 story

Grammar p13

1 1 b 2 a 3 a 4 b 5 b
2 1a ... nine-year-old James Edwards is very talented.
  b ... very talented.
  2a ... is/has been rumoured that Mrs Reed is leaving the school.
  b ... is rumoured to be leaving the school.
  3a ... was thought/felt/believed that the new sports programme had benefited the school.
  b ... was believed to have benefited from the new sports programme.
  4a ... has been suggested that graphic novels could encourage children to read.
  b ... have been made that graphic novels could encourage children to read.
  5a ... is often assumed that an only child will be selfish.
  b ... are often made that an only child will be selfish.
3 (Possible answers) 1 had her camera
  2 is having/getting his washing machine
  3 get/have her hair
  4 had/got our sitting room window
  5 his hand

Listening p14

1 1 visually stimulating 5 stepping stone
  2 novels 6 three
  3 Tokyo/Japan 7 mixed abilities
  4 poetry 8 practical

Use of English p15

1 1 perception 5 method
  2 unconscious 6 entrusting
  3 imbued 7 findings
  4 instincts 8 incentive
2 1 D 2 C 3 A 4 B 5 C 6 B
  7 B 8 C 9 A 10 B 11 D 12 A

Writing p16

1 Underline: 'describing the services it provides'; 'stating whether all the added services are really useful'; and 'saying who you would recommend your choice of mobile phone to and why'.
2 Example b is the best (Example a threatens to be irrelevant by becoming a report and examining 'different types of mobile phone' when the question asks for one; Example c is too informal and vague in style).
3 The sample conclusion is unsuitable because it fails to follow the instructions in the question rubric.

Unit 3

Getting started p17

1 a white water rafting; b yacht racing; c snowboarding;
  d triathlon; e mountain climbing

Reading p18–19

1 1 B 2 D 3 C 4 A 5 D 6 D 7 C

Language development p20

1 a down c down
  b up d up
  e up g down
  f up h up
2 a takes after e taken [you] for
  b take over f take apart
  c take back g took to
  d take on h taken up
3 a lying down e the wind out of my/his/her sails
  b it or leave it f with a pinch of salt
  c the bull by the horns g it out of you
  d hat off to her h it from me

4 game

Grammar p21

1 1 B 2 C 3 D 4 A
2 1 e 2 f 3 a 4 b 5 h
  6 i 7 j 8 d 9 g 10 c
3 a 1 b 2, 4, 5 c 3 d 6, 7, 10 e 8, 9
4 1 a 2 b

Listening p22

1 **certainty:** definite, confident, secure, unambiguous
  uncertainty: doubtful, unconvinced, hesitant, cynical
  positive feelings: exuberant, delighted, elated, thrilled
  negative feelings: frustrated, annoyed, irked, exasperated
2 1 A 2 C 3 B
3 1 A 2 B 3 D

Use of English p23

1 1 against 9 could/might
  2 than 10 which/that
  3 for 11 after/during
  4 with 12 instead
  5 same 13 receive/win
  6 each 14 final
  7 under/within 15 such
  8 be

Unit 4

Getting started p25

1 A Cretaceous, evolution, erosion, fossils, geology, Jurassic, tyrannosaurus rex
  B artificial intelligence artificial life, cells, DNA, genetics, laboratory, microchip, nanotechnology, $E=MC^2$, forensic
  C sci-fi, androids, robotic implants, virtual reality
  D cortex, grey matter, neurology
  E black hole, dark matter, extraterrestrial, supernova
2 a palaeontology f psychology
  b android g cortex
  c nanotechnology h dark matter;
  d extra terrestrial i artificial intelligence
  e DNA j grey matter

Reading p26

1 1 B 2 C 3 A 4 B 5 C 6 D
  7 D 8 A 9 B 10 D 11 A 12 C
  13 B 14 D 15 A

Language development p28

1 a target b cognitive c suppressing
d accomplice e communal f conducive
g hamper h con i testimonial
j calibrated

2
1	began to tell	5	I told you so
2	tell them apart	6	only time will tell
3	tell on	7	never can tell
4	as far as I can tell	8	telltale

3
a	blue	i	black
b	red	j	green
c	green	k	blue
d	red	l	greener
e	blue	m	blue
f	black	n	black
g	red	o	red
h	red	p	blue

4 **red**: in the red; see red; be caught red-handed; red tape; red herring
blue: out of the blue; (talk) till you're blue in the face; feel blue; once in a blue moon; like a bolt from the blue
black: black mark; black humour; be on a black list;
green: green fingers; green with envy; the grass looks greener on the other side

Grammar p29

1 1 a 2 b 3 a 4 b 5 b 6 b 7 a

2 a in ten minutes d as soon as
b in three weeks' time e until then
c by then

3
1 are you going to do about
2 is bound to pass
3 what the future will hold
4 will have been doing/in business
5 'll/will be waiting (for you) outside
6 are on the point of discovering
7 is/will be coming to help us
8 is going to

Listening p30

1 1 E 2 F 3 H 4 B 5 A 6 H
7 C 8 A 9 F 10 G

Use of English p31

1 Gaps 2 and 4

2
1	inevitably	6	living
2	unhealthy	7	typically
3	epidemiologists	8	ceaseless
4	unexpected	9	overreact
5	findings	10	implications

Writing p32

1 Underline: 'Read the extract below and comments from members of the public, and write an article for the magazine, referring to the points raised and describing your own view of the future of shopping'; 'Read them, and send us your views in an article entitled, 'Is high street shopping a thing of the past?'; 'It's so much easier to order my books online'; 'You can find things reasonably priced, and you save time'; 'Shopping is one of my favourite activities, and I love to browse'; 'Online shopping means avoiding parking fees, and crowds'; 'Going shopping gives me the chance to meet up with friends.'

2 (Possible answers) Paragraph 1: Introduction, referring to the survey conducted.

Paragraph 2: refer to comments made in favour of online shopping, and my response.
Paragraph 3: refer to comments made in favour of high street shopping, and my response.
Paragraph 4: Conclusion. My overall view of the future of high street shopping.

Unit 5

Getting started p33

1
1	fraud	9	virus
2	arson	10	convict
3	crimeware	11	implicate
4	sentence	12	murder
5	hacking	13	kidnapping
6	confess	14	victim
7	incriminate	15	charge
8	acquit		

The phrase in the central column is 'forensic science'.

Reading pp34–35

1 1 F 2 C 3 A 4 E 5 B 6 G

Language development p36

1 1 b 2 a 3 a 4 b 5 b 6 b
7 d 8 c 9 a 10 d

2 1 T 2 F 3 T 4 T 5 F 6 T
7 F 8 F

3 1 enforce 3 break
2 obey 4 lay down

4 1 b 2 a 3 c

Grammar p37

1
1	racing	9	to kill
2	to drop	10	seeing
3	to do	11	to find
4	to ram	12	to steal
5	to board	13	chasing
6	to knock	14	to head
7	to tie	15	to continue
8	to defend		

Listening p38

1 1 d 2 b 3 f 4 e 5 a 6 c

2
1	the risk	5	dignity
2	website	6	(unfair) criticism
3	probation officers	7	small
4	regular contact	8	the unexpected

Use of English p39

1
1	instruments	4	conviction
2	law	5	turned
3	profile		

Speaking p39

1 (Possible answers): The facilities: attractive shops, cafeterias, bars, restaurants, and also cinemas, and a theatre, without the chaos of a big city.
The atmosphere: constant buzz of conversation and laughter, without the intrusive noise of the traffic!
Access to other places: it is easy to escape the town to the country.

Writing p40

1 (Possible answers): The notes are irrelevant for this question and too knowledge specific, and there is no organisation of ideas. The student has misunderstood part of the input material, has failed to use it effectively, and has not created headings for each paragraph.

2 (Possible answers): Paragraph 1: Introduction (purpose of the report).
Paragraph 2: Use of mobile phones (approximately 75% of students have a mobile phone; They must switch them off in the classroom).
Paragraph 3: Potential dangers (unknown, but possible brain damage, and increased risk of disease from long-term exposure).
Paragraph 4: Recommendations (teachers give talks advising students on the dangers of using phones too much; students switch off phones as soon as they arrive at school, and only switch them on again when the final bell rings).

Unit 6

Getting started p41

1 a acupuncture   b aromatherapy
   c herbalism   d homeopathy
   e reflexology   f meditation
2 1 herbalism   4 homeopathy
   2 acupuncture   5 reflexology
   3 aromatherapy   6 meditation
3 1 aromatherapy
   2 homeopathy
   3 acupuncture

Reading p42–43

1 Text 1: reflexology;   Text 2: Ayurveda;
Text 3: maggot debridement therapy
2 1 D   2 A   3 A   4 B   5 C   6 B
3 1 complementary   4 potential
   2 consultant   5 infested
   3 superficial   6 yuck factor

Language development p44

1 1 b   2 b   3 a   4 a   5 b   6 b
2 1 lifelong friends   7 a lifetime's ambition
   2 lay down their lives   8 a matter of life and death
   3 life-threatening illness   9 life-jackets
   4 fact of life   10 a new lease of life
   5 have the time of their lives
   6 the life and soul of the
     party

Grammar p45

1 1 If you were to go to America ...
   2 Should you see Garry in town ...
   3 As long as you eat all your green vegetables ...
   4 If you happen to find ...
   5 But for Julian's intervention ...
   6 Had you been invited ...
   7 Even if you had been on time/hadn't been late ...
2 1 had remembered/wouldn't have run out
   2 had/would be able to
   3 walks/will be
   4 hadn't driven/could have got
   5 had taken/would be
   6 comes/will have
   7 was/didn't he fill
   8 runs out/stops

Listening p45

1 1 C   2 B   3 C   4 D   5 A   6 B

Speaking p46

1 These pictures both show ...; ... while the other picture ...; The main similarity/difference between the two pictures is that ...

Use of English p47

1 1 D   2 B   3 B   4 D   5 A   6 A
   7 B   8 C   9 D   10 A   11 B   12 B

Unit 7

Getting started p49

1 1 trip   6 package holiday
   2 safari   7 voyage
   3 excursions   8 flight
   4 ride   9 travel
   5 cruise   10 journey
2 a 2   b 5   c 4   d 8

Reading p50

1 1 C   2 A/D   3 A/D   4 B   5 A   6 C
   7 D   8 A/C   9 A/C   10 B   11 A/D   12 A/D
   13 B   14 A/C   15 A/C

Language development p52

1 1 C   2 B   3 C   4 A
2 1 like the look of it   5 looked him in the eye
   2 much to look at   6 overlook
   3 get a look-in   7 look ahead
   4 look the other way   8 by the looks of it
3 a roadhouse   b road rage   c road test   d roadside
   e road hog   f road map   g road works   h road block
   i road sign   j road show

Grammar p53

1 a the rope would never   b was she aware   c than
   d should you leave   e he had left   f have we seen
   g failed   h had they arrived   i am I to be
   j had finished
2 1 Only later were the details of the scandal made known ...
   2 No sooner had we arrived than ...
   3 Barely had the concert started ...
   4 Seldom do you see ...
   5 On no account must you ...
   6 Never have I seen ...
   7 Scarcely had Gina walked ...
   8 Not only is he a musician, but also ...
3 1 had just come out when
   2 have checked your passport will you
   3 had the plane taken off when
   4 time did Tom apologise
   5 the bus driver stopped did he

Listening p54

1 1 E   2 G   3 B   4 F   5 H   6 C
   7 A   8 F   9 D   10 G

Use of English p55

1 1 not   6 obtaining/gaining/
   2 this/it   acquiring/getting
   3 However/Nevertheless   7 had
   4 eventually/finally   8 one
   5 would   9 although/while

10 but
11 rather/fairly/particularly
12 let

13 this
14 never/previously
15 which/that

Speaking p55

1 (Possible answers): **Package tour operators:** 'suddenly, people from lower social classes could travel abroad. No longer was it reserved just for the rich'; 'this led to more hotels and guest houses being built, and generated business in coastal areas. Of course, the downside of this has been that these areas became very spoilt by overcrowding and pollution'; 'package tour operators tend to flood an area with visitors ...'

The Internet: 'an even wider range of choices, and what was fashionable last year has been replaced this year by another destination'; 'websites promote particular kinds of holidays, and reach more people, since it is a lot easier to sit at home and surf the net looking for a holiday ...'

Writing p56

1 Underline: 'Then, using the information carefully, write a proposal, suggesting the best ways to update the company website'; 'colourful home page with photos from holidays, comprehensive drag down contents list'; 'Holidays separated into 3 main categories – Family Adventure, Extreme Adventure, Expeditions – click on photo for each'; 'Features section, and Last Minute Offers'

2 (Possible answers): **Proposal to update website**
   1 Colourful Homepage: photos from holidays (visually stimulating/appealing comprehensive drag down contents list; give easy access to inexperienced computer users)
   2 Three main holiday categories: Family Adventure, Extreme Adventure, Expeditions (click on relevant photo to go to category page; clear instructions for easy access, so that user knows what to expect)
   3 Special Features and Last Minute Offers section: This section will allow company to focus on particular promotions, or last minute offers on holiday places that need to be sold.

Unit 8

Getting started p57

1 1 The Great Sphinx of Giza
   2 Stonehenge
   3 The Parthenon
   4 The Eiffel Tower
   5 The Statue of Liberty
2 A4   B3   C1   D5   E2

Reading pp58–59

1 1 C   2 B   3 C   4 B   5 D   6 A   7 B

Language development p60

1 1 brought home to me
   2 brought him to his knees
   3 bring your characters to life
   4 brought back to me
   5 bring me to eat
   6 has brought triplets into the world
2 1 bring down   4 bring off
      [the government]   [running a business]
   2 correct   5 bring out [the best]
   3 bring in [enough money]
3 11 times; a 2   b 5   c 2   d 0   e 2
4 7 times

Grammar p60

1 1 by which time
   2 whose cat
   3 correct
   4 neither of whom
   5 who/that you were ...
   6 correct
   7 where I was born/in which/that I was born in
   8 correct
2 1 ND 2 ND 3 D 4 ND 5 D
3 1 point   5 neither
   2 case   6 both
   3 time   7 which
   4 result   8 whom

Listening p61

1 a Speaker 3 b Speaker 2 c Speaker 1
2 1 B   2 C   3 A   4 C   5 C   6 A

Use of English p63

1 1 ventilation   6 survival
   2 organism   7 diligence
   3 inhabitants   8 construction
   4 colony   9 utilisation
   5 harshness   10 estimation

Writing p64

1 1 a brochure for tourists
   2 semi-formal/neutral
   3 a description of a national historical monument in your country and why they are interesting for tourists to visit
   4 Suggestions could include the name of the monument, the area, the history etc.
2 1 amphitheatre   7 mythology
   2 architecture   8 entertainment
   3 construction   9 earthquakes
   4 spectators   10 symbol
   5 spectacles   11 attractions
   6 contests   12 procession
3 elliptical, largest, greatest, ruined, iconic, popular
4 The Colosseum, History, Present condition
   Other headings: Function, Design, Builders

Unit 9

Getting started p65

1 a 2   b 1   c 5   d not used   e 6
   f 4   g not used   h 3

Reading p66–67

1 1 C   2 B   3 C   4 A   5 D   6 B

Language development p68

1 1 c   2 f   3 h   4 b   5 d   6 a
   7 g   8 e
2 1 d   2 a   3 j   4 b   5 h   6 i
   7 f   8 c   9 g   10 e
3 a pay me a compliment   d pay my respects
   b paid through the nose   e paid tribute to
   c pay [you] back
4 1 pay you back   4 paying out on
   2 pay out   5 paid him off
   3 pay this cheque into

Listening p69

1 (Possible answers): 1 pages with simple, clear titles and headings
   2 long texts
   3 information in bullet-pointed lists and use sub-headings etc
   4 using PDFs for general product information
   5 photos of product/prices of product
2 1 D 2 B 3 C 4 A 5 B 6 B

Grammar p70

1 (Possible answer): 'When we are obliged to read, because of computers, we expect the words to be arranged in helpful modules, with plenty of graphics.'
2 1 a2 b1
   2 a1 b2
   3 a1 b2
3 1 How he manages to run six miles after a full day's work
   2 Easy though the job may seem
   3 What you should do is buy
   4 (It's quite simple.) All you need to do is (to)
   5 Where he gets his bad temper from
4 a What did Sarah do? b What did Sarah steal (from the boutique on the corner)? c Where did Sarah steal a dress from? d Who stole a dress from the boutique on the corner? E Who saw Sarah steal a dress? F Where did Sarah hide the dress?

Use of English p71

1 1 all you do is tell him
   2 paid a tribute to
   3 Mandy, it was Peter (not Harry)
   4 though she may be
   5 what I like most (of all)
   6 but for Mr. Smith's
   7 never before have I been
   8 has not/hasn't spoken to her grandfather

Speaking p71

1 First, talk to each other about how each style might attract young people. Then, decide which two would be the most successful.
2 'Don't you agree?'; 'What about this idea of advertising posters from the 1960s?'; 'Do you think young people would be interested in this?'; 'Yes, but isn't that really for smaller kids?'; 'How about this design for the environment idea?'; 'Do you think the Graffiti idea any good?'; 'What do you think of it, Enrique?'; 'So, which ones do you think would make the most successful exhibitions?'
3 'I'm not so sure that many will be interested'; 'Yes, but isn't that really for smaller kids? I can't imagine'; 'I'm afraid I can't agree with you there'; 'Yes, but often too much. Think Green is everywhere'; 'I wonder if it might attract more boys than girls, though?'; 'Do you really think so? I have to say ...'; 'but I'm sure you won't agree with me!'; 'But the adverts don't appeal to me'.

Writing p72

1 (Possible answers): Reason 1: Graphic novels increasingly popular. Justification: More serious graphic novels for adults show that interest in the genre is growing.
   Reason 2: Graphic illustrators have developed exciting styles, and Kishimoto's work is considered among the best.
   Justification: He has developed his own distinctive style.
   Reason 3: The popularity of his graphic books. Justification: The number of websites covering his work stand testimony to his popularity, and many young artists try to emulate his style of manga drawing.

Unit 10

Getting started p73

1 a material wealth   b Good health   c Social standing
   d A good job/career   e A happy family   f Personal success

Reading pp74–75

1 1 F 2 C 3 B 4 G 5 E 6 A

Language development p76

1 1 strains
   2 alarm
   3 up
   4 line
   5 toll
2 a to pull out (of)   b to pull on/at   c to pull off
   d to pull down   e to pull over   f to pull away/out
   g to pull (something) together   h to pull through   i to pull back
   j to pull (something) apart

Listening p76

1 1 E 2 A 3 D 4 G 5 B 6 C
   7 H 8 F 9 A 10 E

Grammar p77

1 1 Jenny told Ed that she wished they could go on holiday the following week.
   2 Michael asked if/whether he could have a salad for lunch.
   3 Mum wanted to know if/whether I/we had any homework to do.
   4 Philip said it was the best meal he had eaten this/that year.
2 1 [It] wasn't me who broke the porcelain vase!
   2 I'm paying for lunch. [Anyway,] it's my birthday.
   3 [You] spoiled the surprise party we had planned for Dad!
3 1 begged Sara not to leave
   2 threatened to tell Mum
   3 advised Jim to get his arm seen (to)
   4 admitted to having [had]/that he had had
   5 mother encouraged her to take
   6 blamed Tony for the fact that
   7 complained that his beer was warm
4 1 decided to wear/put on
   2 dismay that he was
   3 Feeling slightly hurt
   4 he liked
   5 couldn't see what
   6 that she had already decided to wear
   7 that they couldn't go
   8 annoyed
   9 she had a number of dresses
   10 him he was being ridiculous
   11 that if he was going to wear
   12 wouldn't go

Speaking p78

1 **Student 1** Contrast: The second picture is a bit different because ...
   Express an opinion: I don't think she is getting much work done ...; However, if you ask me ...
   Student 2 Compare: They are all pictures of ...
   Describe: This one shows ...; Here we can see ...
   Speculate: I guess it is Switzerland ...; He must be very excited ...; I suppose you would get ...

2 a 2 woman working at home, sitting at a desk with a computer and phone. Behind her the door is open and a child is standing at the door. Toys are strewn across the carpet and a baby is crawling towards her. She is looking at the toddler.
b 1 an alpine lodge, mountains covered with snow, fir-trees scattered around, someone in ski-suit; 2 a [Bedouin] tent in the desert, camels in the background, perhaps an oasis

Use of English p79

1 (Possible answers): She decided to play the songs in alphabetical order; Martin received an order from his Captain; Jesse ordered chicken but was served veal.
The students were presented with the award for Best Dressed Class; I presented my ticket to the guard but he wouldn't let me onto the platform; May I present Lady Smythe, my Lord.

2 1 inch   3 mental   5 range
   2 luck   4 pull   6 shook

Writing p80

1 a explain/give advice/   b local residents
      make recommendations
   c formal/semi-formal

4 a take showers rather than baths, turn off the water while soaping ourselves, use the washing machine less, use washing machines and dishwashers that have good water economy, recycle water used for washing hands; b avoid using a hose in hot weather, avoid watering during the day, avoid washing the car or yard unless essential and use a bucket when doing so, collect rainfall water; c pass the leaflet on to help others save water.

Unit 11

Getting started p81

1 a workaholic   b consumer   c debt
   d identity theft   e expenditure   f transaction
   g accountant   h credit card fraud i finance
   j invest

Reading pp82–83

1 1 C   2 B   3 B   4 D   5 B   6 C   7 C
2 a sequence b spin c fortune d inane e mechanically
   f ostensibly g random h implication i adept
   j incredulous k close shave l composure

Language development p84

1 a your mind b place c money d the blue e luck
2 1 put out   4 hand out
   2 find out   5 sort out
   3 work out
3 a Nouns: outback, outbuilding, outboard, outburst, outcome, outcry, outfall, outfit, outfitters, outflow, outgrowth, outgoings, outhouse, outing, outlay, outlet, outline, outlook etc.
   b Verbs: outclass, outflank, outfox, outgrow, outguess, outgun, outlast, outlaw, outline, outlive, outmanoeuvre, outnumber, outpace, outshine, outwit etc.
   c Adjectives: outgoing, outlandish, outmoded, outnumbered, out of touch, out of date, outlying, outrageous, outright, outstanding, outstretched, outspoken etc.
   d (Possible answers): The school has a large outdoor swimming pool in its grounds; It's such a lovely day that you should be outdoors playing football, not sitting in front of the computer.
4 a raise money   b not made of money
   c pumped money into   d save money
   e money is no object   f put your money where your
                                    mouth is

g have money to burn   h Money talks
i got our money's worth   j throw money

Listening p85

1 1 means   5 income
   2 unforeseen emergencies 6 four
   3 five   7 habits
   4 chart   8 budget

Grammar p86

1 1 resignation   6 criticism
   2 prediction   7 resignation
   3 criticism   8 annoyance
   4 annoyance   9 plan
   5 plan   10 prediction
2 1 might have/could have 4 could
   2 wouldn't be   5 will
   3 would
3 1 will be/is going to be
   2 will buy/get
   3 will (all) have
   4 might have killed/run over/hit
   5 will keep
   6 may/might as well

Use of English p87

1 1 D   2 B   3 A   4 C   5 B   6 D
   7 C   8 C   9 B   10 C   11 A   12 D

Speaking p87

1 (Possible answers): a 'I agree with you to a certain extent, but ...'; 'I think you've got a point, but ...'; 'To a point, you're right, but I have to say ...'; b 'I'm afraid I can't agree with you there'; 'Personally, I don't feel that way'; 'I think there's another way of looking at it'; 'Perhaps, but I think there's another way of looking at it'; 'I don't think that's true for everyone ...'

Writing p88

2 (suggested answer) **Introduction**
The aim of this report is to examine the issues surrounding the workers' complaints, and to make some recommendations for improving the current situation.

Exposure to chemicals in a poorly ventilated environment

It was discovered that due to production demands and recent cutbacks in the workforce, workers are now working for more than three hours at a time without a break, and are constantly exposed to fumes from the paint chemicals. As the ventilation filters are damaged, air is not circulating effectively on the factory floor. We need to ensure that workers have a fifteen-minute break every one and a half hours, during which they should leave the factory floor. The air filters should be replaced, and checked more regularly.

Protective clothing

Furthermore, the clothing currently provided to the workers for their protection is sadly inadequate. The overalls are faded and worn, and the facial masks fail to give workers sufficient protection from the hazardous fumes. Providing workers with new overalls, and masks with air filters would ensure they are not affected by chemical fumes while working.

Conclusion

As can be seen from the points raised above, there are several problems facing workers at present. However, with the implementation of the improvements suggested, the situation will soon improve, to the satisfaction of workforce and management alike.

Unit 12

Getting started p89

1
1 blockbuster	8 plot
2 musical	9 photography
3 screenplay	10 director
4 setting	11 trailer
5 documentary	12 script
6 cast	13 thriller
7 actor	14 lyrics

The word 'cinematography' is spelt out.

Reading pp90–91

1　a irony (n); ironic (adj); ironically (adv)
　　b sarcasm (n); sarcastic (adj); sarcastically (adv)

2　1 C　2 B　3 D　4 C　5 A/D　6 D/A
　　7 B　8 A　9 C　10 A　11 B　12 D
　　13 A　14 C　15 D

3　1 take the reins
　　2 pin (something) down
　　3 a means to an end
　　4 to bridge the gap (between)
　　5 to climb through the ranks

4
1 period-piece	4 genre
2 dot-com	5 apprentice
3 digital	

Language development p92

1　(Possible answers): 1 painful　2 beautiful　3 slow
　　4 dull/boring　5 devoted　6 natural

2　1 d　2 e　3 a　4 c　5 b

3
1 perplexingly named
2 especially under-powered
3 coolly ruthless agent
4 coldly suppressed rage
5 crash-bang Bond
6 deafening episodes
7 similarly powerful vehicle
8 baffling decision
9 thrilling music
10 short, sharp, bone-cracking bursts
11 cool, cruel presence
12 perpetually semi-pursed
13 some new nastiness
14 smart elegance
15 conventional action
16 indefinably difficult task

Listening p93

1　1 C　2 B　3 B　4 A　5 C　6 B

Speaking p93

1　Picture 1: people at the opera
　　Picture 2: someone reading a book
　　Picture 3: people at the cinema
　　Picture 4: young people at a concert
　　Picture 5: people watching TV
　　Picture 6: people playing computer games

Grammar pp94–95

1　1 e　2 f　3 a　4 c　5 g　6 h
　　7 d　8 b

2　1 b　2 c　3 a　4 b　5 a　6 d
　　7 c　8 b　9 a　10 c　11 d　12 c
　　13 b　14 a

3
1 Cynthia and I, both fans of …
2 The film, directed by Woody Allen had received … / Directed by Woody Allen, the film had received …
3 Having been given …
4 Crossing the road …
5 Dick and Isabella, good friends of Cynthia's, who we invited
6 Arriving at the cinema
7 Not wanting to go …
8 Having already seen the film she
9 Not wanting to see
10 nearby restaurant run by an Italian couple

Use of English p95

1　They admire it as an icon.

2
1 preposition of time
2 adjective before noun
3 preposition
4 auxiliary verb
5 conjunction (particle expressing comparison)
6 adjective (preceded by a possessive)
7 particle after noun
8 verb (simple present, third person plural)
9 adjective after noun
10 adverb
11 particle before noun
12 particle (forming phrasal verb)
13 modal auxiliary
14 adjective (defining adjective before noun)
15 relative pronoun

3
1 after	6 own	11 in
2 such	7 of	12 together
3 without	8 is	13 must/should
4 have	9 else	14 other
5 than	10 more/again	15 which/that

Writing p96

3　Points mentioned: an outline of the story, a description of the characters, what you liked about it, background information, the writer, director or actors, how successful it was

4　1 d　2 e　3 c　4 a　5 b

5　1 e　2 a　3 c　4 f　5 d　6 b

Unit 13

Getting started p97

2 publicise

Reading pp98–99

1　1 D　2 B　3 G　4 A　5 E　6 C

Language development p100

1　a to;　b for;　c of;　d of;　e into

2
1 of		5 of
2 to		6 with
3 to		7 of
4 to		8 over

3
1 be settled in certain habits and find it difficult to change
2 don't approve of
3 is due to
4 a fixed choice of food
5 is determined to

4　1 f　2 b　3 j　4 d　5 a
　　6 e　7 g　8 c　9 h　10 i

5 1 set in   4 set back
    2 set off   5 set down
    3 setting aside

Listening p101

1 1 G   2 E   3 A   4 B   5 H   6 D
    7 A   8 F   9 C   10 G

Grammar p102

1 1 playing football, cycling and picking blackberries
    2 the fact that he told the class
    3 the difficulty people have (in expressing their feelings)
    4 the various ways
    5 writing a letter and phoning

2 1 It   4 It
    2 There   5 It
    3 there

3 1 First   9 by
    2 This   10 It
    3 whereas   11 These
    4 such   12 This
    5 They   13 which
    6 of   14 both
    7 which   15 for
    8 This

Use of English p102

1 1 get   4 set
    2 word   5 sound
    3 foreign

Speaking p103

1–2 (Rahul's actual answers):
    1 Yes, but the students can learn a lot of things from the computer, and there are interactive programmes as well ...
    2 I see your point, but I think it's useful for students to have access to computers, and particularly the internet, at school, because they can use them to find out information, and the teachers can show their students clips, etcetera, which can start a discussion in class ...
    3 Yes, I do. For the same reason as the computers. Satellite TV means that students can watch such channels as BBC World. I have this at home, and it's really good, because you can learn things. Again, teachers can use it to give students listening practice, and for discussion. Today, I think students find it easier to respond to pictures – you know? computers, TV – than they do to something they read ...
    4 OK, maybe you're right, but in the language classroom, pictures help students understand certain things, and I think they are easier to respond to. For that reason, I think the computers and the TV are useful tools. What about the group trip to England? That would be fun, wouldn't it?

Writing p104

1 1 b   2 b   3 a
2 1 b   2 a   3 c
3 Teenagers are no longer children, but neither are they completely adults; they have to make decisions about their future; they want more freedom; they have to study, and need advice; parents don't understand them; parents find it difficult to accept that their child has grown up
4 (Possible answers):
Paragraph 1: Introduction/No Longer Children
Paragraph 2: Problems Communicating
Paragraph 3: Practical Solutions/Solutions that Work
Paragraph 4: Conclusion/A Final Word

Unit 14

Getting started p105

1 **Down** 1 primate   **Across** 2 ape
    2 amphibian   5 insect
    3 mammal   6 invertebrate
    4 reptile   8 fish
    7 bird

2 Planet Earth

3 1 f tuna   5 a worm
    2 c snake   6 g pterosaur
    3 h platypus   7 d goose
    4 b spider   8 e spider monkey

Reading pp106–107

1 1 D   2 D   3 C   4 B   5 C   6 A   7 B
2 1 vacuum   5 whopping
    2 cluster   6 diminishing
    3 clutch   7 colossally
    4 frighten the daylights   8 randomly
       out of someone

Language development p108

1 1 out of the woods   4 in deep water
    2 get wind of   5 bogged down in
    3 clear the air   6 the tip of the iceberg
2 1 of   6 about
    2 with   7 with
    3 for   8 about
    4 with   9 to
    5 to   10 of
3 1 c   2 g   3 e   4 h   5 i   6 f
    7 b   8 j   9 a   10 d

Grammar p109

1 1 h   2 j   3 b   4 f   5 g   6 a
    7 i   8 c   9 d   10 e
2 1 I didn't have much money, so I didn't travel around the world.
    2 I did watch a lot of TV, so I didn't read very much.
    3 I studied French instead of Spanish so I went to France/ didn't go to Spain.
    4 He didn't work hard enough so he didn't pass his course.
3 1 hadn't gone   6 stayed
    2 could have been   7 might have got
    3 might/would never   8 could save
       have met   9 had
    4 had never seen   10 got
    5 would probably never
       have got
4 1 is (high/about) time you stopped wasting
    2 wish you had come/could have come
    3 as though he were
    4 had better take some
    5 wish I knew how Sara was
    6 would sooner you called me
    7 only I had gone sky-diving
    8 would rather you helped

Listening p110

1 1 ecosystems   5 6.5 billion
    2 wiped out   6 90 million
    3 viruses [and] parasites   7 policies
    4 five planets   8 side-effects

Use of English p111

1
1. compassionate
2. remarkably
3. climatic
4. prioritise
5. installation
6. joyful/joyless
7. considerably/consideration
8. remorseless/remorseful
9. hesitation/hesitant
10. conservation/conservationist

2
1. seasonal
2. rapidly
3. migration
4. primarily
5. fragility
6. extensive
7. continuously
8. numerous
9. endangered
10. predatory

Writing p112

2 (Answers are clockwise from top centre): earthquakes/tsunamis; species extinctions; desertification/dying forests/threatened ecosystems; rising global temperatures; cities destroyed/millions displaced/famine/disease/conflict; melting ice caps = rising sea levels; polar bears face drowning/starving; hurricanes/storms/forest fires; human deaths/injuries

3 Paragraph 2: how the weather will change
Paragraph 3: how nature will suffer
Paragraph 4: how human civilisation will suffer

Unit 15

Getting started p113

1
1. E
2. G
3. C
4. B
5. H
6. C
7. G
8. H
9. A
10. B

Reading pp114–115

1
1. C
2. D
3. A
4. D
5. B
6. C

2
1. C
2. D
3. A
4. B
5. C
6. D
7. A
8. B

Language development p116

1
1. c
2. d
3. h
4. f
5. g
6. i
7. b
8. a
9. e

2
1. let it pass
2. flying colours
3. pass my lips
4. came to pass
5. pass the buck

3 (Possible answers):
1 a long illness.
2 a drop of blood.
3 post office.
4 travel around the world.
5 employee etc.
6 message that dinner will be at 8.
7 it was clearly her brother's work.
8 mother to child.

4 a pass off as; b pass down; c pass by; d pass out; e pass up; f pass on; g pass away; h pass over

Listening p117

1
1. C
2. B
3. D
4. A
5. A
6. B

Speaking p117

1
1. Fernando, where are you from?
2. How would you describe your home city to someone who has never been there?
3. What can young people do in your country?
4. Claudia, where do you live now?
5. What do you like about it?
6. What are the advantages/disadvantages of living abroad (for a short time)?
7. Fernando, if you could live in another country, where would you choose?
8. Why?
9. Claudia, what are the most popular sports in your country?
10. What do you do to keep fit and healthy?

Grammar p118

1
1. in case
2. Hardly/Barely
3. so that
4. where
5. Consequently/As a result/Therefore
6. In spite of/Despite/Notwithstanding
7. While/When
8. For fear of

2
1. no sooner … than (time)
2. as … as (comparison)
3. so … that (result)
4. if (condition)
5. Nevertheless (concession)

3
1. to her house to talk …
2. Despite being/In spite of being
3. For fear of forgetting …
4. No matter how tough it was …
5. with a view to going …
6. Seeing as you've …
7. Such is the extent of the damage that …
8. do as you're told or else/otherwise …

4
1. For this reason
2. otherwise
3. In order to
4. This is why
5. When
6. with a view to
7. Consequently
8. due to the fact that
9. so as
10. although

Use of English p119

1
1. during/on
2. for
3. where
4. to
5. so
6. them
7. as/when
8. the
9. which
10. such
11. with
12. both
13. from
14. like
15. so/consequently/therefore

2
1. order
2. custom
3. hand
4. belief
5. magic

Writing p120

1 It was the most amazing experience; I won't go into too much detail about; suffice it to say there was; The most memorable part for me was; I was enjoying myself immensely …

2 (Possible answers): 1 Yes, to Cyprus on holiday.
2 Yes, a wedding that went on for three days!
3 Lots of eating and drinking plus the money pinning ceremony.
4 I only had coins in my pocket.

3 Paragraph 1: Where I went (introduction to the experience)
Paragraph 2: General summary of the experience
Paragraph 3: Details of what made it special/memorable
Paragraph 4: What happened at the end.

Unit 16

Getting started p121

1
1. discontinued
2. founded
3. finalise
4. settle
5. launching
6. instigated
7. incited
8. abort
9. generated
10. completed

Reading pp122–123

1
1. C
2. D
3. A
4. B/C
5. B/C
6. C
7. D
8. A
9. C
10. D
11. B
12. A
13. A/B
14. A/B
15. C